DROWNING IN OIL

DROWNING IN OIL

BP and the Reckless Pursuit of Profit

LOREN C. STEFFY

NEW YORK   CHICAGO   SAN FRANCISCO
LISBON   LONDON   MADRID   MEXICO CITY   MILAN
NEW DELHI   SAN JUAN   SEOUL   SINGAPORE
SYDNEY   TORONTO

The McGraw·Hill Companies

1 2 3 4 5 6 7 8 9 0   DOC/DOC   1 5 4 3 2 1 0

ISBN: 978-0-07-176081-2
MHID: 0-07-176081-4

Design by Lee Fukui and Mauna Eichner

This publication is designed to provide accurate and authoritative information in regard to the subject matter covered. It is sold with the understanding that neither the author nor the publisher is engaged in rendering legal, accounting, or other professional service. If legal advice or other expert assistance is required, the services of a competent professional person should be sought.

—*From a Declaration of Principles jointly adopted*
by a Committee of the American Bar
Association and a Committee of Publishers

Library of Congress Cataloging-in-Publication Data

Steffy, Loren C.
  Drowning in oil : BP and the reckless pursuit of profit / by Loren C. Steffy. — 1st ed.
    p. cm.
  ISBN 978-0-07-176081-2 (alk. paper)
  1. Petroleum industry and trade—Mexico, Gulf of. 2. Industrial productivity—Mexico, Gulf of. 3. Oil spills—Cleanup—Mexico, Gulf of. 4. Nature—Effect of human beings on—Mexico, Gulf of. 5. British Petroleum Company. I. Title.
  HD9574.M63S84 2011
  338.7'62218240916364—dc22
                              2010042692

McGraw-Hill books are available at special quantity discounts to use as premiums and sales promotions, or for use in corporate training programs. To contact a representative please e-mail us at bulksales@mcgraw-hill.com.

This book is printed on acid-free paper.

To Laurie, for everything

Culture is forever. Complacency is a great danger.
—U.S. Sen. Slade Gorton, R-Wash., at
the release of the report of the BP U.S.
Refineries Independent Safety Review Panel
(the Baker Commission), January 2007

*This incident that happened on board our rig should have
never happened. There was eleven buddies of mine that perished
and their families deserve to know exactly what happened. "*
—Chad Murray, chief electrician,
Deepwater Horizon

THE VICTIMS

TEXAS CITY
(2004–2009)

Glenn Bolton

Lorena Cruz-Alexander

Ray Gonzalez

William Joseph Gracia

Ronnie Graves

Rafael "Ralph" Herrera Jr.

Daniel J. Hogan III

Jimmy Ray Hunnings

Morris "Monk" King

Richard Leining

Larry Wayne Linsenbardt

Leonard Maurice Moore, Jr.

Arthur Galvan Ramos

Ryan Rodriguez

James and Linda Rowe

Ramon SiFuentes

Kimberly Smith

Susan Duhan Taylor

Larry Sheldon Thomas

Israel Trevino

Eugene White

DEEPWATER HORIZON
(2010)

Jason Anderson

Dale Burkeen

Donald Clark

Stephen Curtis

Gordon Jones

Roy Wyatt Kemp

Karl Kleppinger

Blair Manuel

Dewey Revette

Shane Roshto

Adam Weise

CONTENTS

PREFACE

I first knew BP as a tiny metal truck. It was a green-and-yellow Dodge tow truck with a solitary red light atop the cab and the BP shield logo on the side. My brother had one, too. As children we both played with Matchbox cars, the British-made die-cast replicas of real vehicles. The speedy, durable little cars inevitably had "accidents" that required frequent towing, and the red plastic hooks on the BP wreckers latched beautifully under the wheels of the other cars.

Our collection also included a BP tanker truck and, later, a plastic model of a BP service station. At the time, in the early 1970s, it was about all the contact that anyone in the American public had with British Petroleum.

Even then, BP was among the world's biggest oil companies, but its presence in the United States was largely unseen. It was a partner in the Trans-Alaska pipeline, and it later bought Standard Oil of Ohio; but it remained largely hidden from the American consciousness.

Public distrust of oil companies in the America grew steadily during the final decades of the twentieth century. A blowout from an offshore platform near Santa Barbara, California, gave rise to the environmental movement, and oil companies became its most reliable villain. As prices soared under the foreign oil embargoes of the 1970s, the public began to believe that Big Oil was in cahoots with OPEC, the Middle Eastern cartel that suddenly demonstrated it could bring the world's greatest industrialized nation to its knees with the turn of spigot. In 1989, the *Exxon Valdez* ran aground in Alaska's Prince William Sound, spilling 11 million gallons of oil and cementing the oil industry's demonic public image. BP was the biggest owner of the consortium that operated the pipeline feeding the Valdez terminal.

Still, BP remained little more than a logo on a Matchbox truck to most Americans.

Only in 1998, when it bought Amoco in the biggest industrial merger in history, did it begin to move into the spotlight of American business. Amoco, after all, was one of the fragments of John Rockefeller's Standard Oil, busted up by the U.S. government in 1911.

The Amoco acquisition gave BP a visible presence in America, with a string of branded gasoline stations and the country's third-biggest refinery. Within a few years, BP would be the largest retailer of gasoline in America, and second only to Exxon Mobil in market value among publicly traded oil companies.

BP had moved to the big stage of global business. Under its chief executive, John Browne, it unveiled a bold strategy to push the company "beyond petroleum." BP, whose logo had long sported the color green, would now become "green" in the environmental sense. The familiar shield was transformed into a leafy green-and-yellow sunburst.

Browne, essentially, tried to position BP as the anti-Exxon in the minds of the public. It was a brilliant and, initially, successful strategy. But something was terribly wrong inside BP.

Beneath the green veneer lurked festering and fundamental problems that would, quite literally, explode before a horrified public. The warning signs predate the explosion aboard the *Deepwater Horizon* by more than a decade.

I began covering BP as a columnist for the *Houston Chronicle* in 2005, after an explosion at its Texas City refinery near Houston killed 15 people and injured hundreds. I have watched the company try to move past that disaster, and I have witnessed some of the triumphs shared by its employees as it met the incredible technological challenges of oil exploration and production. I have also seen the terrible cost of BP's troubled culture to employees, contractors, and their families. I've listened to top executives promise change, and I've seen the disturbing patterns that emerge across its operations.

Somewhere, packed away in an upstairs closet, my Matchbox wreckers with their BP shield sit in their case. Like BP's benign corporate anonymity, the childhood innocence with which I once viewed them is long gone.

CHAPTER 1

PIERCING
THE FIRES
OF HELL

Night settled across the Gulf of Mexico about 40 miles from the coast of Louisiana. A sliver of a moon rose above the shimmering water, reflecting off the translucent pillows of jellyfish that bobbed just below the surface. The calm water lapped gently against the giant gray steel pylons that kept the *Deepwater Horizon* drilling rig suspended above an oil well a mile below the surface.

The *Horizon* was a massive feat of engineering, a portable steel boomtown for 126 people. The rig had meandered from ocean to sea to gulf, from one oil hot spot to the next, chasing some of the largest deposits of crude and drilling some of the deepest wells of all time. Technically, she was a ship, with engines that could propel her at about four knots and eight underwater thrusters that kept her positioned over the wellhead when she was at rest. The platform was bigger than a football field, capped by a drilling derrick that towered 20 stories above the main deck. Her owner, Transocean Ltd., had spent a half-billion dollars building her, and she could float in as much as

10,000 feet of water and still drill some 30,000 feet below the earth's surface—deeper than Mount Everest is tall. She was part city and part drilling machine, and she was about to become a flaming tomb.

Maybe 130 other vessels in the world could do what the *Horizon* did. She was special. Built in a Korean shipyard in 2001, she was one of the most advanced weapons in man's insatiable quest for oil. In recent years, she had been working mostly in the Gulf for BP, the British oil company that was developing some of the deepest wells in these waters. She'd hit the Tiber field the previous fall, drilling the deepest well in history at more than 35,000 feet. She had also drilled wells in BP's other two Gulf showcase fields, Thunder Horse and Atlantis, and since February, she'd been positioned over the Macondo prospect.

The Macondo was near a geological formation known as the Mississippi Canyon, an underwater crevasse in the central Gulf about 4 miles wide and 75 miles long. Companies had been drilling in the canyon since 1979, but BP was pushing the technological boundaries, moving to ever-greater depths. The government had issued a permit in March 2009, and one of the *Horizon*'s sister rigs had begun drilling in the fall. A late hurricane, though, had damaged the rig, so that it couldn't complete the job. The *Horizon* had moved in to finish the drilling. At the end of a mile-long pipe that had been fed down from the derrick, a drill bit that looked like three metal softballs made from the soles of cleated baseball shoes, grinding in unison, had punctured the seafloor and churned through the rock beneath. The bit had ground its way through almost two and a half miles of earth until it struck an ancient graveyard of dinosaurs that had long since decomposed into a massive underground pool of petroleum. It had been a rough ride. The Macondo was fussy, like an infant after mealtime, and the pressure and gas rose like burps from deep in the ground, kicking at the drill pipe and causing shudders that could be felt on the rig above. One BP employee, monitoring the drilling process from back on shore, had referred to the well as a "nightmare." Another described it as "crazy."[1] For BP, it was worth it. Macondo had the promise of being a prolific reservoir of oil, the type of huge find that's referred to in the industry as an "elephant." It was exactly the sort of high-risk, high-reward prospect that BP liked, even if the well's crankiness had slowed the drilling process. Macondo and wells like it represent the best hope for finding new oil deposits in America. Unlike the harsh climates of the Arctic, the Gulf of Mexico is warm most of the year, and, aside from hurricanes, it is a relatively easy place to drill. That convenience and the discovery of finds like the Macondo were driving demand for more drilling. For decades, the offshore industry had coexisted with the fragile ecosystem of the Gulf, home to some of the world's most prolific seafood production, without major problems. The last significant spill had been in the late 1970s, when a well in Mexican waters blew out and tainted beaches in south Texas. Tens of thousands of wells had been drilled since then, with ever-improving and safer technology. The need for new oil deposits in friendly waters, combined with the industry's safety record, had eased public concern over offshore drilling. Less than two months after the *Horizon* arrived at the Macondo, President Barack Obama had opened vast new areas of the Gulf, parts of the eastern seaboard, and segments of offshore Alaska to new drilling. The deep water was about to get busier.

As night settled in on April 20, though, none of the crew was thinking about new neighbors barging in on the *Horizon's* solitude. A half-dozen BP and Transocean supervisors had arrived by helicopter earlier in the day to celebrate seven years of impeccable safety on the rig. BP was a company that knew the painful cost of ignoring safety. Just a month earlier, the company had marked a bleak anniversary—a refinery explosion five years earlier near Houston that had killed 15 workers and injured hundreds more. After that tragedy, and after the harsh findings of the investigations that followed, BP had enacted sweeping new safety procedures. A rig operating without an accident deserved special praise. By the time the helicopter ferrying the BP managers had landed, things were winding down on the drilling of the Macondo well. The *Horizon* crew had struck what appeared to be a sizable reservoir of oil, and it was now in the final stages of its task, preparing to cap the well and move the rig to another site. Once the *Horizon* was gone, BP would tie Macondo into a nearby underwater pipeline and begin pumping its oil toward shore. That, however, wasn't the *Horizon* crew members' concern. They just drilled the wells; they didn't stick around for "first oil." Both the *Horizon* crew and BP were ready to move on. The Macondo's crankiness had set them behind schedule by a month and a half, and nowhere was lost time more costly than on an offshore rig. BP was spending about a half-million dollars a day for the *Horizon*, and the delays had pushed the project more than $20 million over budget in rig costs alone.

———— ✄ ————

Stephen Stone was no drilling expert, but even he could tell that things weren't going smoothly. Stone had joined the *Horizon's* crew more than two years earlier, working as a roustabout, which means that he did a variety of jobs and specialized in none. Stone, whose dark beard framed boyish features, mostly assisted crane operators and helped to pump a heavy fluid of clay and chemicals known as "drilling mud" into the well bore. Stone was coming to the end of his two-week stint aboard the *Horizon*. In another day or so, he'd be back on shore and in the arms of his redheaded bride, Sara, whom he had married just six months earlier.

During most of Stone's hitch, the drilling mud had been disappearing in the hole. That wasn't helping the Macondo's budget problems. Drilling mud may sound mundane, but it's a highly specialized mixture designed to lubricate the well and tamp down the pressure. The recipes for mud are carefully guarded by the service companies that make it. For wells like Macondo, BP would be paying about $10 million just for the mud. When a well loses mud, it can mean only a couple of things, and neither of them is good: either the underground formation is unstable, or the well was drilled too quickly, cracking the formation. At least four times during Stone's hitch, the crew had been forced to stop pumping in mud and shoot heavy drilling sealant into the hole, which was supposed to close up any cracks in the formation.

By early afternoon on April 20, the BP "company men," supervisors who were onboard the rig to oversee the drilling operations, decided that it was time to finish the process of capping the well. The drilling crew began pumping mud out of the hole and replacing it with seawater. While not as heavy as the mud, the seawater would help hold back the pressure from the reservoir once the well was capped with cement. Mud was so valuable that companies reused it, and as it came out of the hole, the crew pumped it over to the *Damon B. Bankston*, a supply ship that had arrived that morning. By five o'clock, tests showed a possible pressure imbalance in the well, and the mud pumping stopped. While the supervisors tried to figure out what was wrong, Stone, who'd been working on a nearby crane, wrapped up his 12-hour shift and traipsed down the two decks to his cabin. He crawled into bed and fell soundly asleep.

———∞∞∞———

At nine-thirty, Mike Williams was wrapping up his duties for the day. The chief electronic technician, Williams had spent most of his shift doing routine maintenance and inspecting a crane on the starboard side of the rig. Now, he was sitting at his desk in his small office, logging his maintenance reports and talking to his wife on the phone. Williams had risen through the ranks on the rig, starting as a roustabout like Stone three and a half years earlier. His phone conversation was interrupted by an announcement over the loudspeaker about gas levels on the rig. Did he need to go? his wife asked. No, Williams said. The balky well had been kicking back so much gas, as if it were fighting every step of the drilling process, that Williams had stopped paying much attention to the announcements unless the levels rose high enough that his crew members had to stop all "hot work"—welding, grinding, or anything else that might throw a spark.

As he continued the conversation, he heard a hissing sound that was growing louder, followed by a heavy "thump." Williams's shop was directly below the riser skate. The riser is a large steel tube that descends from the bottom of the rig to the top of the well and surrounds the drill pipe. It's raised and lowered in pieces, and the skate is the device that feeds the pieces into the hole or pulls them out. They must be retrieving the riser, Williams thought, and they backed the skate up too hard. He assumed from the hissing that the force of the impact had ruptured a hydraulic line. He told his wife he'd better go check things out.

As he hung up the phone, he could hear beeping from the engine control room next door as the panels lit up in a chirping choir of warnings and alarms. He tried to make sense of the sounds—the hissing, the thump, the warning lights. What the hell was going on up there? He pushed back from his desk and realized that the onboard diesel engines, which generate power for the rig, were starting to rev. Given where the sound was coming from, he could tell that it was Engine Number Three, and it kept accelerating, revving way beyond anything he'd ever heard. Suddenly, the computer monitor on his desk exploded, and then the light bulbs in the shop began popping in succession, like a chain of firecrackers. As he grabbed the door to his shop, he heard Engine Number Three whining at a higher and higher pitch, rising to a crescendo that heralded disaster. Then it simply stopped. The silence hung in the air, like the moment when a diver first plunges into the water, and then it was ripped away by an earsplitting explosion.

⸺ ∞ ⸺

Moments earlier, and not far from Williams's office, Chad Murray had stepped out of the pump room, which houses the huge machines used to pump mud from the well. Murray, the chief electrician, had been isolating power to one of them so that four other technicians could switch out a valve. The other men were working nearby, between two of the pumps. Murray stepped through the watertight door and latched it behind him. As he returned to his shop, he heard what sounded like a high-pressure noise, a hissing. He walked back to the pump room, and as he reached the door, the rig was shaken by a massive explosion. He scrambled to his feet, grabbed a flashlight from his shop, and spun open the latch on the pump room door. Black smoke billowed out, enveloping him like a shroud. Everything inside was dark. The thick smoke swirled across the beam of his flashlight as if he were driving in fog. All he could see was devastation. Though he couldn't see them, he knew that the four men he'd been speaking with just moments earlier were most likely dead.

———∞∞———

Miles "Randy" Ezell was lying in his bunk watching television when the telephone rang. Ezell was a toolpusher, a senior member of the drilling team, and one of the *Horizon*'s original crew members. He'd spent 33 years working on offshore rigs, and the last 8 on the *Horizon*. Ezell had gone off duty a few hours earlier. The call was from Steve Curtis, the assistant driller on the drilling floor. "We have a situation," he said. "The well is blown out. We have mud going to the crown," which meant that the drilling fluid was shooting from the top of the derrick. Ezell was horrified. He'd left the drill floor earlier in the evening after getting reassurances from his relief that everything was fine. Curtis told Ezell that they were trying to shut in the well. "Randy, we need your help." Ezell grabbed his coveralls and stepped into the hallway. His boots and hard hat were in his office just across the corridor. People were standing around, but he barely saw them. He was riveted by tunnel vision—a singular focus on the danger that he knew faced them all. As Ezell stepped into the doorway of his office, an explosion wracked the room and threw him 20 feet into a wall.

———∞∞———

Stephen Stone awakened with a start. At first, he wasn't sure what had rousted him, only that it had been loud. Then the sleep cleared from his mind, wiped away by the cold realization that the noise had been an explosion. As that thought startled him fully awake, another blast hit. This one shook the platform, and it sounded as if the upper decks were collapsing. Ceiling tiles rained down in a storm of dust and debris. The force blew open the door of his cabin, and, in the hallway, his crewmates were running in the halls, screaming. Stone bolted through the door and made for the stairwell that would take him to the lifeboat deck.

He knew the drill. Everyone on board did. They practiced it every Sunday. Offshore drilling companies trained their crews incessantly on safety and evacuation procedures, yet the entire rig seemed to be gripped in panic. When Stone got to the stairwell, he found that it had collapsed, crumpled like paper discarded in a trash can. He ran back to his room and grabbed a life vest and his shoes, and then, instinctively, snatched his wedding ring.

Back in the electronics shop, the first explosion blew the three-inch-thick steel door off its six hinges, knocked Mike Williams across the room, and slammed him into the far wall. The door followed and struck him in the head. A line containing carbon dioxide ruptured and began spewing gas into the room, clouding his vision. He couldn't see. He couldn't breathe. He crawled along the floor, knowing that oxygen would be more prevalent there, and made it back to the opening where the door had been. As he scrambled through, he pulled a penlight from his pocket, turned it on, and carried it in his mouth, hoping to see where he was crawling. The lights in the next room, like those in his shop and all over the rig, had exploded. Everything was dark. He crawled through the control room, feeling his way, and made it to the door on the far side. As he grabbed the handle, another explosion shook the room.

In the hallway outside his cabin, Stephen Stone spotted a crane operator he worked with who was running toward the other end of the living quarters. Stone followed him. Together, they made their way up the stairwell at the far end of the rig from Stone's cabin. They were now one deck below the rig's surface, but the lifeboats were at the opposite end. They raced through the upper deck of living quarters, and as they reached the other side, a collapsed ceiling blocked their path. The air was thick with black smoke and grit, as if someone had turned on a fan in an ash bin. Debris was strewn everywhere. Still following the crane operator, Stone picked his way through the rubble, and together they pushed through onto the lifeboat deck.

As he stood up on the deck, Stone turned around and looked up. The towering derrick was ablaze, a forest fire of metal soaring skyward and turning the night sky to day. He stood mesmerized by the flames until his reverie was shattered by a call to muster. Someone was trying to rally the crew and get a head count before they moved into the lifeboats. That, too, was a well-rehearsed procedure. Many of the crew members gathered on the lifeboat deck, though, continued to stare at the burning derrick, unable to move, unable to look away as the horror slowly sank in. The nightmare well, with its mile-long conduit into the belly of the earth, seemed to have tapped into hell itself.

Chad Murray was supposed to report to the engine control room on the other side, but with the inklike smoke filling the pump room, he knew he'd never make it there. Besides, the explosion had come from the engines. There probably wasn't anything left back there. This wasn't an emergency drill; this was outright crisis. Murray knew that the rig had to be evacuated. He began making his way forward toward his muster station, where he was supposed to gather for an evacuation. He picked his way through the galley. The floor was littered with broken ceiling tiles. Blown-out wall panels were scattered everywhere. It looked like the scenes on the news after a tornado had ravaged a trailer park. As he made his way across the galley and down a corridor, he came upon four of his fellow crewmen huddled on the floor.

The first thing Randy Ezell remembered after the blast was that he was covered by parts of the ceiling and other debris that had rained down on him after he hit the wall. He tried to get up, but he couldn't move. He tried again, but he lacked the strength. He told himself, "Either you get up or you're going to lie here and die." He summoned a burst of adrenaline and pulled himself free. He stood up and sucked in a lungful of smoke, which was billowing through the room. Remembering his safety training, he dropped back to the floor and began to crawl. He tried to remember the direction of the door. He thought he felt a puff of air and headed toward it. It must be the way out. He clambered over the shattered remains of his office. As he made it to the door, he realized that what he had thought was air was actually methane. He could feel the droplets on his face. Everyone was in danger. Another explosion could doom them all. As he crawled down the hallway, he came across Wyman Wheeler, another toolpusher, who was covered in debris. As he cleared it off, a flashlight approached, bobbing around like a bouncing ball of light. It was Murray. The hallway was chaos. A few people came and went; several people were injured, and others were trying to help them. Ezell and another worker tried to lift Wheeler, but he was in too much pain. Ezell asked Murray to go to the bow and get a stretcher. Ezell promised Wheeler he'd stay with him. Somehow, they'd get him out.

———— ∞∞∞ ————

Mike Williams was angry. He shoved the door aside. At that moment, he hated doors. Two of them had hit him in the head and pinned him against walls. "They were beating me to death." He couldn't see anything. Something was in his eyes, but only later would he realize that it was blood running down his forehead. He couldn't move one arm, and his left leg was useless. He was choking on the CO_2 that was still flooding the room. He knew he had to get outside, to fresh air, if he was going to survive. The explosion had blown him back 30, maybe 40 feet. He began to crawl once again toward the doorway.

The control room had an elevated floor, like a computer room. The floor tiles were suspended a few inches above the subfloor to allow cabling and wires to run underneath, connecting all the control panels that lined the room. The explosion had shaken the floor panels out of their supporting grid, and as he crawled, Williams had to pick his way through the mesh of supports, like a football player doing tire-training drills in slow motion. As he crawled, he came upon the bodies of at least two men. They weren't moving, and they weren't responding. He assumed that they were dead. Even if they weren't, in his condition, he was unable to help them. He wasn't even sure he could help himself. As he continued to make his way across the room, he saw a dim light and headed toward it. Eventually, he pulled himself outside. He still couldn't breathe, and as he got to his feet, he turned toward the starboard side of the rig. Earlier in the day, when he had been working on the crane, he recalled that the wind had been coming across the starboard side. His training had taught him to stay upwind of smoke and fire. His vision began to clear, and he started to move forward. As he was about to take a step, he realized that there was no walkway in front of him, no handrails. "One more step and I would have been in the water." The exhaust stack, the housing for Engine Number Three, and the walkway that went past it were all gone. He turned around and headed in the other direction, toward the lifeboat deck. Realizing that the situation on the rig was worse than he'd expected, and not knowing how many others were alive, he thought about getting into the lifeboat and launching it himself.

Then Williams remembered the emergency procedures. He had responsibilities. He was supposed to gather at an emergency station, but his station was the room he'd just left. His secondary muster point was the bridge, on the opposite side of the rig, and, strapping on a life vest, he decided to make his way toward it. As he crossed the main deck, the hissing sound he'd first heard when he was on the phone with his wife had grown to a full-blown roar. As he picked his way through the debris, making his way forward, he could see that the derrick and the driller's shack—the derrick's control room—were engulfed in flames. He knew then what had happened. It was the worst thing that could occur on any well, but especially on one that was being drilled 40 miles from shore. One word echoed through his mind: blowout.

———— ✕✕✕ ————

As Stephen Stone stared up at the flaming derrick, it seemed to intensify, burning more brightly as if someone had thrown another log on a giant campfire. The heat rose in intensity from ovenlike to an uncontrolled blast furnace. Workers who had been too shocked to move flipped into full-blown panic, scrambling for the lifeboats. Stone strapped himself into Lifeboat Number Two, but nothing happened. The red boat stayed on the deck while the voice that had been calling for muster was still hoping vainly for a head count. The lifeboat, which was more like an enclosed metal pod, began to fill with smoke. Strapped in and frozen in time, Stone realized that he was about to die. The flaming derrick above him would melt and crumble, raining molten death down on him. Or the entire rig would simply explode in one last, cataclysmic blast, a final inferno enveloping them all.

At the moment when he thought death was upon him, Stone felt the lifeboat lurch as it was lowered on its cables toward the water. The sea, too, was on fire by then. The *Horizon* had begun to break apart, and bits of it were tumbling into the water, spreading over the surface like a sense of dread. The lifeboat was still under the platform, floating in a flammable sea surrounded by burning debris. Finally, the boat was cut from its cables and motored toward the nearby supply ship, the *Damon B. Bankston*.

Mike Williams reported to the bridge and told the rig's captain that the vessel had no propulsion and no electronic control. Engine Number Three was gone, and the others might have blown, too. The bridge was a nest of controlled confusion as the rig's leaders tried to figure out what was happening.

Jimmy Harrell was the *Horizon*'s offshore installation manager, essentially the senior officer when the rig was connected to the well. Harrell had spent the better part of the day talking to the visiting managers from BP and Transocean; then, after doing some paperwork on the bridge, he'd returned to his quarters and was taking a shower when the first explosion hit. His quarters were blown apart by the blast. He stumbled from the remains of the shower, grabbed a pair of coveralls, and headed into the hallway without any shoes. Randy Ezell was kneeling beside Wyman Wheeler, moving debris off him. Harrell managed to crawl through the debris, making his way to the main deck and eventually to the bridge. As he got there, he heard the subsea engineer telling the rig captain that he was disconnecting from the well.

By the time Williams arrived, other workers had begun to reach the bridge. Noticing the blood pouring down Williams's head, a supervisor told him to sit down. Williams kept repeating his assessment of the damage he had seen. "We need to abandon ship now" he said. The supervisor looked for a medical kit to treat the gash on Williams's forehead, but all he could find was a roll of toilet paper to stop the bleeding. Several people gathered around Williams began talking about the standby generator. If they could get that running, they could get lights and some minimal functions back. But reaching the generator meant heading back toward the fire.

The supervisor turned to leave. Williams stood up. If this had any chance of working, it would take more than one person. They couldn't send a man back into the maw of the flames alone. Williams grabbed the supervisor by his shirt and told him that he wasn't going by himself. Paul Meinhart, a motorman who'd joined Transocean just three months earlier, went with them. The three men headed back across the main deck and into the generator room. For 10, or perhaps 15, minutes they frantically tried to start the generator. The generator had a battery starter, and Williams was reading a 24-volt charge on the battery, but the engine wouldn't start. Were they doing something wrong? They fumbled around the darkened room and found an instruction manual. By flashlight, they read the starting procedures. They were doing everything right. After five or six futile tries, they gave up and headed back toward the bridge.

Back on the bridge, alarms were shrieking, and the captain knew that they were running out of time. The subsea engineer had hit the emergency disconnect for the well, and although the control panel showed that the rig should be free, it wasn't. The hydraulics were dead. Fire continued to shoot from the top of the derrick. The rig had no power, and without power, it had no pumps for the firefighting equipment, no way to shut off the flow of gas from the well, and no way to disconnect the rig from the flaming umbilical that had it tethered to the wellhead. All they could do was leave. The captain gave the order to abandon ship.

As they made their way back toward the bridge, Williams felt a sickening feeling wash over him. Lifeboat Number One was descending from the rig. Without power, there'd be no way to raise it again. Meanwhile, Chad Murray and Randy Ezell emerged from below deck, carrying Wyman Wheeler on a stretcher. They joined up with the group, as did David Young, the chief mate who'd been helping to get other crew members to the lifeboats. By the time the bridge crew got to the lifeboat staging area, the second one was gone, too. There were about 10 of them in all, probably the last crew members still aboard. They stood in stunned silence as the heat from the flaming derrick swatted at them and debris swirled around them. All the lifeboats on their side of the rig were gone. Someone suggested that they try to make it to the aft boats. Williams looked up at the derrick, an inferno of twisted metal. Flames were now shooting out of the top, fueled by the flow of gas rushing up from a mile below them. Little explosions were going off everywhere, and things were popping and shooting past them. Projectiles were flying in every direction, but it was impossible to tell what they were. Trying to reach the other lifeboats would get them all killed for sure.

Young grabbed for the only option they had left: an inflatable life raft. Like the lifeboats, the rafts were covered, with a small opening for people to climb through. The rafts were hooked to a winch with an arm like a small crane that swung over the side of the rig and lowered the raft to the water. As the raft inflated, it became entangled with the arm of the boom. A blizzard of smoke whipped around them, and heat seemed to be coming from below the rig. Williams feared that the fire was creating a backdraft that was wrapping around under the vessel, between the legs of the giant rig, and coming back up the other side. So much heat was rising from below that he feared the raft would pop or melt and cook the people who were getting inside.

Young climbed in, followed by Murray and Ezell. Once they were inside, they guided Wheeler's stretcher through the opening, then several other members of the group jumped in. Watching from the deck, Williams worried that the raft would swing out and dump the stretcher into the water 100 feet below. They waited for breaks in the swirling heat before scrambling into the raft a few people at a time. Then, when it came Williams's turn, the raft inexplicably deployed before he could get in. He was left on the deck with two members of the bridge crew, a woman named Andrea and Curt Kuchta, the captain.

———❦———

To steady the raft as people climbed in, one of the lines securing it had been tied off to a handrail. As the raft descended, the line pulled taut, jerking the raft sideways in midair and causing everyone inside to tumble to one end. The force of the impact pulled the line loose, and the raft snapped back, flinging the crew back against the opposite side. As they hit the water, disoriented from being tossed around and trying to work around

Wheeler's stretcher, they knew that they had to get free of the rig. Murray and several others scrambled out of the raft, hoping to pull it through the water and away from the flaming platform above them. The raft wouldn't move. The line on which they'd been lowered was still connected, holding it in place. Transocean, the *Horizon*'s owner, had a policy prohibiting crew members from carrying pocketknives. In the cramped, darkened interior, the frantic occupants of the raft couldn't find the cutting tool that was stowed inside. Overhead, the flames shot ever higher into the night sky. Flames licked the surface of the water, moving closer to the raft.

Back on the deck, Mike Williams looked up at the derrick. It was burning hotter than ever, like a giant funeral pyre. Given his injuries and the time it had taken to wrestle with the life raft, he knew that they didn't have time to inflate a second one. They had a choice: They could stay on the rig and die, or they could jump.

Jumping, too, was something that they had trained for. It was the last-ditch survival technique: Wrap your hand around your life vest, step off, cross your legs, look straight ahead, and fall. But if they fell straight down, they would probably hit the life raft that had just descended. They and the people in the raft would all be lucky to survive such an impact. Williams turned to the woman beside him and told her that they'd have to run and jump. She said she couldn't. She couldn't jump. She couldn't. Kuchta ran and jumped over the edge. Come on, Williams urged. He just did it. You've got to do it. She couldn't, she said. She just couldn't.

Time was running out, literally burning away. The deck was getting hotter, as if they were standing on a griddle that was getting warmer by the minute. Finally, Williams said, "Well, watch me, then," and he jumped, plunging 10 stories into the water below. He hit the surface and sank deep, coming back up to find that calamity had followed him from the rig above. The water was coated with something: oil, hydraulic fluid, diesel fuel—he couldn't tell what it was, but it was covering him and burning his skin. What had he done? The deck might have been a raging inferno, but at least he hadn't been swimming in acidic sludge. He looked at the flames nearby. The fire, he realized, would come across the water and burn him up just as surely as if he'd stayed above. He was under the rig now, its massive legs rising above him like darkened skyscrapers. Fire rained down, and flames danced along the surface of the water.

Williams began to backstroke, using his one good arm and one working leg. He kept pushing himself forward until he felt no pain and the heat subsided, fading into blackness. He was just conscious enough to think that he might be dead, that the flames had caught him and he'd burned up. Another explosion above him jolted him back. He was still in the rig's shadow, and he could see the glow from the fire raging on the deck from which he'd jumped. He told himself that he had to swim, willing his broken body forward. He heard something in the distance—a voice calling, "Over here! Over here!"

He swam as hard as his one exhausted arm and leg could move him, floundering forward until the pain and the heat once again began to fade and the blackness returned like a blanket. Suddenly, he was being lifted out of the water. He flipped over into a small orange rescue boat, and as soon as he could speak, Williams tried to tell anyone who could listen that they had to get away.

But there were others in the water. The boat operators could see the flickering of the emergency lights from their life vests. Instead of leaving, they headed closer to the flaming rig, back toward the inferno that now loomed above them. They stopped and pulled in another survivor floating in the water. It was Andrea, whom Williams had been unable to coax from the deck moments earlier. Finally, he thought, the ordeal was over. She had been the last one off as far as he knew. Now they could make their way to the *Bankston*.

Lying in the boat, though, he could feel the heat intensify. They weren't pulling away, they were heading closer to the rig. Williams protested, but the boat driver told him that there was a life raft under the rig. The bridge crew was still stuck there, bobbing in the underbelly of the flaming giant above. The raft was drifting farther under the rig, toward the fire. The rescue boat crew threw a line over in hopes of towing the raft, but as it tried to pull the raft away, Williams could feel the rescue boat moving sideways. Something was holding them back. As they looked at the raft, it was tilted at a 45-degree angle, pulled taut against the line that was still connected to the rig. Kuchta, the captain, who had jumped just before Williams, was in the water near the raft. He swam to the rescue boat, got a knife from the pilot, and swam back to cut the raft free. The rescue crew hauled him into the boat, and they all headed toward the *Damon B. Bankston*.

Eleven men aboard the rig, many of them on the drill floor or working near the engine room, didn't survive. The roll call for the dead would come later: Jason Anderson, Dale Burkeen, Donald Clark, Stephen Curtis, Gordon Jones, Wyatt Kemp, Karl Kleppinger, Blair Manuel, Shaun Roshto, Dewey Revette, and Adam Weise.

About half an hour after Stephen Stone was pulled aboard the supply boat, the Coast Guard arrived and began flying the injured to a triage station on another rig 14 miles away. Some were flown directly to hospitals on shore, depending on the severity of their injuries and whether they could handle the helicopter flight to land. The *Bankston* stayed at the scene all night as the remaining *Horizon* crew members watched their floating city burn. "That was one of the most painful things we could have ever done—stay on location and watch the rig burn," Ezell said. "Those guys that were on there were our family. It would be like seeing your children or your brothers or sisters perish in that manner." Ezell wished the Coast Guard had allowed the *Bankston* to move away from the disaster site to some place where they wouldn't have had to keep staring into the burning maw of death that had been the *Deepwater Horizon*. Not until eight o'clock the next morning did the *Bankston* finally make for shore.

Four hours later, the ship pulled alongside another platform and Coast Guard investigators came aboard, interviewing survivors. Everyone had to give a written statement before leaving, they were told. At one-thirty, about 28 hours after the explosion that had awakened him, Stone stepped on shore, but he wasn't going anywhere. By then, Transocean had amassed a response team, and as the survivors disembarked from the *Bankston*, they were told to line up for a drug test. Battered, exhausted, and overwhelmed by the events of the past day, Stone had survived a disaster only to be made to feel like a criminal by the very company that had put him in harm's way.

As the survivors arrived, they were ushered into a big room, told that they couldn't contact families or attorneys, and presented with a paper that they were supposed to initial and sign before they could leave. One of the statements said: "I was not a witness to the incident requiring the evacuation and have no firsthand or personal knowledge regarding the incident." Finally, Stone was allowed to call his wife, Sara. She'd flown from Houston to New Orleans and had gotten word that Stephen was safe, but she'd been frustrated at not being allowed to speak with him. After another three hours, Stephen was taken to the Crown Plaza hotel in New Orleans, where he finally was reunited with her, given a room, and allowed to sleep—the first sleep he'd had in more than 30 hours.

A week and a half later, a Transocean representative met Stone at a Denny's restaurant and again urged him to sign a waiver saying that he wasn't injured. In exchange, he would receive a check for $5,000 that was supposed to cover personal possessions lost on the *Horizon*. After 10 days of nightmares, memory loss, and flashbacks of the blast, he refused to sign anything saying that he'd suffered no injuries.[2]

Hours before the sun rose on the flaming wreckage of the *Deepwater Horizon*, news of the disaster had crossed the Atlantic, reaching the inconspicuous brick building on London's tony St. James's Square. The building lacked the ostentation that might be associated with Britain's most prominent company and one of the world's biggest oil producers. In his fifth-floor office, Tony Hayward, the short, slight chief executive with a tangle of black hair, was in shock, stunned by the reality that was slowly beginning to sink in. Hayward, just three years into his tenure as chief executive, was supposed to be the reformer, the leader who understood BP's internal problems and was leading it to a new era of safe operations. He wanted to make the company's operations an example for the entire global energy industry.

His record had reflected that. His time as chief executive had been marred by none of the calamities that had plagued the final years of his predecessor, John Browne. In fact, BP had largely faded from the headlines, which had been Hayward's plan. He didn't court the spotlight the way Browne had. He was determined to run things smoothly, and if operations ran smoothly, they weren't newsworthy. Now, the flaming rig in the Gulf of Mexico would draw headlines and television cameras to BP like moths to headlights.

BP didn't own the rig, but regardless of what had happened, it owned the problem. Under its lease agreement with the U.S. government, it was responsible for any oil that leaked from the well. That was true even if Transocean's equipment had failed—the equipment that was supposed to prevent this sort of thing. Whatever the cause, Hayward and BP would be forced to face the consequences. This would become BP's crisis, and it was BP that would have to fix it. Hayward, who'd managed for years to avoid getting caught in BP's fatal legacy, was now fully ensnared. The company's past, which he thought he had buried, had come roaring back.

He'd gotten the job after the disasters of 2005 and 2006, which included the deadly refinery explosion in Texas City and oil spills from BP-operated pipelines on the Alaskan tundra. When he took over, Hayward vowed sweeping changes, and he'd been making them. Safety had improved. He could cite the numbers to prove it. He'd slashed BP's bloated bureaucracy, clearing out offices throughout the building in which he now paced. Had he instead been simply an errant guide, leading his company in circles as if lost in a wilderness of its own failed culture? How the hell could this happen? That was the question the entire world asked as the *Deepwater Horizon* burned, then sank, breaking off the riser pipe and unleashing a flow of oil that in a week would already create a slick the size of Delaware off the Louisiana coast. For three months, the well would spew oil and the slick would grow, staining not just one of the world's most important bodies of water but the reputation of the company that Hayward now ran. For Hayward, the end was beginning. He didn't realize it yet, but his 28-year career with BP was descending rapidly into disgrace. Like his predecessor, he would be forced from the company, knocked from the highest pedestal of British business. His name would never be forgotten, forever linked with one of the industry's greatest failures. Few remembered who ran Exxon when the *Valdez* tanker ran ashore and sullied the coastline of Alaska's Prince William Sound in 1989. But few would forget who was running BP when the *Deepwater Horizon* exploded.

How the hell could this happen? Hayward demanded. Left unspoken was the final word of the question, the word that put the latest and largest of BP's disasters into its fatal context: *again.* How the hell could this happen *again?*

CHAPTER 2

DAWN
IN THE
DESERT

By the time of the *Deepwater Horizon* explosion, the outer continental shelf of the Gulf of Mexico had become the energy industry's new frontier. While drilling here was vastly expensive—BP had spent more than $150 million on the Macondo well beneath the *Horizon* wreckage—oil companies were drilling almost three dozen similar projects at the time. In the industry, such wells are often referred to as "ultra-deep"—in more than 5,000 feet of water, as opposed to deepwater, which runs from about 500 to 5,000 feet. Less than 500 feet is considered shallow water. Some 50,000 wells have been drilled in the Gulf during the past 60 years, but only 700 of them have been in water 5,000 feet or deeper. Ultra-deepwater drilling represents a new technological threshold, one in which the pressure at the seafloor can equal more than 30 atmospheres and in which all the work at the wellhead must be done by remotely operated robot submarines. It's an exclusive club, and BP produces more oil there than any other company.

While ultra-deepwater drilling remains at the forefront of
man's engineering capabilities, offshore oil exploration in shallower areas has become almost as routine as shrimping in the
Gulf. As far back as the 1930s, the Gulf's waters were plied by
drilling equipment, although in the early days, the wells were
so close to shore that the crews literally waded to the well sites.
Even before that, platform drilling had been tried in Louisiana
lakes, and derricks had been set up on fishing piers off Santa
Barbara, California, in the late 1800s. Those projects, though,
produced scant amounts of oil and bore little resemblance to
modern offshore drilling. Offshore rigs, as we now know them,
were first developed by Kerr-McGee, an Oklahoma-based oil
company that gambled on a technology that many larger companies deemed impossible. It built a platform more than 10
miles off the Louisiana coast and struck oil in 1947.[1] In a touch
of historical irony, Kerr-McGee would eventually be bought by
Anadarko Petroleum, which owned a one-quarter interest in
the Macondo well that the *Deepwater Horizon* was drilling.

Despite Kerr-McGee's success, other companies didn't rush
to follow it offshore. While Kerr-McGee's well was a technological achievement, offshore wells cost more than five times as
much as land wells, and the expense was simply prohibitive for
many companies. At the same time, the federal government was
squabbling with coastal states over control of drilling rights for
the continental shelf. Huge potential tax benefits were at stake,
but the uncertainty that resulted, combined with the high costs,
made it cheaper to import oil from petroleum-rich nations in
the Middle East.[2] By the middle of the twentieth century, the
Middle East had become a vital source of oil for the West. One
of the biggest producers in the region was Iran, whose oilfields
were first discovered by a Londoner named William Knox
D'Arcy, the founder of the company that became BP.

At the turn of the last century, oil was beginning to capture
the fancy of the world. In 1901, on a windswept hillock on the
plains of southeastern Texas, a creaky, steam-powered wooden
derrick punched a hole in the ground and unleashed a shower
of black petroleum. Spindletop, as the hill and later the discovery itself became known, gave birth to the modern age of
liquid fuel and established the oil industry as the foundation for
a century of global industrial growth. Spindletop captured the
fascination of the world in a way that only gold had previously
done, and soon prospectors the world over were trading their
pans and pickaxes for derricks and drill pipes.

By then, D'Arcy had already made his fortune. A specula-
tor, he'd set out from London to strike it rich in Australia's gold
rush, and once he had done so, he returned, planning to retire
to his home in Grosvenor Square and enjoy the trappings of his
newfound wealth.[3] He ensconced himself among the London
aristocracy. Portly and balding, with a drooping gray mustache,
he married an actress after the death of his first wife, and they
threw lavish parties. D'Arcy owned two country estates and
nurtured a love for horse racing that he had developed during
his prospecting days in Australia. Like many men who become
rich, D'Arcy found that wealth brought with it a desire for more
wealth. He became a financier of sorts, always on the prowl for
new and lucrative investments. The allure of oil drew his attention. It was called "black gold," after all, and the similarities between petroleum and the precious metal didn't end with
their value. The process of extracting oil and the financial risk
involved had many parallels with gold mining. Oil was gaining
importance by the late 1800s, as it proved to be a more efficient
and cleaner fuel than coal. In the rising demand, D'Arcy saw

opportunity—and profit. He would gamble much of his sizable fortune to capitalize on it.

Getting wind of a report by French geologists about possible oil amid the limestone formations of Persia's Zagros Mountains, he dispatched two representatives to negotiate a drilling concession with Mozzafar-al-Din Shah.[4] D'Arcy's men were able to secure almost a half-million square miles, an area twice the size of Texas, for £20,000, a stake in D'Arcy's new company, and 16 percent of the net profits. To develop the concession, D'Arcy hired George Bernard Reynolds, a self-taught geologist and engineer who had already drilled for oil in Sumatra. Reynolds was 50 years old by then, a scrappy loner who had little time for city-bound dandies. For three years, he persisted in drilling exploratory wells for D'Arcy in the searing heat of the Chiah Surkh, a plateau near the present-day Iran-Iraq border. However, his efforts were largely unsuccessful, revealing only scant signs of oil.[5]

This was no gold mine, and D'Arcy found his thirst for the gambler's share tested by the sheer magnitude and expense of the endeavor he'd undertaken. Reynolds blew through £200,000, and D'Arcy feared that his tony lifestyle would be compromised if he spent any more. "Every purse has its limits," he wrote in 1903, "and I can see limits of my own." What little oil was flowing wasn't enough to cover the drilling costs, and D'Arcy's banks were threatening to seize the concession. His dreams of making a second great fortune in Persian oil were crumbling.[6] However, D'Arcy wasn't prepared to give up. He began searching for other investors, approaching first the British government, then other oil companies. Eventually, he secured the help of Burmah Oil, a well-financed company founded by a Scottish millionaire who had made his wealth in Canadian railroads. Burmah Oil kicked in additional capital, and Reynolds shifted his drilling program to the central Persian plain. The new money, though, came with certain strings attached. The investment meant that Burmah Oil executives were now calling the shots, and Reynolds, who had kept drilling operations going for years despite impossible conditions, had nothing but disdain for his new bosses. D'Arcy, too, bristled under the control of his investors, who were growing increasingly impatient with the rising costs and lack of progress. They wanted D'Arcy to put up more money, but he didn't have it to spare, so he simply ignored the requests from Burmah's board. By May 1908, Burmah executives had had enough.[7] They sent Reynolds orders to close the drilling operation. When the telegram arrived, Reynolds was furious. He'd spent six years in the dusty, sweltering deserts of Persia, and D'Arcy had forfeited a sizable piece of his fortune, only to be told to return home in defeat. Reynolds decided to stall. He couldn't rely on a telegram for orders of such importance. Who knew what errors might have been typed into the message? He would need written confirmation, which, he hoped, would take at least a month.

Two weeks later, while most of the drilling crew was sleeping, they were awakened at four in the morning by a rumbling and then the sounds of shouting. A gusher of black crude shot 50 feet in the air, and oil rained onto the plains of Persia. Reynolds sent the news back to London—via telegram. Now it was D'Arcy's turn to await confirmation, but he couldn't help but express his relief. "If this is true, our troubles are over," he said.[8] The dawn of petropolitics was nigh.

After the discovery, D'Arcy and Burmah Oil formed the Anglo-Persian Oil Company and sold shares to the public. The offering created a mob scene at the Bank of Scotland's Glasgow office as investors clamored for shares, each hoping to buy a small piece of the oil frenzy that was now gripping the industrialized world. Throughout the day, the lines were five or ten people long, and at times it was impossible to get inside the bank.[9] The company grew rapidly, employing a couple of thousand people. It built the first pipeline in the Middle East, transporting its crude from Persia's central plains to the coast, where it was shipped by tanker to Europe.

In just a few years, though, Anglo-Persian was again in financial trouble. To get the most oil out of the fields, more wells had to be drilled, creating a seemingly insatiable hunger for capital. The financial burden was taking its toll, and the company's board feared that it would be acquired by Shell, its Anglo-Dutch rival. Winston Churchill had other ideas. Churchill became First Lord of the Admiralty, the civilian head of the Royal Navy, in 1911. He had grown concerned about the threat of war from Germany, and he worried that the navy was unprepared for an attack. Churchill championed a plan to convert the naval fleet from Welsh coal to oil. As a more efficient fuel, oil would enable the navy to commission faster and more powerful ships, but it came with a dangerous trade-off: much of Britain's military would depend on fuel from foreign countries. Churchill argued before Parliament that the government had to own or at least control the sources of oil needed to power its defenses. Rather than buy oilfields itself, the Admiralty paid £2 million for a controlling stake in Anglo-Persian. The deal required that the company remain an independent British concern and that all its directors be royal subjects. The government also appointed two directors with veto power.

In exchange for the steady flow of government funding, Anglo-Persian and its successor companies sold oil to the Royal Navy on generous terms—so generous that the details were kept secret for more than 50 years.[10] British Petroleum, as the company would later be known, remained a quasi-government enterprise for much of the century. The investment proved immensely beneficial to the British government, and to the British people as well. Most government pensions were invested in the company's stock. For much of the century, the company was intertwined with the British identity, operating under a blurred distinction between government office and private corporation. "This great enterprise has played a notable part in the history of the past 50 years, and has contributed to our national prosperity in peace and our safety in war," Churchill wrote in a foreword to the company's history, published in 1959.[11]

Government control, though, had its side effects. BP took on many of the characteristics of a nationalized company, including a ponderous bureaucracy. In foreign countries, BP often found itself resented as an arm of the British government. The company's formation became a template for the rest of the industry. Just as D'Arcy found that he was unable to shoulder the huge capital investment needed to extract oil alone, so, too, would oil companies large and small partner with others to share the risk of future ventures. The government's stake in BP also served as a blueprint for other countries that were developing their own oil wealth. By the end of the twentieth century, independent companies found themselves at a disadvantage. When it came to finding new oil reserves, they were often beaten by nationalized companies that would lock up new finds.[12] BP's mergers in the late 1990s were, in some ways, an indirect result of the very nationalization movement that it had helped start.

⸺⸺

Persia, which became Iran in 1935, remained BP's primary source of oil into the 1950s, but the foreign company's control of Iranian oil reserves was a source of growing agitation for Iranians. Ever the wheeler-dealer, D'Arcy, who died in 1917, had negotiated terms that left Iran with scant revenue from its own oil. The concession was revised several times, but it remained skewed in the company's favor. Mohammad Mossadeq won election as prime minister in 1951 by threatening to take back the country's oil reserves. As soon as he took office, Mossadeq nationalized the country's oil assets, essentially kicking BP out of Iran.[13] Mossadeq was part of a growing movement among Third World countries whose economies were being transformed by oil wealth. The pattern began in Mexico in 1938, when President Lázaro Cárdenas seized the assets of foreign oil companies and made oil revenue the basis for the country's economic revolution.[14] Mossadeq was no revolutionary, although his election and his later ouster were to sow the seeds of revolution. The son of a Qajar princess and the shah's finance minister, Mossadeq grew up in a rarefied lifestyle in mid-twentieth-century Tehran. At age 16, he took his first government post, as a chief tax auditor of his home province, and he rose to political prominence despite an undiagnosed medical ailment that left him prone to fits of fainting, crying, or uncontrolled laughter. His rise to power was marked by his outrage at the D'Arcy agreement and his contempt for the Iranian royal family, including Mohammad Reza Shah Pahlavi, who had ascended to the throne during World War II. The new shah, like his predecessors, generally supported the D'Arcy concession. Mossadeq believed that monarchs should leave politics to elected officials.[15] The British, though, had other ideas. They responded to Mossadeq's seizure of BP's assets with an embargo on Iranian oil, assembling a Royal Navy flotilla in the Persian Gulf. The Russians and the British had squabbled over Iran since the turn of the century, and now, American and British intelligence agents worried that the embargo would drive Mossadeq closer to the Soviets. In 1953, the Central Intelligence Agency and the British Secret Intelligence Service led a covert plot to overthrow Mossadeq as prime minister and restore the shah as the ultimate ruler.[16]

The coup enabled BP to reclaim its Iranian assets, but it changed the course of Middle Eastern history. Rather than allowing democracy—perhaps what would have become the first democratic state in the Muslim Middle East—the West's thirst for oil prevailed. Many Americans had forgotten the coup by the late 1970s, when it was the oil-producing countries of the Middle East that enacted an embargo against *them*. The Iranians didn't forget. In the 1979 revolution that finally overthrew the shah, many protesters carried posters of Mossadeq, and the new revolutionaries once again seized the assets of foreign oil companies.

—❦—

No one, of course, worried about that in 1954. With the pro-West shah firmly in control, the oil companies returned. The D'Arcy agreement, with its onerous terms, gave way to a consortium of foreign companies that had a stake in Iranian oilfields. The biggest was BP. The consortium split the profits from the oil fifty-fifty with the fledgling National Iranian Oil Company. The return of the Western oil businesses brought a new wave of executives, many of whom moved their families with them. Among the children who arrived with their parents was a nine-year-old boy named Edmund John Phillip Browne.[17] Almost 40 years later, he would become the chief executive who orchestrated BP's transformation into both a global powerhouse and a perpetrator of disaster.

CHAPTER 3

RISE
OF THE
SUN KING

John Browne was the polar opposite of the stereotypical oilman. Short and reserved, he lacked the swagger and braggadocio of legendary wildcatters. He had a love of opera, ballet, and the arts; relished his standing among the London gentry; and basked in international media attention. He was more like BP's founder, William Knox D'Arcy, than like H. L. Hunt, the Texas gambler and card player who turned oil wells into one of the world's greatest fortunes. Browne fancied himself a problem solver (he studied physics at Cambridge) and considered pursuing a career as a researcher. His father convinced him that the ever-changing challenges of business would present a better outlet for his skills, and Browne took an apprenticeship with his father's former employer, BP, in 1966.

By the time Browne took over as the company's CEO in 1995, BP was shaking off the vestiges of its past as an arm of the state. The British government had sold its remaining stake in the company to the public in 1987, but BP was still a staid and stodgy place. If Browne wanted to solve problems, he had plenty from which to choose. Enrico Mattei, head of the Italian oil company ENI in the postwar years, coined the term "Seven Sisters" to refer to the world's biggest oil companies—Exxon, Gulf, Texaco, Mobil, SoCal, BP, and Shell. BP, once among the proudest of the Sisters, had become something of a stepchild. Browne wanted to restore the company's grandeur, to make it a true global competitor. In the process, he would become something of a rarity—a rock star of British business.

Browne was born a child of the realm, but he spent little time in England as a boy. His parents met in Germany shortly after World War II, and Browne was born in Hamburg in 1948. His father was a British army officer. His mother, Paula, was a Hungarian of Jewish descent who had spent a year in Auschwitz and who had lost most of her family during the war. As a boy, his parents had young John in tow as his father was posted to Germany, England, and Singapore before taking a job with what was then Anglo-Iranian Oil and moving to Iran.[1] At the age of 11, John's parents sent him to boarding school in London, the King's School Ely, which he would later liken to "*Lord of the Flies* for real." He bristled under the harsh regimens and rote learning, and because he was short and chubby, he was easy prey for bullies. When he was about 12 years old, Browne began to realize that he was different from the other boys. It wasn't just his interest in theater or his experiences living in Iran; he *felt* different. He realized that he was gay. He said nothing; he was terrified both because homosexuality was illegal in Britain at the time and because the school curriculum had underscored the immorality of it. Boys who were revealed as homosexual were expelled. His fear of being found out was deeply rooted, and Browne kept his sexuality closely guarded for almost 50 years, even from his mother, who later in life became his constant companion.[2]

His secret wouldn't have been any more welcome in the oil business. In the late 1960s, it was still a rough-and-tumble industry, populated by wildcatters and roughnecks and often requiring negotiations in countries where homosexuality was either illegal or unwelcome. The oil business's male-dominated culture created what Browne saw as an "unpleasant bravado" that, like boarding school, carried its own elements of William Golding's famous novel. During one early stint at a BP refinery, Browne was doused with crude oil as an initiation rite.[3] Had he come out as gay, especially as a young man, he almost certainly wouldn't have risen to lead BP. "You had to remove yourself from conversations, from play acting, from the macho talk. You became very good at avoidance."[4] Nevertheless, Browne pursued his career plans, joining BP full-time after graduating from Cambridge. He was posted to Alaska. Anchorage in the late 1960s was an oil boomtown, not unlike those that had populated Texas in the early days of its oil rush. Browne arrived at his hotel on his first day in town to find that "the noisy smoke-filled bar was crammed with burly, beer-swilling men, with 'working' women loitering at the entrance."[5] Like most boomtowns, it was rowdy and crawling with opportunists looking to make a fast buck. Oilfield work was hard in the best of conditions, but in the frozen climes of Alaska, companies had to pay top dollar to get even unskilled labor to the job site. Those who could endure the harsh conditions could make a lot of money quickly. When they weren't earning it, they were spending it, often in the sawdust-floored bars that, besides oil, were the town's other major enterprise. Binge drinking was the favorite pastime, and bar fights were as common as snow flurries. Thrown into this environment as a fresh-faced college graduate, it's little wonder that Browne kept quiet about his sexuality.

He spent a few obligatory months working on BP's exploratory wells, but he soon joined the team working with other oil companies to solve the problems that they all shared in producing oil in such a difficult place. Alaska had become the new great hope, the energy frontier, for the entire industry, and no company was relying more on its promise than BP. Concerned about the instability of the Middle East, BP executives had begun diversifying the company's reserve base. In 1964, the company bought a concession in Alaska, where U.S. oil producers had been scouring the geology for years. Atlantic-Richfield and Humble Oil—which later became part of what is now Exxon Mobil—struck oil in Prudhoe Bay four years later, and BP made its own discoveries in the area a year after that.

If living in Anchorage was a stark contrast to Browne's school days in Cambridge, so too was working with U.S. oil companies. BP was still British Petroleum at that time, and it operated more like a government agency than like a private enterprise. While the engineering team was a collaborative effort, it was also bound by the rules of competition, and Browne was struck by the intensity with which the oil companies vied against one another. They guarded their strategies closely, each trying to figure out the best drilling prospects before the others, so that they could lock up the choice leases. His exposure to this competitive fire shaped his views of how business should operate, a view that decades later would transform BP and bring an American competitive flavor to a British institution.

Seeing the vigor with which the U.S. companies squared off, Browne came to a more immediate realization: BP was at a disadvantage. Using computer skills that he'd learned at Cambridge, he began writing FORTRAN programs and wangling mainframe computer time at night to improve BP's technology for assessing and mapping the Alaskan geology, which he thought would give BP an advantage over its American rivals.[6] It was exactly the sort of problem solving he had hoped to do when he joined the company, and it proved to be the springboard for his career.

Browne rose through various posts at BP, which moved him to New York, San Francisco, Calgary, and back to London. But he was drawn to America, to its thirst for competition, and he found that he missed it when he was back in the head offices of the government-controlled BP.

During his time in San Francisco, he earned a business degree from Stanford, having been selected by BP to study as a Sloan fellow. Studying business in America only underscored Browne's belief in competition and efficiency, and made him more aware of BP's plodding, risk-averse culture. That feeling intensified when he moved to Cleveland in 1986. Cleveland isn't typically thought of as an oil town, but it was home to Standard Oil of Ohio, one of the dismembered pieces of John D. Rockefeller's former monopoly. Cleveland had been Rockefeller's starting point, the launchpad from which he had slowly gobbled up his competitors and built the greatest oil empire in history.

BP bought into Sohio, as the company was known, in 1970, using the company as a retail outlet for its Alaskan oil. By 1986, though, Sohio was a mess. BP's ownership had increased to 55 percent of the company, and it was proving to be a lousy investment. Sohio had been generating weak returns, and it was losing a billion dollars a year. It had squandered $6 billion in profits from its Alaska assets on a disastrous copper-mining venture, and it was drilling one dry hole after another. As group treasurer in the early 1980s, Browne developed a plan for BP to buy Sohio outright, using its controlling stake to replace the Sohio board with directors who would support the acquisition by BP. It was the heyday of hostile takeovers, when corporate raiders like T. Boone Pickens were prowling the oil patch looking for undervalued and poorly managed companies, but BP's chairman, reflecting the company's timid heritage, decided that Browne's plan was too heavy-handed.[7] Instead, BP pressured Sohio to remove its three top officers and replace them with BP executives, including Browne.

Ultimately, BP wound up buying out the remaining piece of Sohio anyway, paying almost $8 billion for it, and Browne and the other executives implemented a turnaround plan that included huge job cuts in an effort to generate more than a half-billion dollars in profit in two years.[8] By the time his Sohio project was complete, Browne had become convinced that the only way BP could compete globally was to shake off its stodgy culture and embrace American-style management. Between his Stanford education and his experience at Sohio, Browne began to develop another idea that was to define his leadership at BP: companies could save money by replacing their own experts, such as engineers, with outside consultants. Public companies, after all, exist to make money for their shareholders. The amount of oil that they had in the ground didn't matter if it couldn't be sold at a profit. Engineers and designers always seemed to be doing things that cost money rather than earning it. The company could save a lot of money by getting highly skilled employees off the payroll and hiring technical expertise when it was needed.

———— ∞ ————

The third major lesson of Browne's education as an executive came, once again, from Alaska.

Browne hadn't been stationed there in more than a decade, but the state remained vital to BP's strategy. The company had helped develop the Trans-Alaska Pipeline during his time there, and it continued to pump millions of gallons of crude hundreds of miles across the frozen tundra from the Arctic Ocean to the southern port of Valdez. Browne was running BP's U.S. exploration division and was on the verge of a promotion to lead its global operation from London when the *Exxon Valdez* tanker ran aground in Prince William Sound. Browne was on Alaska's North Slope at the time, at a base camp, when he was awakened at five in the morning with the news. He flew over the spill in a small plane and was struck by the slow response to the crisis, thinking that more boats and containment booms would be deployed more rapidly.[9]

Ironically, BP controlled the industry consortium that was responsible for containing spills around the Valdez terminal. Officials with the consortium, the Alyeska Pipeline Service Co., were notified within minutes of the spill, but it took seven hours to get the first helicopter airborne with a Coast Guard investigator. The first barge with containment equipment didn't arrive for 12 hours. The consortium lacked the proper skimming equipment and generally fumbled the response, state investigators later found. A day into the crisis, Exxon officials realized that the consortium was botching the cleanup and took over the operations itself.[10] The poor response to the *Valdez* spill is legendary, but BP's role was overshadowed by Exxon's emergence as America's newest environmental villain.

Environmentalists had been at war with the oil companies since 1969, when the blowout of a Unocal well off the coast of Santa Barbara had stained California's famous beaches. The *Valdez* spill was like handing them a new round of ammunition. Whatever trust the general public had left in Big Oil would be washed away, mired in the black goo oozing from the gash in the side of the massive tanker. As Browne saw it, "The industry was now measured by its weakest member, the one with the worst reputation. That oil company was now Exxon."[11] Two decades later, Exxon and others in the industry were saying much the same thing about BP. The *Deepwater Horizon* disaster quickly eclipsed the magnitude of the *Valdez* spill, and unlike in the Alaska disaster, BP's involvement was at the forefront.

Six years after the *Valdez* spill, Browne was promoted to chief executive. In 1995, BP was still among the world's elite oil companies, but it was struggling. Debt and government influence had left it a lumbering and narrowly focused giant. With the Iranian oilfields long lost to a revolution, the company's oil reserves were concentrated in the North Sea off the coast of Great Britain and in Alaska's Prudhoe Bay. To keep pace with its bigger rivals, BP would have to find more oil in more places.

As Browne ascended to the CEO's job, the global oil industry was undergoing another fundamental change. Large independent companies like BP were increasingly finding themselves shut out of major new discoveries. Emerging nations were keeping their oil wealth for themselves, and foreign companies weren't able to finagle their way into the oilfields the way William Knox D'Arcy had done in Persia almost a century earlier. The majors desperately needed to find new sources of oil. For a decade or more, none of the Seven Sisters had increased its reserves significantly, and major fields were showing signs of depletion. As prices fell during the 1990s, the majors began to realize that their way of doing business was becoming obsolete. They needed a big change, and that change came from the smallest and least likely among them: BP.

Browne was determined to push BP into a leadership role among the major oil companies, and the first step in his plan was to indulge an idea that he'd been nurturing since he'd run Sohio in Cleveland almost a decade earlier. He wanted BP to buy Mobil.[12] Faced with the threat of declining reserves, he argued, the majors needed to boost profits and cut costs, and the best way to do that was to combine. A century earlier, the U.S. government had broken apart John D. Rockefeller's Standard Oil trust. Now, Browne would set in motion a series of deals across the industry that would draw the fractured pieces of Rockefeller's empire back together, and no company would wind up holding more of them than BP.

Browne's hopes of buying Mobil never materialized, but he quickly moved on to his next target: Amoco. Then the fifth-largest U.S. oil company, Amoco had been the refining arm of the Standard Oil monopoly, and it owned five refineries in the United States, compared with BP's one. Unlike BP, though, Amoco was a failure at finding oil. It had spent billions on new prospects, only to come up empty-handed. Pushing into international markets like Uganda and Pakistan, Amoco found itself locked into multiyear work agreements in countries that had little infrastructure to support drilling. That made the company's prospects more expensive to undertake, which just added to the losses when the wells didn't produce oil. Amoco drilled dozens of dry holes around the world, leading to one of the worst drilling records in the industry's history. With no new reserves being found, the company was rapidly depleting its reserve base. By the late 1990s, as the price of crude fell toward $10 a barrel, Amoco represented a chance for BP to pick up a major refining and retail presence in the vital U.S. market at a bargain price.

Amoco also offered something else: a chance for BP to rework some of the company's poor drilling programs, much as Browne had done with Sohio. BP's strength was exploration, which was Amoco's weakness, but Amoco had some promising prospects, including acreage in the Gulf of Mexico. BP had put its toe in the waters of the Gulf in 1988, when it bought a 29 percent stake in Shell's Mars project. Shell, facing budget cuts because of weak oil prices, couldn't afford to fund on its own a project that many of its engineers and geologists thought was questionable economically. Like the fateful Macondo project years later, Mars was drilled in the Mississippi Canyon formation. At the time, it was the deepest water in which any company had drilled, almost 3,000 feet. Mars was a successful project for both companies, as it held some 500 million barrels of oil, but it proved a boon for BP and a tactical blunder for Shell. Until then, Shell had been the leader in deepwater technology and had more leases in the Gulf than any other company. By bringing in BP, Shell allowed its bitter rival to learn from the inside how to conduct deepwater projects. "It basically allowed BP to go to school on Shell technology," said deepwater historian Tyler Priest. "That's where BP really sank its teeth in deepwater." With the acquisition of Amoco and its portfolio of Gulf leases, BP began an aggressive drilling campaign in the deep waters of the Gulf, and by 2004, it was the biggest leaseholder in the region, ultimately producing more oil from there than any other company. [13]

The $52 billion Amoco acquisition was announced on August 11, 1998, as the "largest ever industrial merger." It created a company with a market value of $120 billion, making BP third, behind Exxon and Shell among the biggest publicly traded oil companies. It was billed as a "merger of equals," but as is so often the case with corporate combinations, the label was just public relations spin. Browne had no intention of sharing power—or, for that matter, even keeping the Amoco name for long. Within a few years, BP Amoco was again BP, and Amoco's CEO, Larry Fuller, was long gone. Browne wasted little time in making it clear what the merger was about. He planned to save $2 billion a year by adopting Amoco's strategy of concentrating exploration on "elephants"—the giant oilfields that meant taking big risks, but that paid big rewards when they succeeded. He would cut additional costs by firing thousands of workers, including many of the company's engineers.[14] Blind to the technical challenges of pushing the frontiers of energy exploration, Browne saw the engineers as cost centers. The bigger, emboldened BP would focus on new discoveries, on making the big finds, not just on solving problems like squeezing more oil from aging reservoirs. To make the strategy work, Browne brought in legions of accountants determined to help him meet—or beat—his promises to Wall Street of increasing profits.

———— ∞∞∞ ————

BP stock began an upward climb that would continue, with few setbacks, through 2000, more than tripling during Browne's first five years as chief executive. Wall Street loved what he was doing. Investment banks always cheer mergers because they mean big advisory fees, even if the deals are ill-conceived or destined for failure. But the prolonged slump in oil prices during the 1990s meant that the major oil companies had to get bigger so that they could weather the downturn. At the time, most forecasters believed that oil would remain cheap, and that oil supplies were abundant. The majors, then, had to find a way to increase their production without increasing their costs, and Browne knew that a company of BP's size wouldn't survive if it didn't find a way to increase its oil reserves quickly. With oil prices low, the stock of struggling companies like Amoco was cheap, and this enabled BP to buy reserves at a discount while bolstering its ability to find bigger oil deposits.

"The rationale at the end of the '90s was about companies that had truly global scope and scale," Tony Hayward said later. "BP was a little company when we merged with Amoco, and we couldn't do everything. We often got opportunities that were too big for us, and therefore, we got someone else to help us."

As long as BP needed other companies' help, it was vulnerable. Browne's strategy of focusing on elephants was aimed at solving this problem. It was cheaper to drill into one big reservoir and pump as much oil as possible than to tap lots of smaller ones. Wall Street saw Browne's grab for Amoco as exactly the solution that the industry needed, and analysts began clamoring for more deals. They even coined a term, "supermajors," to describe the pending marriages among the Seven Sisters. They didn't have to wait long. Exxon bought Mobil later the same year, before BP's deal for Amoco had closed. Chevron then bought Texaco, Conoco bought Phillips, and France's Total bought Petrofina and Elf. Browne's ambition had transformed Big Oil and elevated BP to the global stature he'd long sought.

Even as other companies were following him, Browne cued up another merger. The head of Atlantic-Richfield (Arco) had approached him about a deal, fearing that his company was a takeover target. As the seventh-largest U.S. oil company, Arco was too small to compete with the supermajors, yet too large to be considered an independent. Like Amoco, it had had a string of humiliating dry holes, and its losses were mounting. The Amoco acquisition had awakened something of a deal lust in Browne. Snapping up Arco would enable BP to challenge its longtime global rival Shell as the industry's number two behind Exxon Mobil. What's more, without Arco on the market, Shell would be left without a merger partner, a wall-flower among the Big Oil brethren. That would make it vulnerable to Browne's endgame: BP's takeover of Shell. By swallowing Shell, BP would catapult ahead of Exxon, making Browne the world's most prominent energy executive.

The Arco purchase enabled BP to essentially double down in Alaska. Arco and its predecessor company had been the first to find oil there in the 1950s, and it, like BP, was part owner of the Trans-Alaska Pipeline. Politicians in Alaska disliked the concentration of power in BP's hands. Arco was known to take care of its employees and the environment. BP, in contrast, even then had paid millions in fines for lapses in pipeline maintenance that led to spills. Its role in the *Valdez* spill response may have been obscured in the rest of the country, but Alaska officials hadn't forgotten.

Federal regulators also opposed the deal on antitrust grounds, ultimately suing BP to block it. To break the stalemate, Browne agreed to sell half of Arco's Alaska production and its stake in the pipeline to Conoco, just prior to that company's merger with Phillips. To get the deal done, Browne was forced to surrender the main reason for doing it in the first place. The whole point had been to strengthen BP's position in Alaska. Without those assets, the Arco purchase made far less sense, especially given the $27 billion that BP was paying. As is often the case with mergers, the deal itself became the goal, and the reasons for it no longer seemed to matter. Browne was determined to get it done and move on with his plan to acquire Shell. It might have been a costly mistake, undermining Browne's strategy and causing its soaring stock price to stumble, but Browne caught a lucky break from the markets. The Arco purchase made BP the biggest producer of natural gas in the United States just before the price tripled.[15]

———∞∞∞———

With both the Amoco and Arco deals completed, Browne faced the arduous task of combining three major oil companies into one. Two of those companies had been money-losing operations. Integrations are always tricky, but Browne was determined to make these deals pay off quickly. Once again, he turned to cost cutting. It was a crucial moment in the evolution of Browne's BP. One executive later remarked that BP had had a chance to set itself on the right course. It could have created a new culture for its North American operations, choosing among any of the three companies. Arco's worker-friendly environment, which made safety paramount, might have changed BP's culture before it had a chance to take hold, steering the company away from the disasters to come. Instead, BP focused on the financial integration and, in the process, wound up with the penny-pinching mindset of BP and the lawyer-driven mentality of Amoco. The thing that was lost—Arco's operating culture— was the thing that should have been kept. Browne, though, had his own ideas about the culture he wanted to create, and few outside the company questioned what he was doing. BP's board, too, was enamored with his leadership. After all, he'd taken a moribund nationalized company and turned it into a global powerhouse. By 2001, just two years after the Arco deal, BP had become the third-largest oil company, and it was closing in on Shell's number two spot. It had sales of almost $150 billion and an annual profit of $12 billion. Along the way, Browne had earned a spot as one of the greatest industrialists in British history. He was seen not only as a brilliant deal maker, but as a man who would literally transform the global oil business, much as John D. Rockefeller had done in his own time.

Browne viewed himself as a new visionary leader for the oil industry, and to cement that role, he laid out a controversial new direction for BP that he encouraged the rest of the industry to follow. By the late 1990s, scientists had begun raising concerns about global warming. Some argued that man's use of carbon-producing fuel, especially coal and oil, was the primary cause. The oil industry had long been at odds with environmentalists, and global warming had all the makings of a new battleground. Since the Santa Barbara spill in 1969, environmentalists had cast the oil industry as the environment's biggest foe. The 1989 *Valdez* spill cemented in the public consciousness the industry's image as a pillager of the earth. Shell executives worried that the new findings would lead to stricter regulation of oil companies, and they began to develop a program for investing in sustainable energy—low-pollution fuels such as solar and wind power.

＊＊＊

About six months before Shell unveiled its project, Browne stole his rival's thunder. On an uncharacteristically sweltering day at Stanford University in 1997, Browne outlined a plan that would redefine BP. Speaking at an outdoor amphitheater, surrounded by solar panels made at a recently acquired BP factory, Browne called for a change in the oil industry's attitudes toward the environment.[16] Rather than refute the emerging science linking man-made carbon emissions to global warming, he embraced it. The possibility of a link between greenhouse gases and climate change could no longer be ignored, he said. He pledged that BP would put $20 million into a California solar plant and fund research into sustainable energy.[17]

It was a token gesture—$20 million was a pittance for a company BP's size—but it was the first step in positioning the company as different from the rest of the oil industry. What's more, solar power is among the least economical of alternative fuels. Though it is favored by environmentalists, it produces some of the most expensive electricity on earth. "It's not a business, it's a social program," said John Hofmeister, the former president of Shell Oil, who runs the grass-roots group Citizens for Affordable Energy.

Lee Raymond, the chief executive of Exxon, was furious. Browne was getting a little too uppity. As head of the industry's trade group, the American Petroleum Institute, Raymond would have none of it. He believed that alternative energy was folly, and he didn't like to see the major oil companies breaking ranks.[18] The competition among major oil companies that Browne had first seen in his early days in Alaska was a limited thing. It wasn't the same sort of competition that existed between Wal-Mart and Sears. Oil companies competed for leases, but they also collaborated. Almost every company in the industry partnered with another at some point. All oil companies operated under the same government regulations and tax structures, and they almost always presented a united front on policy issues. Browne's insouciance was a major breach of industry protocol.

Browne didn't care. He was redefining the role of British executives, inspiring a generation of young leaders. He was making bold predictions and sticking to them. Later that same year, he pushed for an internal trading scheme that BP could use to reduce its carbon emissions by allocating quotas of pollution permits to the company's business units worldwide. The company's divisions could then trade the permits. A unit that came in below its emission targets could sell its excess permits, while one that exceeded its targets could buy them. The system enabled BP to cut its carbon emissions by 10 percent through efficiency programs and reducing the flaring of natural gas at its refineries. Browne was so taken with the idea that he used his political connections to pitch it to the Clinton administration in the United States and to a friend of his, British Prime Minister Tony Blair. The United Kingdom embraced the plan, creating a private market for carbon trading in 2002.[19] In the United States, where it has become known as "cap and trade," it remains a controversial idea. Critics say that it punishes refiners and coal producers while benefiting companies with large reserves of natural gas, chief among them BP.

Browne continued to milk the "green" agenda, basking in the global media attention that came with it. After a few years, BP had invested less than $100 million in alternative energy, compared with the $10 billion it invested annually in its oil and gas business, but it didn't matter. Browne used alternative fuels as the foundation for rebranding the entire company. He got the idea from serving on the board of Intel, the California microprocessor manufacturer.[20] Intel's chips were buried deep inside personal computers, and few computer buyers were aware of them. The company launched an aggressive ad campaign, slapping labels on PCs declaring, "Intel Inside." It made flashy television ads with dancing tech workers in colorful "bunny suits," the dust-free protective gear worn inside clean rooms. Within a few years, Intel became one of the best-known consumer brands, and Browne was captivated. "People don't ask whether BP is inside. Maybe some day they will," he declared in an article in the *Harvard Business Review*.[21] He set about changing BP's image, starting with the name itself. At the time, BP was really a nickname, an abbreviation of the official "British Petroleum." Now, it *became* the name. Next to go was the company's shield logo.

An advertising agency developed a symbol of a yellow helios surrounded by what looked like leaves, using BP's traditional green and yellow colors. It also added a slogan. BP now meant "beyond petroleum." Some in the industry accused Browne of "greenwashing," hyping alternative energy to make the company appear to be something it wasn't. But the campaign worked, raising BP's profile around the world, and especially in the United States. BP reflagged Amoco stations as BP, a move that Browne was later to say was a mistake.[22] Amoco's torch logo was well known, with a loyal following. After the *Deepwater Horizon* accident, with BP's corporate image sullied by the worst oil spill in U.S. waters, the red, white, and blue Amoco oval might have muted some of the backlash against BP as a foreign oil company. Many of BP's independent retailers, some of whom became targets for boycotts and vandalism, would have preferred just about any brand name to BP at that point.

—— ◦◦◦ ——

The new image pushed Browne, already a star in financial circles, to new heights of celebrity. In 1998, he was knighted by Queen Elizabeth II, and in 2001 he became a life peer of the House of Lords, assuming the title of Baron Madingley. He enjoyed fine wine and smoked four Epicure No. 2 cigars a day, at a cost of £20, or about $31, each. His Cambridge home was featured in *Architectural Digest* and included a banquet table that could seat 30 people. The designer, Timothy Gosling, referred to Browne—identified in the story merely as "the client"— as "having an opinion and always being willing to take risks."[23] If Browne enjoyed the trappings of executive life in the grandest sense, he was also doted on in the press. While his homosexuality was known or at least suspected by many BP executives, nothing ever reached London's raucous tabloids. In 2002, the

Financial Times ran a lengthy profile, branding him "the Sun King of the oil industry."[24] A few years later, *Vanity Fair* featured Browne in its annual "green" issue, declaring him "the oilman with a conscience."[25]

On the front lines of BP's operations, though, Browne's conscience was less evident. Warning signs, subtle at first, were piling up. Beneath the veneer of fawning media coverage, BP's oil operations, which generated most of the company's revenue but far fewer headlines, were beginning to fray. From the waters of the North Sea to a refinery in Texas, workers were fearing for their lives.

CHAPTER 4

"FLYING
CLOSE
TO THE
WIND"

The North Sea is the stuff of Gothic legend. Its weather is cold and terrifying, roiled by relentless gales and massive undulating waves that roll toward the coast like a giant gray blanket unfurled by an angry maid. Its bitter, powerful currents and frequent storm-force winds can make the most hardened sailor or pilot anxious. Against this inhospitable backdrop 250 miles north of Scotland, BP found oil in 1965. Five years later, it discovered the Forties field, touching off a North Sea oil boom and enabling BP to shift its reserve base from the Middle East, where countries were nationalizing their oil fields. The Forties, along with Alaska, became the cornerstone of BP's reserve base. By 2003, however, the Forties field was in decline. Production had peaked in 1979, and most of the easy oil had been pumped out long ago. Now it was costing more and more to get less and less from the reservoir deep below the tumultuous seas. It wasn't the sort of field that BP wanted to hang onto. Under John Browne, the company wanted big new discoveries with fast payouts. It didn't want to squeeze reluctant reserves from old, lingering fields. BP planned to sell its interest in the Forties field and all its platforms to Apache Corporation, a Houston-based oil company.

———∞∞∞———

Early in the afternoon in late November 2003, as winter loomed on the North Sea, Oberon Houston sat in his office below the helicopter landing pad of the oldest of BP's five platforms in the Forties field, the Forties Alpha. The *Deepwater Horizon* was a rig, a mobile piece of equipment that drilled exploratory wells. The Forties Alpha was a platform, fixed in place, to pump oil from under the sea. The Alpha, far smaller than the *Horizon*, represented the cutting-edge technology of a past era, the oil-drilling equivalent of a Betamax videotape player. Houston was the sort of hotshot young engineer that BP cultivated under Browne. He'd joined the company in 1999, and was placed in the fast-track leadership program. Four years later, he found himself in training as an offshore installations manager, the second in command of an aging platform with a crew of almost 200. He was working on maintenance plans for a major overhaul of the platform in the weeks ahead, a process referred to on the rig as the "scrap-heap challenge" because of the magnitude of the maintenance and the limited resources available to complete it.

As he pored over maintenance schedules, a call came across the rig's loudspeaker for a technician to fix a compressor that had tripped offline. On an old platform like the Forties Alpha, such maintenance problems were annoyingly routine—another glitch that would chip away at the falling revenue from the declining field. Suddenly, Houston's office was shaken by what felt like "an artillery shell [that] had just hit the platform." He staggered to remain upright in his office as debris crashed around him.

It wasn't an explosion. It was a sonic boom. Because of the broken compressor, an aging gas line became pressurized and, weakened by corrosion, ripped apart. Natural gas was shooting from the gash in the line at supersonic velocity. The entire platform was one spark away from becoming a floating inferno. That scenario was what had happened on another North Sea platform, Occidental Petroleum's Piper Alpha, in 1988. Gas from a ruptured line had ignited, engulfing the rig in flames and killing 167 men. Only 59 crew members survived. Even after the *Deepwater Horizon* explosion, Piper Alpha remains the industry's shorthand for horror—its worst offshore disaster.

Fortunately, the Forties Alpha had a different outcome. No one died that day, thanks in part to the high winds of the blustery late autumn in the North Sea. Disaster was averted by what Houston attributed to "sheer luck." BP later admitted to breaching health and safety regulations and was fined £200,000. Houston left the company a few months later, disenchanted with a senior management that seemed to see safety as a game. The company and its executives were "focused so heavily on the easy part of safety, holding the hand rails, spending hours discussing the merits of reverse parking and the dangers of not having a lid on a coffee cup, but were less enthusiastic about the hard stuff, investing in and maintaining their complex facilities."

What Houston saw aboard the Forties Alpha, though, went beyond a misplaced understanding of safety. As BP prepared to sell the depleted field, it began to resist spending money to maintain the platform. "They flew very close to the wind," Houston said. "It was being run for the minimum cost and the maximum profit right up until the sale." John Browne may have fancied himself a problem solver, but by the time he became chief executive, his concerns were primarily financial. He responded to the siren call of market analysts who cheered a rising stock price and strong quarterly earnings but understood little about the difficulty of running machinery as complex as an offshore drilling rig.

—— ◦◦◦ ——

Managers like Houston were constantly under pressure to cut costs, and this message overrode all other concerns. "The focus on controlling costs was acute at BP, to the point that it became a distraction," Houston said. "They just go after it with a ferocity that's mind-numbing and terrifying. No one's ever asked to cut corners or take a risk, but it often ends up like that."

Browne appeared blind to the technical challenges the company was embracing, seeing all the engineering and design work involved as overhead—a roadblock impeding the company's progress toward his singular focus, the big payout. He built a management structure that reinforced his message, running off many of the experienced managers who might have challenged him. As one rival put it, "Browne didn't want a strong bench." He assembled a group of young executives who would implement his agenda without question. Known as "the turtles"—after the Teenage Mutant Ninja Turtles cartoon characters—they were on the fast track to succeed Browne as CEO. The turtles were shifted frequently, often staying in charge of a particular division for as little as a year or two. The constant shuffling kept any one of them from assembling a power base that could challenge Browne directly, but it also reduced their accountability. They did what had to be done to meet the cost-cutting goals for a particular division and then moved on. The consequences were the next guy's problem. Among the turtles was a young geologist with the looks of a British schoolboy named Tony Hayward, who not only would inherit the consequences of

Browne's management, but would become the most hated man in America.

The influx of youthful managers came at the price of experience. They micromanaged without the background of years in the field. "I saw mistakes being made. I saw too many inexperienced people getting too much power too quickly," said one former Arco manager who stayed through the acquisition.

The top-down demands to cut costs created a stifling environment of intimidation. Employees were given contracts, with incentives that were tied to meeting specific goals. Those who came up short worried about losing their jobs. In another nod to his Stanford training, Browne set up "business units," each of which operated like a separate little company within BP, with its own profit-and-loss reports, and led by what amounted to a mini-CEO. The idea was that each unit could operate autonomously, creating an entrepreneurial zeal that would benefit the larger corporation. After the Amoco and Arco mergers, though, the number of business units ballooned to more than 300. The structure became unwieldy. Each unit leader was focused on meeting his own goals but wasn't concerned with how those goals fit into the bigger picture. Known as "BULs," the business unit leaders, like the turtles, were moved around frequently. Each time they achieved the goals stated in their contract, they were shuffled to another unit.

⸻ ◦◦◦◦ ⸻

Within the units, decisions tended to be made by committee, with input injected haphazardly up and down the management chain. Contractors who were hired to do work for BP often found it difficult to determine who was ultimately in charge of a project. "They have a fundamental cultural issue of people not being used to making decisions," said one. "There's no single-point accountability." The lack of accountability also frustrated the lead Coast Guard investigator probing the *Deepwater Horizon* accident, who declared, "If everybody's in charge, nobody's in charge."

One contractor noted that he'd seen such a lack of accountability in only one other place: Enron. It wasn't a coincidence. Enron's failed management model had been the work of Jeff Skilling, a veteran of the consulting firm McKinsey & Co., who pushed Enron's freewheeling strategies so far that they became fraudulent, ultimately destroying the company. Skilling was sent to prison for 24 years for his role in the company's 2001 collapse. During his time at Stanford, Browne became enamored with McKinsey and frequently brought the company in as an advisor to streamline BP operations. The arrival of the McKinsey teams frustrated the BP engineers, who felt that the consultants had little technical expertise. One team that arrived on Forties Alpha during Houston's time there had just come from a stint at a Toyota plant. Offshore drilling was about as far removed from auto manufacturing as a candy store, yet the McKinsey recommendations were central to Browne's plans.

Having so many businesses within the business, each focused on its own goals, created a fractured and shortsighted outlook, with managers being motivated more by their immediate self-interest than by the long-term interests of the overall company. Above all the units was Browne, pushing as relentlessly as ever to control costs. He wanted to adopt the financial discipline of Exxon Mobil, but he overlooked one key element of Exxon's success. After the *Valdez* spill, the company had to change dramatically. Safety was now paramount throughout its operations. The company was a financial machine, the envy of the industry, but as closely as Exxon's management watched costs, it also made it clear to every worker that the one cardinal sin was skimping on safety. At BP, Browne would never catch up. BP's management talked about safety and monitored slips and falls, but it glossed over the importance of instilling a safety culture—a system that would analyze how disparate events such as a bad decision could combine with others, such as under-funded maintenance, to spark catastrophe.

Browne pushed forward, not appreciating that BP's rapid growth meant that it lacked the experience of having been a larger company for many years. For a while, it worked. Browne vastly expanded BP's reserve base just in time to catch a surge in world oil prices that surprised even him. Most experts in the 1990s expected oil prices to remain in the $10 to $15 a barrel range for a decade or more, ushering in an era of cheap oil. Instead, prices rose steadily. By the time BP had completed its purchase of Amoco and Arco in 2000, oil was averaging more than $27 a barrel, pushing BP to the $12 billion record profit that made the mergers appear to be a stunning success. Browne had made it look easy, and investors cheered.

Then the market turned on him. A recession hit the United States in 2001, cutting into oil demand, and prices began a two-year slide. The decline only intensified the cost-cutting fervor within BP. Browne slashed budgets while demanding that BP find enough new oil to replace depleting reserves. His strategy became known by the simple mantra "more for less." The constant squeeze on budgets spawned a backlash against Browne, who failed to notice that the rest of the company wasn't keeping up with his vision for where BP was headed. In the hallways of One St. James's Square, workers sometimes referred to the spritely CEO by the nickname "Elf"—"evil little fucker."

Beneath the veneer of what he fancied as his visionary leadership, Browne's cobbled-together business empire was warping
and buckling like a cheap coffee table left in the rain. The signs
of financial starvation were beginning to affect safety, and
one of the earliest signs came in mid-2000. Within a two-week
period, BP's Grangemouth refinery in Scotland experienced
three separate accidents, beginning with a power failure that
forced an emergency shutdown of part of the facility. A week
later, a steam pipe ruptured, and the resulting jet-engine-like
roar scared a pedestrian walking nearby, causing her to trip
over her dog and crack her ribs. Three days later, as a unit was
being restarted from the power failure, a fireball erupted, send-
ing workers scattering and shaking the surrounding town.
Other than the dog walker, no one was injured, but the accidents resulted in a record criminal fine of £750,000. Government investigators found that an emphasis on short-term costs
and production compromised safety and that BP's fractured
management structure inhibited development of a "strong,
consistent overall strategy for major accident prevention."[1]
The regulatory response was swift and fines were large for a
noninjury accident. BP claimed it had gotten the message, and
that it had shared the lessons it learned with its 11 other refineries throughout the world.[2] It hadn't. Later investigations would
find that BP largely ignored the causes of the Grangemouth
accidents, which would set a pattern for BP safety lapses.[3]

In the United States, however, where BP's worst lapses
were to occur, its operations failed to attract much regulatory
scrutiny. If accidents like those at Grangemouth had occurred
in America, BP would not have been required to report them to
safety regulators because no workers were injured. Workplace

safety inspections at refineries had become woefully inadequate, as regulators lacked the staff to carry them out with any frequency. Meanwhile, BP's offshore rigs were monitored by the Minerals Management Service (MMS), which was more a promoter of new drilling than a watchdog. If lessons were learned at Grangemouth, they weren't shared with BP's American refineries, which seemed to operate in a different world. Despite Browne's global accolades, few BP workers in the United States knew who he was. They might be working for BP, but many still thought of themselves as working for Amoco or Arco. Browne had integrated the companies financially, but he'd failed to integrate the cultures—a classic pitfall of big mergers.

One of the assets that BP acquired in its purchase of Amoco was a refinery in Texas City, Texas, about 40 miles south of Houston. The refinery, which sits on the edge of the Houston Ship Channel in Galveston Bay, was originally built in 1934 and is the third-largest in the country. It can produce 10 million gallons of gasoline a day, or about 3 percent of all the gasoline sold in the United States. However, Amoco had let maintenance of the refinery slip in the years before the sale, and upgrades had been deferred. That wasn't uncommon in the oil business. After all, BP would do much the same thing with its Forties Alpha platform. When companies bought these complex, industrialized assets, they typically set out a budget for beefing up the maintenance and factored that into the cost analysis for the deal. BP, though, never put money into the refineries it bought from Amoco. Rather than investing in new equipment, it continued to cut costs, further stretching the already overstressed equipment. Covering more than 1,200 acres, the refinery is like a small city, with an intricate system of pipes and containment tanks, all of which are subject to deterioration as a result of age and corrosion.

Once again, the markets' fluctuations came into play. By 2004, oil prices were averaging more than $37 a barrel, having risen 65 percent in two years. For BP's exploration division, that was good news. Higher prices meant more revenue. For the refining operation, though, it had the opposite effect. Refineries buy crude oil to process into gasoline and other fuels. A buyer the size of BP wasn't paying full market price, but the cost of raw materials for its refineries soared. To maintain its profit margin, it had to slash costs. The order came down to the refinery offices to cut expenses 25 percent across the board.

⸎

The cuts came just as deadly accidents at the refinery seemed to be rising. In March 2004, a ruptured pipe in an ultraformer unit, which provides blending components used to boost the octane of gasoline, triggered a series of explosions and fires. The Occupational Safety and Health Administration (OSHA), the government agency that polices workplace safety, cited the BP subsidiary that ran the refinery for 14 serious violations and fined it $63,000.[4] No one died in the blasts, but two months later a worker, Israel Trevino, fell to his death inside a storage tank. In September, a seal ruptured on a water pump, spraying 500-degree water and steam on three longtime refinery workers. Robert Kemp, who received burns to 70 percent of his body, was the only survivor. A day after the accident, Maurice Moore Jr. died from his injuries. Ray Gonzalez, a pipefitter who had worked at the refinery for 33 years, lingered in the hospital for more than two months. He endured daily, painful skin cleanings and numerous skin graft surgeries to repair the burns that covered 80 percent of his body. He died after spending his thirty-fifth wedding anniversary in the burn unit of a local hospital. Refineries are, as many people in the industry point out, inherently dangerous places. Workers are surrounded by thousands of gallons of hazardous and explosive chemicals, by hot gases and liquids under high pressure. The tiniest leak and a single spark can lead to catastrophe in seconds. That's why refinery operators stress safety. Hours are spent training employees, meetings routinely begin with "safety moments," and companies typically monitor the frequency and type of accidents. Yet BP didn't seem to have done any review of past accidents.

The plant's manager, Don Parus, had recently joined BP. He wasn't "legacy Amoco." During 2004, his concern at the mounting fatalities grew. He attended the funerals of workers who died, and made frequent appearances in Gonzalez's hospital room. Parus began looking into the death rate for the refinery during the previous three decades. His findings were alarming. Twenty-three workers had died at the plant, giving the refinery one of the worst safety records in the industry. Even more upsetting, no one in the company seemed to know the plant's fatal history. Parus put together a presentation for BP officials entitled "Texas City is not a safe place to work." He hired a workplace safety consultant, the Telos Group, to assess the safety culture, instructing the firm not to spare him the "brutal facts." The consultants surveyed more than a thousand workers, from low-level employees to top managers, and found the facts to be brutal indeed: many workers believed that each day on the job could be their last. The report included 56 pages of raw quotes pertaining to almost every aspect of the refinery's management and operations. Workers surveyed for the study overwhelmingly cited "making money" as the refinery's top priority. Second was "cost/budget," and third was "production." "People" came in last, in ninth place.

The worker comments by themselves should have been a wake-up call. Asked if they had ever been injured on the job, workers gave responses such as: "No, I run like hell and have ducked and dodged every hazard in this dump." Another answered, "Yes, I have been hurt and had management punish me and make a fool of me. Need I say more?" A third indicated that he had been hurt in a mechanical failure. "I was blamed in the end. I was not the root cause." Workers also said that their operational concerns about the aging refinery had been ignored since BP bought the plant. "It seems like it all comes down to money. We tell them we need it. They tell us they don't have the money. As soon as it blows up or someone gets hurt, there's all sorts of money."

Many of the respondents expressed fears about old pipes thinned by years of corrosion that might burst, similar to the accident aboard the Forties Alpha platform in 2003. BP had refused to modernize the pipe system. "We will have our most profitable period in years, but will not reinvest in the plant," one respondent said. Other workers said that routine maintenance was deferred without regard to the risk. The Telos investigators concluded: "We have never seen a site where the notion of 'I could die today' was so real for so many hourly people."[5]

Ralph Dean didn't need surveys. The plant gave him the creeps: "Every time I walked into that place, the hair on the back of my neck would stand up." Dean was a rigging supervisor who worked for a contracting firm hired by the refinery. Just as he had done with engineers, Browne had shifted much of the refinery work off the company's payroll, hiring outsiders instead. Dean's 16-hour shifts meant that he and his wife, Alisa, who also worked there, would arrive in the dark and leave in the dark, each day shrouded in a twilight of dread. "That particular refinery was the worst one I had ever been in. It was falling apart at the seams. They did just enough to keep the product flowing." He noticed a sign in one of the control rooms that reminded workers to "keep shutdowns to a minimum." Shutdowns cost money.

Despite the rise in oil prices, though, BP's refinery was making $100 million a month by late 2004, Parus would later testify. Alarmed by the Telos findings, Parus requested that his budget be increased to upgrade the facility and make it safer.[6] Instead, London once again insisted on budget cuts. As 2004 drew to a close, the refinery's health, safety, security, and environment division drew up its business plan for the following year. Among the key risks it listed was that the refinery "kills someone in the next 12 to 18 months."[7] It wouldn't take that long.

CHAPTER 5

"THERE'S NOTHING LEFT"

D eath unfolded before Glenn Alexander's eyes almost as if it were a dream. Unable to stop it, all he could do was watch in horror.

Alexander, an electrician, was walking along a catwalk about 70 feet above the ground at the West Plant of BP's Texas City refinery. It was late March 2005, and spring had come to South Texas. The Easter weekend was just a few days away, and the sun shone clear against the cloudless blue bowl of the sky. Even along the industrialized coastline that defined the 25 miles of the Houston Ship Channel, it was one of those days that could make the busiest refinery worker pause and take notice.

It had, until that moment, been a good day. BP managers had catered a lunch of fajitas from Gringo's Mexican Café, a local favorite. The meal was a reward for workers—most of them contract employees—who had completed another week without injuries. Now, they were returning to their posts. They climbed ladders and filed back to control rooms. Dave Leining, a stocky construction supervisor, and about 19 others headed for a portable office building nestled among the jungle of pipes and conduits. They were scheduled for a routine meeting to discuss the final steps to complete a turnaround of the ultra-cracker, which makes high-octane liquids that are blended into gasoline. The work had been going well, and the project was coming in on budget. Leining sat down in the office of Morris King with his back against the outside wall of the double-wide trailer, which was about 40 feet across and 80 feet long, divided into small offices with a larger meeting room at one end.

Outside, just after 1:15, Alexander began crossing the cat-walk, and the radio on his belt crackled with the alarmed voices of other workers.

"What's that coming out of that stack?"

"I hope that's water. God, I hope that's water."

Several hundred feet away, a clear liquid was spewing from a 100-foot-tall ventilation stack. The rusted pipe reached sky-ward, venting an isomerization unit, which processes chemicals used to boost the octane of gasoline.

—⊗≋⊗—

Crews had shut the unit down for maintenance weeks before. A refinery is a cluster of small factories. Each part of BP's 1,200-acre complex performed different functions that, when combined, resulted in the production of gasoline and other fu-els. But at any time, one or more of those factories might be shut down. The rest of the city would continue to bustle. Re-starting an operating unit, though, is one of the most dangerous moments in refining operations, and it is usually done during off hours, when fewer workers are around. Instead, the isom unit was being restarted on a busy Wednesday afternoon. Back in the trailer, Leining and his coworkers had no idea that the unit was being restarted. If they had known, some said later, they wouldn't have shown up for work.

The BP refinery, parts of which were 70 years old, had been expanded over the decades, and now included 30 units. Combined, they processed 460,000 barrels of oil a day, turning it into gasoline, jet fuel, diesel, and petrochemicals that might be used in BP's neighboring chemical plant to produce plastics. Only two other refineries in the United States were bigger—one in nearby Baytown, Texas, and one in Baton Rouge, Louisiana, both owned by Exxon Mobil.

As the Texas City refinery workers watched a geyser of liquid erupt from the isom unit, they knew almost instantly that it wasn't water. A vapor cloud began to form and billow from the spout, a sign that whatever the stack was belching forth, it contained hydrocarbons. That meant that it was combustible.

"Turn the equipment off!" a voice crackled over the radio.

The liquid ran down the sides of the vent stack, pooling on the ground. The vapors followed the flow of the liquid. As Alexander and others around the nearby workplaces began to grasp the mounting danger, they watched in horror as a truck started backing unwittingly toward one of the pools of newly formed liquid.

An image flashed into Alexander's mind. His wife, Lorena, was among the workers in the trailer with Leining and the others, less than 150 feet from the isom unit. He'd said good-bye to her just moments earlier, and now, like a nightmare in which he was helpless to prevent disaster, he knew what was about to happen.

———∞∞∞———

The trailer was made of flimsy fiberglass and aluminum, designed to be light and easy to move. BP had plunked it down in the middle of the refinery, a convenient location because workers wouldn't have to walk very far from the job site for meetings. It was never meant to withstand a blast of the magnitude it was about to endure. Few materials known to man could. Inside the trailer, Lorena Cruz-Alexander and her colleagues had no idea of the fireball that was about to engulf them.

Leining heard a bang that reminded him of a tailgate on a dump truck slamming shut. He turned to King. Was a delivery of dirt or something expected that day? Before King could answer, another boom burst through the conversation, and Leining stood up and turned toward the window. He got only halfway around before the floor began to shake violently.

———∞∞∞———

Outside, workers from around the area screamed at the truck driver to stop and get out. The hood of the truck blew open like the top of a teakettle that had been left on the stove too long. The engine revved, and flames danced from the undercarriage like angry fingers.

The driver and a passenger darted from the cab of the truck. Workers who had been frozen in terror only seconds earlier began to dash for whatever safety they might hope for in the instant before the bowels of hell opened.

On the catwalk, Alexander heard an ear-piercing whistle. Air was being sucked toward the ventilation stack with the roar of a freight train. He turned and ran back along the catwalk in the direction he had come from, away from the blast. It felt like running into a hurricane as he struggled against the vacuum building behind him.

The force of the explosion hit a millisecond later, launching him into the air. He fell forward and tumbled along the catwalk. He stumbled to his feet and ran—perhaps it was three steps, maybe only two, before he was flattened again by a massive explosion three times more powerful than the first.

Fire and debris flew in all directions, like some violent, tumultuous whirlpool of destruction. The explosions—as many as five of them all together—were heard and felt five miles away, on the island city of Galveston and amid the hubbub of downtown Houston. The blasts shattered windows of homes across Texas City as an acrid black cloud rose from the metal forest of the refinery.

Alexander could feel the seething maelstrom that had erupted behind him, but he kept running. As he looked over his shoulder, he saw a roiling fireball envelop the trailer where his wife was working. He knew that she was in grave danger. They all were. From his 70-foot perch, he was staring into the gaping maw of every refinery worker's worst fear.

Then it hit. A shock wave shot toward him from where the isom unit had been. As it raced forward, it seemed to warp the very air. "I've never seen anything like that. I have never seen air buckle and move like that," he would recall later.

The impact slammed him to the floor of the catwalk again. He pulled himself up and looked back at the trailer—at Lorena's trailer—but there was only a concrete slab blown clear by the force of the blast. A couple of twisted ribbons of steel were all that remained of the supports that had held the trailer in place. "It was completely gone. There was nothing but the floor. The desks, the file cabinets, the bodies were all scattered outside."

With the help of a coworker, he managed to make his way to the ground. He stumbled, dazed, through the flaming battleground that had been his workplace. Metal pipes were twisted like bread ties. Buildings were swatted aside like models smashed by an angry child.

He moved toward the inferno, toward the still-burning isom unit and the flaming vestiges of what had been the trailer where Lorena worked. He mumbled something about wanting to help her, but a coworker pulled him back. Safety procedures required all surviving workers to get to safe zones, designated places away from the disaster to protect them in case of another blast.

Once there, Alexander fell to his knees and prayed. He prayed that Lorena had somehow survived the explosion, the searing heat, and the concussive force of the shock wave that had come from, essentially, next door. But even then, he knew that his prayers were in vain.

Workers wandered into the safe zones, bloodied, their clothes in tatters. Some were choking or vomiting. Others had shards of glass embedded in their faces from the force of the blast.

Back in the trailer, as he stood and began to turn around, Leining was knocked to the ground as debris from what had been the trailer wall swirled around him as if someone had opened the door of an airplane at 20,000 feet. He could feel the pressure crushing him, and the noise made him feel as if he were standing in the backwash of a jet engine. David Crow, who'd been standing in the doorway to King's office, was blown off his feet, thrown across the hallway, and slammed into the floor of his own office. In the torrent of debris that followed, the men were battered by pieces of the trailer wall, by airborne filing cabinets, by chairs and papers and an unidentifiable litany of office contents.

Everything became dark and silent as Leining was overcome by pain. Gradually, the light came back, and he began to see images that looked like "little figurines." As his vision returned, he realized that he was on his back, staring at what had been the trailer ceiling. A red fireball was rolling overhead, followed by a shroud of smoke as thick as tar.

Moments later, as the smoke cleared, he heard his cell phone ringing in his pocket. He later learned that his wife, also a worker at the refinery, was frantically trying to call him, but he couldn't reach his phone. His right arm was pinned behind him by the debris that had fallen on top of him. Across what had been the hallway, Crow lay amid a pile of debris and heard what he believes was a divine voice telling him to get up. "I felt God had his hand on my shoulder," he said.

He pulled himself from the rubble. Looking toward the isom unit, he saw a huge fire raging at the base of the vent stack. Bleeding from his head and disoriented, he managed to stumble to a nearby road and clamber into the back of a pickup truck as another worker drove him to safety.

Jack Skufca, who had also been in the meeting in King's office, found himself lying near the top of piled-up rubble. He could hear the moans of injured workers under him. He spotted a radio a few inches away, just close enough for him to reach. The blast had fractured his skull and ruptured his aorta. He managed to pull the radio toward him and call for help, giving rescuers his location.

Leining, meanwhile, remained pinned by the debris, unable to move. He could see that the remnants of the trailer were on fire; flames leaped around him. His left hand was pressed close to his chest. Realizing that the microphone of his two-way radio was still attached to his collar, he fumbled until he found the mike button and squeezed, calling for help. Nearby, a fire roared, making it difficult to hear.

"This is Dave Leining," he said. "We're in Morris King's office. We're trapped in this trailer."

Seconds later a voice responded: "You can't be. There's nothing left."

Ralph Dean was working on a forklift when the blast churned through the refinery like a tornado in midtown Manhattan. He raced to the scene, arriving before any rescue workers. His wife, Alisa, and her father were both inside the trailer. He tried to dig for her, pushing aside the burning debris, but he was overwhelmed by the heat. Just a few feet away, in a makeshift parking lot for the trailer staff and others working nearby, a line of cars and trucks was burning. He knew that they would explode when the flames reached their gas tanks. The scene reminded him of a combat zone. "There were all kinds of things coming out of the air. Balls of fire. Pieces of pipe. Wood. Pure destruction. It was like someone had made a bomb run on us," he said. He jumped in a forklift and began moving the vehicles away, pushing five of them free of the site. Some of them blew up anyway, but at least they didn't rain more destruction down on the trailer. If Alisa was still alive, maybe, just maybe, he'd bought her some time.

Buried beneath the rubble, Leining could see Dean, and called for him on the radio. He picked up a two-by-four and began waving it, telling Dean to look for it, but Dean couldn't see it. Dean kept digging as rescue workers arrived, and eventually they reached Leining. As he was pulled from the pile, Leining realized that what he'd been waving was little more than a nub of wood, six inches long at most. Battered, dazed, and weakened by the blast, he had thought he was waving a plank that would tower above the rubble. Rescuers put Leining on a Life Flight helicopter to a Galveston hospital with two broken ankles. It would be almost a year before he could walk again.

At the site of the decimated trailer, Dean kept digging, frantically searching for Alisa. He found Skufca and pulled him out, then continued his search. As he tried to pry apart the shattered remains of the trailer, he uncovered a body. It took him a moment to recognize who it was. "It turned out to be Pop" (his father-in-law, Larry Thomas). "He had already passed." While he was devastated, Dean knew that he had to keep digging. He had to find Alisa. When he finally reached her, crumpled under a bookshelf in what had been her office, he thought she was dead, too, looking limp and lifeless among the charred debris. Miraculously, though, as he pulled her out, he found that she was alive. He rushed to rescue workers, who took her to the hospital. She suffered a range of injuries, including a broken back and severe lung damage from heat and smoke inhalation.

Crow, who was also pulled from the remains of the trailer, had a fractured ankle and a broken back. They were among the lucky ones, the seven workers inside the trailer who survived. Fifteen others, including King and Lorena Cruz-Alexander, didn't. Beyond the 15 deaths, the disaster injured almost 200 workers, many of them severely. Many were burn victims; others lost limbs.[1]

―――― ∞∞∞ ――――

Outside the refinery fence, in downtown Texas City, everything had been quiet at the main fire station that morning. After lunch, firefighters had begun doing routine chores around the station when they felt the blast and immediately knew that something had gone wrong at one of the refineries in the area. Within minutes, they could see the smoke rising above the BP

complex. Under a long-standing arrangement, city firefighters were to assist the refineries' own response teams as needed.
Captain David Teverbaugh, a 22-year veteran of the department, led his men to where BP was supposed to have a command post. Instead, they were greeted by chaos as terrified
workers poured out of the refinery gates.

Unsure of the situation, Teverbaugh got a BP worker to
drive him into the refinery. As the van made its way through
the devastation, Teverbaugh felt as if he were witnessing a nu-
clear holocaust. Fires burned everywhere, and the wounded
wandered around like zombies. He was dropped off about 200
feet from the exploded isom unit, and the driver left. None of
the BP response teams were in place. Everyone was still reel-
ing from the blast. Teverbaugh found himself standing, alone,
at what felt like the center of an apocalypse. He called back to
his firefighters and told them to bring everything they could.
They went to work looking for victims. Everywhere he looked
he saw debris, and it was impossible to distinguish one pile from
another. As he worked, BP's own firefighters began to arrive.
Teverbaugh found one kneeling on the ground, and as he approached, he realized that the man was holding the head of
an unconscious worker, trying to keep it out of the water and
chemicals that were flowing on the ground. The BP firefighter
pointed to two other injured people nearby. Teverbaugh hadn't
even seen them as he approached because they were covered
in debris. "You just couldn't see them until you were right on
them," he said.

They continued to dig for what seemed like hours, sifting
through the charred detritus of the trailer. Teverbaugh believes
that he found the body of Lorena Cruz-Alexander, although to
this day he still isn't sure. Gradually, it became clear that the
few survivors that they'd found were all they were going to find.

"We just dug and dug until finally one of my firefighters just said, 'Captain, there's nobody left. This is a body recovery now.' It was pretty horrific," Teverbaugh said. "The people we found were just burned up."

Firefighters and rescue workers pulled hundreds of victims from the site, straining the resources of local hospitals. Two helicopters worked in shifts to evacuate the wounded. As one took off to shuttle victims to nearby hospitals, another would land to take on more wounded. With each trip, the workers still standing were left, amid the debris, to wonder why it happened.

As soon as it became clear that all the survivors had been recovered, Teverbaugh and his crew were escorted off the premises, and they returned to their station. For the next eight days, BP retained sole control over the blast site before federal investigators and police were allowed in. In the weeks that followed, as the first answers began to emerge, injury gave way to anger and eventually to outrage. While determining the cause of the blast would take months, a few facts began to trickle out even as the northeast corner of the refinery complex still smoldered.

The first was that the dead had died unnecessarily. Twelve of the fifteen who were killed were, like Lorena Cruz-Alexander, in the temporary trailer. Among them were James and Linda Rowe, who were both killed in the trailer, and who left behind a daughter, Eva, who would relentlessly pursue BP through the courts. Many of those who were killed or injured in the trailer were attending a meeting that could easily have been held outside the refinery fence or even around a table at a local restaurant. They were what are known in refinery parlance as "nonessential personnel." In other words, they didn't need to be there. Indeed, two years later, BP used a converted

Walmart store in a Texas City strip shopping center for many of its training and management meetings.

But at the time of the explosion, despite the common industry practice of keeping trailers far from operating units, convenience was the prevailing concern. Trailers were brought as close to the operating units as possible to make it easier for personnel to move from the work site to the meeting rooms.

⸎

The problem, though, wasn't the trailer. The problem was what was happening about 120 feet away, in the isom unit. The facility had been shut down for maintenance, and, with the repairs finished, workers were restarting the unit. The hours-long process involves gradually filling the unit with the volatile chemicals used to make gasoline. Gauges are supposed to monitor the levels to make sure that the unit restarts safely. A key monitor, the transmitter that measures fluid levels inside the isom unit, wasn't functioning. Workers began filling the distillation tower in the isom unit anyway, unaware that the readings from the fluid-level indicator weren't accurate. An alarm that should have warned them of an excessive fluid level in the tower didn't sound. Normally, during a restart, the tower is filled with 3 to 10 feet of liquid hydrocarbons. Inside the isom unit's control room, the operator thought the level of hydrocarbons was decreasing when it was actually about to overflow, rising to 120 feet. The final fail-safe, a level sight glass that lets workers actually see the fluid level, was so dirty and unreadable that the person manning the tower couldn't see the brewing catastrophe.

Meanwhile, workers heated the fluids too quickly, causing them to expand and overflow the tower. They spilled into an antiquated "blowdown drum," basically a large metal reservoir at the base of the 100-foot-tall vent stack. The over-heating caused some of the fluid to evaporate, forming the gas cloud that workers saw just before the blast. Another alarm that should have alerted workers to the high fluid levels in the vent stack also failed to sound. Investigators later found that BP managers knew that the level alarm needed repair, but decided to defer the maintenance until after the unit had been restarted.[2] The mechanical failures, though, paled in comparison with the bitter realization that the dead had died needlessly, victims of a procedure that never should have been done when they were around. "If they were going to start something up, they should have [had] all of those people go home to have a nice Easter weekend," A. J. Ramos Jr., whose father, Art Ramos, died in the trailer, told the *Houston Chronicle* in the days after the explosion. Ramos, like others in Texas City, spent the Easter weekend of 2005 planning a funeral. Many more sat at the bedsides of loved ones who were recovering from burns and other injuries.

Later that day, in his hospital room in Galveston, Dave Leining watched the television coverage of the fire and shook his head in disbelief. The TV reporters didn't even know what they were filming, he told his wife. They were showing pictures of the coke pit, a flat, open collection area for carbon deposits that are a by-product of the refining process. The more he looked at the image, though, he began to realize that what he had thought was the blackened hole of the coke pit was actually the concrete slab for the trailer where he'd been sitting, chatting with Morris King. All that remained were a few twisted metal struts. There really was nothing left.

—————

The Texas City refinery had, indeed, killed again, as the health and safety division had warned could happen months earlier. Government investigators would find that, for years, the refinery had languished as BP cut budgets, which translated into delayed maintenance and deferred upgrades.

The disaster put BP atop a dubious list. It now led the nation in refinery deaths, accounting for more than a quarter of all deaths industrywide and more than 10 times the number at Exxon Mobil.[3] John Browne's dream of building the world's biggest oil company, of surpassing Exxon Mobil, was beginning to unravel.

CHAPTER **6**

IMMINENT HAZARD

The ground was fresh with Easter funerals. The holiday weekend, normally a celebration of renewal and redemption, had instead become a bitter indictment. Easter eggs went unhunted, candy uneaten, brightly colored dresses unworn. A sense of mourning hung over the holiday. The first of the victims was laid to rest the day after Easter. The funerals stretched from the cities interspersed among the sprawling industrial complexes south of Houston to as far away as North Carolina. Glenn Bolton, Lorena Cruz-Alexander, Rafael "Ralph" Herrera Jr., Daniel J. Hogan III, Jimmy Ray Hunnings, Morris "Monk" King, Larry Wayne Linsenbardt, Arthur Galvan Ramos, Ryan Rodriguez, James and Linda Rowe, Kimberly Smith, Susan Duhan Taylor, Larry Sheldon Thomas, and Eugene White. They were mothers and fathers, sisters, sons, daughters, husbands, and brothers. Now they were gone, simply from trying to earn their daily bread in a place where warnings went unheeded and maintenance was ignored until it became an open invitation for death.

———&&&———

Texas City, Texas, knows tragedy. Most of its residents live in the shadows of the huge chemical plants and refineries that line the Houston Ship Channel, the man-made waterway that has become an aquatic freeway between America's fourth-largest metropolitan area and the Gulf of Mexico. Residents also know the dangers of refinery work; they know that the sprawling industrial complexes mix dangerous chemicals, and that sometimes things go terribly wrong. For decades, Texas City residents have made that bargain—weighing the risks against high-paying jobs. Sons and daughters follow their fathers and mothers to the refineries, knowing that something as simple as a spark could turn them from workers to victims in an instant.

———&&&———

Long before the explosion ripped through BP's refinery, Texas City bore the scars of industrial disaster. On a different clear spring day, almost 58 years earlier, a French-flagged freighter, the SS *Grandcamp*, floated beside the Texas City wharf, having taken on a load of ammonium nitrate. The *Grandcamp* had been a Liberty ship, serving in the Pacific during World War II. After the war, it was given to the French to help in efforts to rebuild Europe. Part of that rebuilding process included supplying Europe with vast amounts of ammonium nitrate, a powerful fertilizer. It's also a powerful explosive. The terrorist Timothy McVeigh used it in 1995 to blow up the federal building in Oklahoma City.

Longshoremen loaded more than 50,000 of the 100-pound bags into the belly of the *Grandcamp*, fuel to help Europe re-plant, to help feed a war-ravaged continent. A few of the bags seemed warm to the touch, but the longshoremen continued with their work. Before long, smoke began billowing from the cargo hold, and attempts to extinguish the smoldering fire in the hold were in vain. The water around the ship's metal hull began boiling from the heat as bag after bag of the fertilizer ignited. The members of the town's fire department boarded the *Grandcamp* and tried to put out the flames. Moments later, they were all dead.

The explosion wiped away a thousand buildings in the area—homes, offices, chemical plants—like someone clearing a table with a sweep of an arm. The first explosion set off a chain reaction as other ships, some also carrying ammonium nitrate, erupted, followed by waterfront chemical tanks and refineries. Shock waves were felt as far away as Louisiana, and in Galveston, 14 miles to the south, pedestrians were knocked off their feet. The final number of the dead was impossible to determine because many were vaporized, but the best estimates put the loss of life at 567. More than 5,000 were injured.[1]

It remains the worst industrial accident in American history, and on the afternoon of March 23, 2005, it was still a painful enough memory that some in Texas City feared that history was repeating itself.

This time, however, the blast was much smaller; the fatalities, mercifully, far fewer; and the blame far easier to assess. Even in this city that knew disaster far better than any community should, even in a place where danger was embedded in so many paychecks, anger began to simmer.

David Teverbaugh, the fire captain, had stood in the blast zone, looking at the burned remains of a woman whom he believes was Lorena Cruz-Alexander. She was so covered in debris that at first it had been impossible to distinguish her body among the rubble. "Those people who make the decisions to cut corners, to maximize profits, to compromise safety, will never see what I saw," he said. "They will never allow themselves to be exposed to the chemicals we crawled around in to save the few that we did. They will never talk to me, to the other responders, or to the families that they devastated. The message was clear to me that we are expendable if there is a chance to profit." Soon after the explosion, Teverbaugh moved his family out of Texas City.

Five years after the blast, Alisa Dean, one of the few who survived from the trailer, still suffers from chronic back pain and breathing problems that will continue for the rest of her life. Her burned lungs work at half the capacity they did before the accident, making it impossible for her to hike, camp, hunt, or enjoy most other outdoor activities the way she and her husband, Ralph, did before the accident. The Deans reached a settlement with BP, but Ralph says that he would "give them every nickel back if they gave me back my father-in-law and made my wife whole."

As the *Deepwater Horizon* disaster unfolded, with the incessant coverage focusing on the growing spill, Dean found himself thinking of the victims, especially the families of the 11 who died. "You hear about the clean-up, but you don't hear about the victims. You don't hear about what they're going through, but I have a real good idea what those families are going through. I am sure they are having trouble like we did."

⸺⸻◈⸻⸺

Residents who live in the shadows of Texas City's refinery row are accustomed to fires and explosions, to the warning sirens and the procedures for "shelter in place": Close windows and doors, turn off the air conditioning, stay indoors, and await evacuation orders. Refinery fires were common enough that when Teverbaugh and his crew first heard the explosion on March 23, they knew instinctively that they should jump in their trucks and head toward the east side of town, toward the swath of massive industrial complexes that rise like steel forests along the Houston Ship Channel.

Gradually, though, it became clear that the explosion at the BP refinery wasn't just the result of a dangerous working environment. Many workers who'd survived the blast, such as Ralph Dean, never returned to the plant. Dave Leining wasn't one of them. Like many who worked at the plant, Leining came from a refining family. His father and other family members had all worked at the plant, and they had all grown up with the risks. His cousin was to die at Texas City two years later in yet another accident. It took Leining a year to recover from his injuries, to be able to walk again, but when he finally could stand on his own feet, he returned to work for BP. Only then did he realize there was no going back. After a few months, he resigned after what he described as a dispute over safety. There's a difference, Leining said, between working in an environment that's inherently risky and working in what the BP refinery had become. "It's a dangerous place to work, but it shouldn't be a hazardous place to work." BP officials didn't seem to understand that distinction. Companies that operate dangerous workplaces have a responsibility to make safety paramount. At BP, safety too often seemed to be viewed as overhead.

Few at the refinery knew who John Browne was when the soft-spoken Englishman showed up in Texas City the morning after the explosion. He'd arrived late the previous evening from California, where he'd been attending an Intel board meeting.[2] The next morning, he went to the refinery, meeting with workers and listening to their "harrowing stories."[3] Browne, who had been to Texas City only once before,[4] assured them that BP was responsible for what happened on its property, but he brushed aside reporters' questions about whether the company had pushed the refinery beyond its limits to capitalize on rising gasoline prices. "We do not produce day to day just to make a quick buck," he said, insisting that BP always had "safety first in mind."[5] Then, with the press conference over, Browne quickly left town.

Browne and his handlers had debated whether he should bother coming to Texas City, and some of his top lieutenants had thought it wasn't worth the trouble. The head of BP's worldwide refining operations, John Manzoni, was vacationing in Colorado and later complained in an e-mail to a colleague that he was summoned to accompany Browne "at the cost of a precious day of my leave."[6] In keeping a low profile, Browne was following the advice of BP's public relations staff, who suggested that the explosion would quickly fade from the national headlines. After all, it was a long weekend because of the Easter holiday, and the nation's attention was focused on Terri Schiavo, a Florida woman in a vegetative state whose husband had gone to court to end her life, sparking a national political battle. During his brief time in Texas City, Browne assured the surviving workers that BP was committed to doing what was right, and that he would launch an investigation to determine what had caused the explosion.

Like all oil company executives, Browne was aware of the fallout from Exxon's disastrous handling of the *Valdez* tanker spill in 1989. He remembered how slow Exxon officials were to arrive on the tainted shores of Alaska's Prince William Sound, and how unconcerned they appeared to be about the environmental impact. By going to Texas City quickly and vowing to investigate the cause of the accident, Browne hoped to set a different tone.[7]

⸺⸺

In the days after the disaster, though, BP angered outside investigators with its eight-day lockdown of the site. Refinery officials said that the area wasn't safe because of structural damage and a benzene leak, but investigators worried that the company might be tampering with evidence. They never found any proof to support those concerns. Less than two months after the explosion, BP released the preliminary findings of an internal probe (known as the Mogford report, after BP's safety chief at the time) as proof that the company was taking responsibility for the disaster. It outlined revisions to procedures for starting up refinery units after maintenance, but it blamed low-level personnel for a series of failures that led to the blast. Unit managers and operators "greatly overfilled and then overheated" the raffinate splitter, a cylindrical tower that separates light and heavy components of gasoline. The investigation also acknowledged that the number of deaths and injuries had been "greatly increased" by the location of the temporary trailers. However, it was quick to note that the trailers had been placed near the isom unit because BP's hazard reviews "did not recognize the possibility that multiple failures by isom unit personnel could result in such a massive flow of fluids and vapors to the blow down stack."[8]

It was still early in the investigation, but the report showed the direction in which BP investigators were heading. Human error—or workers not following the rules—meant that BP itself wasn't to blame. This wasn't some broader failure of Browne's leadership; this was a few bumbling workers who just hadn't followed the rules. "The mistakes made during the start-up of this unit were surprising and deeply disturbing," said Ross Pillari, the head of BP America at the time.[9] The attempts to blame workers for the accident infuriated the United Steelworkers union, which represented workers at the plant. "We knew it wasn't operator error, it was in fact a failure of process," union president Leo Gerard said. Federal investigators were disappointed. They'd hoped that Browne's statements the day after the explosion had meant that the company would take a hard look at the management lapses behind the accident. "The level that they are trying to put blame on is too low. This is something that should be looked at higher up," Glenn Alexander said at the time.

BP was in full damage-control mode. Browne, once the media darling, dodged interview requests while the company floated the trial balloon of the internal investigation. No one was fooled. Blaming employees as the cause of industrial accidents is a "premature stopping point" in any investigation, according to guidelines developed by the Center for Chemical Process Safety. Errant employees aren't the root cause of an accident but rather a symptom of the cause, the center said.[10] Ironically, the committee that developed those guidelines was chaired by a BP executive who was involved in the internal probe into the Texas City explosion.

However, BP didn't get the final say in the investigation. That fell to a little-known federal agency, the Chemical Safety and Hazard Investigation Board (CSB). The CSB was created under the Clean Air Act, an antipollution law passed in 1990. The board was designed to conduct independent investigations of chemical accidents, much the way the National Transportation Safety Board (NTSB) investigates airplane crashes. Like the NTSB, the CSB can't issue fines or citations. All it can do is make recommendations on how similar accidents can be prevented. Even in that limited role, though, the CSB struggled. For the first eight years of its existence, it received no funding. President Bill Clinton almost abolished it before Congress pressured him to give it a meager budget of $4 million in 1998. Even after that, the CSB had a rocky start, marked by political infighting. What was then the General Accounting Office (GAO) blasted it in 2000 for an unacceptable backlog of investigations, questionable spending, and a lack of defined procedures and policies.[11] The GAO report led to changes, and the CSB's activity began to pick up. While it had done only two investigations in 2001, by the time of the Texas City explosion, the CSB had 11 active cases under way.

While the CSB began its investigation, lawyers for the victims' families were already uncovering disturbing information. BP had twice considered equipping the vent stack with a flare, which would have burned off excess gases before they reached a critical level, but had declined to do so. Company officials must have thought it was a good idea, though. Documents revealed in the civil litigation found that before the blast, BP had submitted a permit application to the state environmental agency indicating that a flare had been installed. BP also claimed that relief valves were being monitored when they weren't. One expert testified that he believed the omissions and inaccuracies were intentional, which BP denied. A former state technical expert called BP's representations in the permit application "incorrect" but said that BP still would have received an emissions permit if it hadn't declared that it had the flare.[12] While it may have been irrelevant to government bureaucrats, a flare might have saved the lives of the 15 who died. The excess hydrocarbons would probably have burned away safely at the top of the stack, and the accident would have been avoided, the CSB found.

Despite BP's frequent public statements about its commitment to safety, workers and contractors grumbled that inside the refinery, little was changing. Just two months after the blast, refinery managers knowingly operated an ultraformer unit with thinning and eroding pipes for three days, acknowledging that doing so was "a serious safety risk."[13] It was the same ultraformer that had been the site of the explosions in March 2004 that resulted in the $63,000 OSHA fine. Those explosions, too, had resulted from thinning pipes. Four months after the March 2005 explosion, another blast rocked the Texas City plant. This one was far less severe, and no one was killed, but because it had come so soon after the earlier fatal accident, Carolyn Merritt, the head of the CSB, was incensed. BP had been reluctant to cooperate with the board's investigation. As far as Merritt was concerned, BP didn't seem to be getting the message. She worried that the accident rate at the refinery was accelerating and that whatever lapses had led to the fatal blast in March would be repeated, with even more disastrous consequences. The second blast could indicate a systemic failure within BP. In an unprecedented move, the CSB declared that BP's management lapses presented an "imminent hazard" to its workers and to the public at large. It called on BP to assemble an independent panel that would examine the safety culture at the company's five U.S. refineries. The CSB, a tiny government agency with a minuscule budget, was determined to force changes on one of the biggest energy companies in the world. The watchdog had found its teeth, and it was about to sink them into the Texas City refinery investigation.

As its lead investigator, the CSB chose Don Holmstrom, a refining industry veteran, lawyer, and union leader who was known for his expertise on safety issues. Holmstrom had left the CSB during its political turmoil and was working with community groups in Colorado to develop safer working environments. His earlier work for the board, though, had left him with a reputation for thoroughness, and his 18 years in refining made him uniquely qualified to lead the Texas City investigation. He tabled his love for outdoor adventure, from whitewater kayaking to buffalo hunting, and moved from Colorado to Texas City.

As the CSB's scrutiny mounted, Browne's vision for BP was showing other signs of stress. Two weeks before the second blast at Texas City, the company suffered another embarrassment. Hurricane Dennis roared into the Gulf of Mexico in mid-July, an unusually powerful storm for so early in the season. Dennis churned through the oil-producing areas of the Gulf with winds of as much as 140 miles an hour, and companies cleared crews from the rigs ahead of the storm. The timing couldn't have been worse for BP. Three months earlier, it had hauled its massive Thunder Horse semisubmersible production platform into position in about 6,000 feet of water about 150 miles southeast of New Orleans. Just getting the massive platform there had been an ordeal.

Built in a South Korean shipyard, Thunder Horse's construction had run behind schedule and crews had worked furiously, finishing the work as the platform piggybacked on a special heavy-lift vessel plodding its way from the Pacific, around Africa's Cape of Good Hope, to the Gulf. BP had invested $5 billion in building the platform, the largest ever constructed. The size of three football fields, it weighed almost 60,000 tons and could support a crew of almost 300, more than twice as many as the *Deepwater Horizon*. While the *Horizon* was designed to drill underwater wells, Thunder Horse would sit over wells that had already been drilled, tethered by 16 massive anchors embedded in the sea floor, and pump the oil from the reservoirs deep in the earth. Thunder Horse was the vanguard of Browne's exploration strategy—finding only the biggest and most lucrative oil reserves. The Gulf represented a unique opportunity. Geologists believed that vast oil deposits lay untapped along the outer continental shelf, but finding them meant pushing the limits of drilling technology. BP had discovered the Thunder Horse field in 1999, and it quickly became mired in controversy. It was originally named Crazy Horse, after rock singer Neil Young's backup band, but descendants of the Lakota Sioux warrior and spiritual leader had protested, claiming that use of the name was sacrilegious. The Lakota tribe had filed lawsuits against companies that had used the name on everything from beer to strip clubs. BP agreed to the tribe's request and changed the name.

Bob Malone, who was to become chairman of BP America in the summer of 2006, replacing Ross Pillari, would later participate in an official ceremony to make amends. A plaque bearing the platform's name was buried in a sacred area of tribal land in South Dakota, and Malone made an offering of sweet grass and smoking tobacco. Tribal leaders wrapped him in a ceremonial blanket and proclaimed him an honorary Lakota. The ceremony was so moving that Malone's wife, who is half Navajo, was in tears by the time it was over, and Malone himself would recall it as one of the most moving and emotional experiences that he had during his 30-year career with BP.

———— ∞ ————

With both the field and the platform renamed, BP began drilling multiple wells, some at depths of more than 25,000 feet below sea level. In all, 25 wells were to be drilled, dotting the sea floor with "production trees" of wellheads that looked almost like small villages. They were spread across an area about four times the size of Manhattan, and each was connected to the huge platform floating overhead, which would pump the oil to the surface. It was an unprecedented undertaking, and much of the technology had to be either modified from existing well designs in shallower water or designed specially to account for the unique challenges of drilling at such depths and pressures. Thunder Horse, then, would be the proof that BP was now at the forefront of the global search for oil. It wasn't producing oil yet, but it was in place over what BP hoped would be one of the most prolific fields in the Gulf. Company officials predicted that the field held one and a half billion barrels of oil. Oil prices had been climbing steadily for several years and were nearing $60 a barrel. At those prices, the total bounty of the Thunder Horse field could be worth more than $90 billion to BP over several decades. When the platform reached its full pumping capability, it would more than double BP's oil output in the Gulf, producing 250,000 barrels of oil a day. If that oil were converted to electricity, the Thunder Horse field by itself would generate enough energy to power six and a half million homes—more than all the households of New York, Los Angeles, Chicago, and Houston combined.

———— ∞ ————

In the late summer and fall, the Gulf of Mexico lives up to its nickname, Hurricane Alley. Its warm waters and prevailing winds make it a prime breeding ground for massive storms that build in circulation and intensity as they move westward from the Atlantic. In decades of offshore drilling, the oil industry has perfected a routine for handling the storms, narrowing the time that crews must be gone from the rigs to a precise window. For platforms such as Thunder Horse, production continues even after the crew leaves, until moments before a storm arrives; then the platforms are shut down by remote control from shore.

Hurricane season officially starts at the beginning of June, but the most intense storms typically don't form until September. The 2005 season, though, wasn't typical. It was to become the most active season of Atlantic storms on record, starting with Tropical Storm Arlene—which swirled into existence just a week after the season began—and ending with Tropical Storm Zeta, which dissipated in January 2006. The season produced 28 storms—so many that the National Weather Service ran out of letters for naming them and began working its way through the Greek alphabet as well. Of those, 15 became hurricanes, and 7 of them were major, including two of the costliest and most intense ever—Hurricanes Katrina and Wilma.

Hurricane Dennis was among the seven major storms, though not nearly as severe as Katrina. It formed in the eastern Caribbean in early July, ripping across Grenada and building in ferocity as it churned across the waters toward Cuba. It struck the island nation with Category 4 force, the strongest storm ever so early in the year, then moved on to Haiti, swung through the Gulf, and came ashore in the Florida Panhandle. It left 89 people dead and as much as $6 billion in damage. BP's crew had left Thunder Horse two days ahead of its approach, and when they returned just hours after it passed, the vision that greeted them was like a kick in the stomach. The massive monolith was listing to its port side like a torpedoed ocean liner, its upper platforms leaning into the water. Years in the making, the symbol of BP's newfound exploration prowess was in danger of sinking.

———◦◦◦———

Browne was on his way to a gala at the Greenwich Maritime Museum when he got the call from Tony Hayward, his "turtle" who was running BP's exploration operations. Hayward told him that something had gone terribly wrong with Thunder Horse. "I don't fully understand what's happened," Hayward said.[14] He soon would, and the answer pointed to a much deeper problem within BP.

Dennis was a fierce storm, but its path took it far to the east of Thunder Horse. The platform had to endure high winds and rough seas, but waves never topped 30 feet, and it never took anything close to a direct hit. Even if it had, the platform had been designed to withstand the fiercest gales and roughest seas. Something else had happened. Within days, underwater inspections determined that the hull hadn't suffered any storm damage. A salvage crew of more than 900 workers and 15 support ships was dispatched to right the platform. They slowly began pumping seawater from its pylons. At first, the platform's list was so extreme that the port side of its top deck, which was supposed to be 15 stories above the surface, touched the water, and workers could clamber onto it directly from the ships.

Eventually, Hayward had his answer to what happened. The huge platform had been hobbled by a six-inch line of pipe that was improperly plumbed, allowing water to flow freely between ballast tanks that help keep the platform level. As the

platform tipped, one-way valves that had been installed back-
ward were forced open. Rather than blocking the flow of water
into the bilges, they pumped more water in, filling the huge
port-side legs with water. The inflow of water ruined 30 giant
motors and corroded miles of electric cable on the platform.

Thunder Horse had been hobbled by careless mistakes.
The platform had to be hauled to a Texas shipyard for repairs,
which cost almost $250 million. By May 2006, it was once again
on the verge of "first oil." After all the maintenance work, BP
engineers prepared for a routine test of the subsea system, the
network of pipes and conduits connecting the treelike villages
of wells spread out across the seafloor. The test showed a leak.
This was a different problem, unrelated to the platform issues
that engineers had been wrestling with. The wellheads in the
Thunder Horse field were far too deep for any human diver to
reach. All the work had to be done by undersea robots, known
as ROVs (remote operating vehicles). The ROVs scoured the
array of pipes and pumps, looking for the source of the leak,
which could have been as small as a single valve or a cracked
seal on a pipe. Crews injected ink into the system, then sent
a robot down to send back video. In the closet-sized control
room aboard the platform, the ROV operators spotted the ink
pouring through an inch-long gash in a piece of pipe leading to
a "manifold," a junction that pulls together lines from dozens
of wellheads. As the submarine moved on, the operators found
another leak, and then another. Across the entire system, welds
were corroding and pulling apart.

As BP was later to be reminded when it tried to cap its runaway Macondo well after the *Deepwater Horizon* explosion,
the extreme pressure a mile below the surface complicates

everything. In the case of the Thunder Horse field, the equipment on the seabed had sat idle while repairs were completed on the platform above. The intense pressure had forced hydrogen atoms into the alloys used to weld the pipe joints. The hydrogen made the welds brittle, and the pressure from the tests had caused them to break down.

About three-fourths of the underwater network, stretching out for miles from the area below the platform, had to be hauled back to the surface and repaired. It would be a long time before Thunder Horse would see first oil. The delay angered BP's partner in the project, Exxon Mobil, whose executives had always viewed BP with disdain and believed its engineering capabilities to be inferior. Lee Raymond, Exxon's chairman, was still bristling over Browne's "green" agenda, and he'd decided that enough was enough. BP's bumbling was costing Exxon money. He sent engineering teams to the Gulf to oversee the repairs to the subsea network. This wasn't a job he was willing to trust to the number crunchers at BP.

Hayward now had his answer. He now knew what had happened to Thunder Horse, and the answer wasn't pretty. It went far beyond the fact that the company's technological flagship had been unable to weather a storm. BP's failures were ones of basic engineering and oversight. The Thunder Horse project had begun in the late 1990s, when oil prices were hovering near $10 dollars a barrel and BP was acquiring Amoco and Arco, hoping to wring profits from the deal by cutting costs. Browne's strategy had been to fire huge swaths of engineers in favor of accountants. Rather than being a symbol of BP's oil-finding prowess, Thunder Horse had become a monument to its lack of engineering skills.

"When we started Thunder Horse, the reality is we didn't have sufficient depth and competence of engineering skills,"

Hayward was to say later. "So we set off on what was for the oil industry putting a man on the moon without really the engineering underpinning to achieve that. I think if you step all the way back, you'd say that's the real root cause of all the issues we've had at Thunder Horse."

⎯⎯ ⚬⊗⚬ ⎯⎯

That lesson, though, seemed lost on Browne. Known for jetting around the world giving speeches, he continued to tout his "Beyond Petroleum" strategy, seemingly ignoring BP's traditional petroleum operations to such a degree that crises were imminent. Browne and his lieutenants saw no connection between the problems with Thunder Horse and the Texas City explosion. After all, they had happened in two completely different divisions, operations that were autonomous and that had little contact with each other. One was a tragedy that BP wanted to blame on worker error; the other was an engineering mishap. It would take another crisis or two before the common cause became clear.

CHAPTER 7

THE
PRICE
OF
FAILURE

B ob Malone missed his own celebration. After years of working for BP in Alaska and London, Malone was finally returning to his native Texas. To celebrate, he'd planned a weekend gathering of family and friends at his ranch near the west Texas town of Sonora in the summer of 2006. Less than a day after he'd arrived, he got the call. A BP pipeline on Alaska's North Slope was leaking. It was a small feeder line, and the leak was tiny, but Malone knew that the fallout would be as loud and as bitter as if he had personally piloted the *Exxon Valdez* onto the rocks. After all, it was an oil spill. It was Alaska. And it wasn't the first time this had happened. In fact, BP's oil was coagulating on the tundra for the second time that year. Malone made his apologies, ditched his own party, and headed to Alaska.

Malone had been running BP's global shipping business, but he was well aware of the company's faltering record in the United States. In 2005, he'd been at the Greenwich Maritime

Museum with Browne when Tony Hayward called about Thunder Horse. In fact, Malone had been giving the speech that night. The next day, he was supposed to leave for a family vacation, a photo safari in Africa, but instead, he wound up flying to the United States to help with the maritime issues involved in the platform's salvage operation. Now, Thunder Horse was just one of the items on a growing to-do list. Five weeks earlier, Browne had asked Malone, who resembles a rugged version of newsman Jim Lehrer, to take over BP's U.S. operations. Malone's job was to repair BP's tattered corporate image. Things hadn't gotten better for BP after the Texas City fires and the Thunder Horse fiasco. Even before the platform problems were resolved and before the corrosion of the subsea manifolds had been discovered, a new crisis had ensnared BP's U.S. operations.

Federal regulators accused the company of having used its aggressive trading operations to manipulate markets for gasoline and propane as far back as 2002. BP's trading operations were a sore spot with other oil majors. Typically, the big oil companies trade futures contracts to protect them against price swings on oil they produce or that they buy for their refineries. In many cases, integrated oil companies don't refine the same oil that they pump out of the ground. Instead, they rely on the global markets for buying and selling oil, locking in prices by using futures contracts to protect themselves against swings. These contracts are traded through in-house trading desks, but all of the transactions are tied to oil that the company is actually buying or selling. This is known as "physical trading," rather than speculation, which is the buying and selling of contracts purely for profit.

BP's trading, however, went beyond physical trades. Its traders aimed to make money by buying and selling futures contracts across a range of products and speculating in the markets. Its trading floors were much more aggressive than the typical in-house shops of other oil companies. Its traders were paid on short-term contracts that offered big bonuses for quick returns, creating a profit-driven culture that was focused on the near term. BP also had another advantage: It produced oil in key markets around the world, it bought crude for its refineries, and it sold gasoline and other refined products in many of the same markets. In other words, BP was intimately connected to every level of the petroleum economy. This insight gave BP a powerful source of information that few other companies could match.

Traders are notoriously jealous of others' success, and BP had long drawn the ire of its competitors. It began to draw scrutiny from regulators, too. In 1998, London's International Petroleum Exchange fined BP £125,000 for conducting a false trade, which can affect market prices.[1] Some competitors saw this as a slap on the wrist. Then, in 2003, BP again came under fire for allegedly manipulating the price of light sweet crude, better known as West Texas Intermediate, a grade of oil preferred by many refiners. The company didn't admit to any wrongdoing, but it paid the New York Mercantile Exchange $2.5 million to settle claims of deceptive trade practices. It was hardly a deterrent. BP spent ten times as much on its initial solar project to kick off Browne's "green" program. None of the traders involved in the violations were disciplined.

The government claimed that in 2004, though, BP's propane traders in Houston crossed the line. Propane is a by-product of crude oil and natural gas refining that is sold as a fuel for everything from outdoor grills to agricultural equipment. BP traders attempted to corner the market as propane prices rose, driving prices even higher for some seven million consumers. In

2006, just before Malone took over his new job, the Commodities Futures Trading Commission moved in, bringing an indictment against the company. The evidence was damning. Traders' calls had been recorded, and on one, a BP manager told the head of the propane desk, "Dude, you're the entire [expletive deleted] propane market."[2] BP tried to dismiss the comments and others like them as traders' braggadocio, but it had been only three years earlier that prosecutors had released tapes of Enron's traders cheering California wildfires and laughing at the idea of little old ladies left in the dark, deprived of electricity by their greedy actions. BP's culture of compliance was suspect, but internally, the whole matter was dismissed as "rogue traders." After all, they and their superiors knew that their calls were being taped. How could the company have condoned such a blatant attempt at market manipulation? From Browne on down, BP executives insisted that the trading debacle, the Thunder Horse incident, and the Texas City explosions were unrelated.

It was an increasingly incredible argument, but BP officials stuck to it. Now, on his way to Alaska, Malone knew that he was headed into tricky territory. BP had been operating in Alaska since the 1960s, and John Browne and other top executives, including Malone, had trained there. The producing fields of Prudhoe Bay, on Alaska's frozen, remote North Slope, had been the company's cash cow in the years before BP bought Sohio. Internally, the Alaskan properties were often referred to as "the green mountain of cash."

The Trans-Alaska Pipeline had been approved by one vote, and ever since, it had remained a hotly debated project. Now, much of the infrastructure was 30 years old, and parts of it were showing signs of corrosion. Workers for both BP and Alyeska, the consortium that operated the pipeline, began to see signs of neglect. When they tried to warn their supervisors, they felt that their concerns were ignored or belittled by supervisors who didn't want to deal with the problems. Feeling as if no one inside the company would listen to them, they turned to an outsider named Chuck Hamel, a former oil broker who had become an activist for pipeline workers. Over the years, workers had learned to trust Hamel, and what they were telling him about corrosion along the transit lines that transport oil from the wells to the main pipeline worried him.

In the fall of 2005, Hamel contacted Scott West, the lead investigator for the Environmental Protection Agency's office in Seattle. Eventually, West flew to Alaska to hear the workers' concerns firsthand. "They spoke authoritatively. They spoke from positions of knowledge and expertise," West said. They were concerned about the level of sludge building up in the transit lines and the corrosion that was eating away the pipes underneath the sludge. Oil pipelines collect silt and debris carried in the oil, which is deposited along the lines. Over the years, the sludge builds up, like an artery clogging with cholesterol. To fight the sludge accumulation, pipeline companies typically run a cylindrical device called a "smart pig" down the line. Smart pigs travel inside the pipeline and use electronic scans to test the wall for corrosion or weakness. The pig clears out the sludge and takes readings on the integrity of the pipeline walls. Done periodically, it's a good preventive against decay.

Just as in the Texas City refinery, though, BP's pipeline operations were under pressure to cut costs every year. Smart pigging was expensive, and it required shutting down the pipelines. The sludge cleared out by the pig had to be cleaned up in accordance with the strict environmental rules covering the Trans-Alaska Pipeline. Rather than pig the line, BP put corrosion-fighting chemicals into the pipeline flow and used metal tags, called "coupons," to measure the level of corrosion. Coupons, though, float in the flow of the oil inside the pipe. The corrosion that the workers were most worried about was occurring under the blanket of sludge that was building up along the pipeline walls, so the bacteria that were eating away at the pipe went undetected. BP also visually inspected the outside of the pipelines for signs of corrosion. Rather than maintain its equipment, BP tended to wait until it broke down, then repaired it. "The company was saving pennies but risking tens of millions of dollars in a catastrophe," West said.

Still, there was little that West could do. The EPA didn't have jurisdiction over the pipelines. However, by meeting with the workers, West established that BP managers knew about the workers' concerns. Just a few months later, in March, one of the BP transit lines finally gave way, spewing 270,000 gallons of crude onto the tundra and into a frozen lake nearby. A BP worker on the line called West in Seattle and told him, "There's oil everywhere."

Had transit line breakage happened in the summer, when the ground was thawed, it could have been a major environmental disaster. In March, when the tundra was still frozen, the oil was easier to contain. Because it had soiled a lake, West intended to prosecute BP under the Clean Water Act, which assesses fines based on the amount of oil spilled. Meanwhile, the U.S. Department of Transportation, which regulates pipelines, ordered BP to begin using smart pigs to inspect all the transit lines.

When it did finally send pigs down the lines, the results were stunning: 16 miles of pipe had corroded to the point where leaks were a serious threat. Then came the second, far smaller leak in the summer of 2006 that sent Malone off to Alaska. He'd run BP operations in Alaska before moving to London to take over the shipping business, and he knew he'd better get to the North Slope and see the problems for himself. John Browne had asked him as a personal favor to take on the new job as chairman of BP America, and Malone, somewhat reluctantly, had agreed. He'd planned on retiring soon, and now he was being asked to tackle some of the company's biggest problems. He thought he knew what he was walking into. He'd known, of course, about the disaster in Texas City, about Thunder Horse, and about the earlier Alaskan spill. He knew that the company faced years of rebuilding, both of its facilities and of its public image. The latter effort, though, couldn't begin as long as problems kept erupting. Malone was loyal to Browne, but he wasn't a turtle, and he'd already been making plans to retire to Texas. Perhaps better than any other executive at BP, Malone understood that the company's culture had to change in order to fix what was so badly broken. He could fix BP's problems in America, but Browne would have to trust him.

In some ways, Malone's new job only added to BP's unwieldy bureaucracy. Technically, he was the highest-ranking BP official in the United States. Browne designated him the public face of BP in America. With West's case, BP was now facing three separate criminal investigations: Texas City, Alaska, and the trading scandal. This just wouldn't do. Browne was busy building his image as the twenty-first-century oil executive, the newer, greener face of energy. How would it look to have BP's oil staining the tundra in the same state where the *Exxon Valdez* ran aground?

While the day-to-day operations still reported to the heads of their respective business units, Malone had unique authority to intervene when it came to safety, compliance, and ethics. He may have been BP's public face, but he also served as its corporate conscience. Malone had sole discretion to spend money or do whatever he felt was necessary to prevent another accident.

Even before he reached Alaska, he had a pretty good idea of what the problems were. He was familiar with the operations there, and he knew the friction between the workers and management. Toiling in the frigid climate and the perpetual darkness of the Alaskan winter might make pipeline workers prone to complain, but Malone knew that at least some of the concerns that the workers had raised with Hamel had merit. The warnings were there, and the company didn't listen. He knew, too, how BP created incentives for managers. As in other parts of the company, they were on a rotation that was more like a Mixmaster. They might be in their supervisory role for six or ten months before moving on to another job. If they wanted their bonus, they had to meet the specified goals, and those goals almost always involved money. Scott West saw the same thing as he pressed his investigation. "There was always this attitude that the managers would come in and cut, cut, cut, then get out and leave the consequences to their successors," he said.

Surveying the damage on the North Slope, Malone didn't take long to decide that the only possible decision was to shut it down. Turn off the spigot on America's biggest domestic oil flow. Browne, who was in Venice at the time, thought that shutting down the entire field "seemed a little extreme."[3] But he had declared Malone the top BP decision maker in the United States, and publicly he backed Malone's call. Such singular accountability was rare within BP's fragmented management structure, but this time, Malone made it clear that he was in charge. Until BP could figure out what was wrong, until it could be sure of the pipeline's integrity, no oil would get through, he decided.

The sudden drop in oil supply had immediate repercussions. The next day, crude oil futures jumped more than $2 dollars a barrel on the prospect that the Prudhoe Bay oilfield could be shuttered for weeks. The summer driving season wasn't over, and gasoline prices had been steadily creeping up from just over $2 a gallon at the start of the year. After the shutdown of Prudhoe Bay, they topped $3 a gallon. Analysts warned that a prolonged shutdown would be devastating to the economy. Soon, the entire country would pay the price for BP's neglect.

CHAPTER 8

THE
FIXER

The morning was cold and overcast, with a wet wind whipping among the glass-and-steel office towers of downtown Houston. The weather contradicted Texas stereotypes, but it fit the solemn mood of the proceedings. The 11 members of the Baker Commission sat behind a long table in a conference room of Houston's Four Seasons hotel. Led by former secretary of state James Baker III, the panel had been commissioned, and funded, by BP in an attempt to forestall more federal backlash and find answers to the causes of the Texas City explosion—answers that were more objective and believable than the findings of BP's earlier internal investigation. Union leaders and even some federal investigators were skeptical.

BP's internal investigation had placed most of the blame on low-level workers. This time, the investigation dug deeper, analyzing the cultural and management failings that led to the accident. The Baker panel studied not just Texas City, but all five of BP's U.S. refineries, and it found a disturbing pattern among all of them. BP assembled the panel in the fall of 2005, after the second explosion at Texas City that summer prompted the warning by the Chemical Safety and Hazard Investigation Board of an "imminent hazard" at the plant.

--- ∞ ---

The decision as to how the independent review should be structured and who should conduct it was left to BP. Browne called Baker and asked him to lead the group.[1] The two men had met through political channels, and Browne considered Baker a "proper and correct person." Baker was exactly what Browne wanted. He was "a man of considerable standing to undertake that investigation,"[2] but also someone who, as a prominent Texas lawyer and perennial political appointee, understood the oil business.

Baker is the walking definition of a tall Texan and is a long-time friend of President George H. W. Bush. He served as Ronald Reagan's chief of staff and later as treasury secretary, and Bush named him secretary of state in 1989. Baker also became a key operative in Republican party politics, earning the nickname "the Fixer." When there was a problem, Baker could find a solution. He oversaw George W. Bush's 2000 campaign and led the fight for the Florida recount that ultimately got Bush elected. In Houston, Baker is a civic icon whose name adorns one of the city's most prominent law firms. At 80 years of age, he still maintains an office high atop One Shell Plaza, one of downtown's landmark skyscrapers, and often can be seen walking in the pedestrian tunnels that link Houston's office buildings or spotted dining at his favorite Chinese restaurant.

Baker vowed to pursue the BP investigation even if it led all the way to St. James's Square, and he warned Browne that the panel's findings might require costly remediation by BP. In an interview the day he officially agreed to lead the panel, Baker punctuated his comments with words like "thorough," "credible," and "let the chips fall where they may." He insisted that neither he nor the commission was "in the tank for BP."

BP's expanding base of critics still wondered how impartial Baker would be. After all, he had deep ties to the oil industry, and he had some indirect connections to BP. His law firm had done some work for the company, although Baker personally hadn't, and Baker's public policy institute at Houston's Rice University had named John Manzoni, the BP refining executive who complained that the Texas City explosion had cost him a day of vacation, to lead an energy task force.

Completion of the study took more than a year. As the commission members took their seats behind the long hotel conference room table with its clip-on pastel skirt, thick three-ring binders were handed out to the press. The findings in their glossy 300 pages were pointed. Inspections were long overdue; near catastrophes were never investigated; known equipment problems such as pipes thinning from years of use had been left in disrepair for more than a decade. Tests of alarms and other emergency shutdown systems either weren't done or were done improperly. What attention BP did pay to safety was focused on preventing personal accidents, avoiding slips or falls or vehicle accidents. When BP officials such as Browne talked about the company's stellar safety record, they were looking at individual injury statistics. The bigger problems—making sure that processes like starting an isom unit were done safely—weren't emphasized, the panel found. Managers weren't measured on process safety, only on reducing the number of personal injuries. Worker surveys showed a pervasive sense that safety wasn't a priority in the refineries.

The same "entrepreneurial culture" that Browne prided himself on having infused into BP was at the core of the problem. It didn't hold managers sufficiently accountable for process safety. Nor did it create an adequate avenue for workers' concerns to be heard. Long before the explosion, worker surveys had found persistent concerns about safety, but even after the blast, BP hadn't implemented an system for responding to those concerns.

What's more, any concerns about safety that managers had were lost in a maze of feel-good, consultant-driven programs and policies, many of which overlapped when they were articulated to employees. BP had 18 "group values." Only one mentioned health and safety, and even that was rather vague: "no accidents, no harm to people, and no harm to the environment." BP also had four "brand values"—being performance-driven, innovative, progressive, and green—that made no mention of safety. The only policy that addressed safety directly was BP's code of conduct, which included a host of other company policies. The myriad values and priorities diluted any message about safety, the panel found.

The blame for that lack of emphasis went all the way to London, to Browne himself. "Browne is generally noted for his leadership in various areas, including reducing carbon dioxide emissions and developing the use of alternative fuels," the study found. "In hindsight the panel believes that if Browne had demonstrated comparable leadership on and commitment to process safety, that leadership and commitment would likely have resulted in a higher level of process safety performance in BP's

U.S. refineries." The tone for safety, the report noted, has to come from the top.

—∞∞∞—

Browne accepted the report on BP's behalf and vowed to embrace the ten recommendations it offered for making the company's refineries safer, including appointing an independent safety monitor to oversee the company's operations for five years. In Texas, it was seen as an important first step. In London, though, the report was viewed more as an attack. While BP's track record in America was foundering, Browne was still considered a business celebrity in the United Kingdom. The BBC referred to the Baker Commission report as "extremely savage," and the Sky News cable channel called it a "devastating blow to the oil giant's reputation." The *Telegraph* newspaper, which typically takes a pro-business stance, spoke of "BP's Day of Shame."

Financially, though, the report had little impact. BP's share price had little reaction; the company's finances remained strong, and its operating profit would end the year 7 percent higher than 2006. Many investors had feared that the market reaction might be worse. As one London stock analyst noted at the time, however, the financial sector doesn't care about an industrial accident or a few workers getting killed. For Browne himself, the report was a bitter referendum on his tenure as chief executive and the price he was willing to pay for his expansive strategy to transform BP. He had planned to retire at the end of 2008, but just days before Baker's panel released its report, Browne said that he intended to step down in the summer of 2007, about 18 months sooner than he had planned. Although his decision had little to do with the Baker Report, the timing seemed curious. As the Baker panel's meeting ended, BP held a press conference of its own at another hotel a few blocks away, carefully timed to allow reporters to get from one session to the other. The BP meeting began with a briefing from a public relations representative discussing the location of the hotel's emergency exits, as if to show reporters how safety-conscious the company had become. BP, Browne told reporters by video feed from London, understood that it needed to put a higher priority on safety, and he called the report a "hard-hitting critical analysis."

Then Browne fired up the spin cycle. As critical as the report was, he said, it should be noted that it was "about *an* aspect of BP." Baker's panel had looked only at U.S. refinery safety, and nothing in the report indicated that there were any wider problems in BP's global organization. The refinery issues, he insisted, were unrelated to the pipeline corrosion in Alaska or the rogue trading operation that had attempted to corner the propane market. Manzoni, the refining chief, sat stoically beside Browne, who professed his confidence in his lieutenant.

———❀———

As critical as the Baker Report was of BP and of Browne himself, it was still preferable to what BP officials knew was coming. By then, they had a sense that the CSB's report would be far more scathing. While the CSB hadn't released all its findings yet, two months earlier it had publicly expressed concerns about the deep budget cuts for the Texas City refinery that had been mandated by BP's London headquarters. The board echoed what plaintiff's attorneys pursuing the company on behalf of the victims had been saying for months—that the legal fight was uncovering troubling documents related to cuts in maintenance and training costs.

The Baker panel was limited in its scope from the beginning, which had created a critical shortcoming in its findings. In keeping with BP's segmented management structure, the Baker panel looked at only one aspect of the business, not at how broader events might have conspired to promote safety lapses across the enterprise. As a result, the panel said that it didn't uncover evidence of deliberate cuts in safety funding. Browne latched onto the findings and redefined them, saying that there was no evidence that cost cutting had resulted in safety lapses.[3] The panel, though, had chosen its words carefully. Baker himself noted later that the scope of the investigation didn't extend to the impact of broader cost cutting, merely stating that no safety programs had been cut. The fragmented corporate structure and the frequent shuffling of key managers meant that while safety might be talked about, or even emphasized, managers were rewarded for meeting budget goals. Documents unearthed in the thousands of civil lawsuits related to the explosion revealed internal e-mails showing management's almost pugilistic attitude toward cost cutting. After some refinery managers questioned another round of cost cuts in 2004 and the impact that it might have on already stressed operations, a supervisor responded: "Which bit of 25 percent don't you understand?"[4]

Nevertheless, Browne persisted in using the Baker Report to beat back any criticism linking cost cutting to the deaths in Texas City or the lapses in other parts of the company.[5] The report also noted that Browne had improved his attitude toward safety and that he had confessed to BP's employees that he hadn't been "sufficiently passionate" about the issue.

During the press conference, Bob Malone sat silently at the front of the room. Most of the questions were directed at

Browne. It was the first time he'd openly addressed reporters since the Texas City disaster. Yet much of the responsibility for implementing the commission's recommendations would fall to the soft-spoken Malone. Later, pressed on Browne's insistence that there was no connection between the refinery explosion, the Thunder Horse problems, and the pipeline corrosion, Malone acknowledged that he saw some overlap. In the months since he'd taken over BP's U.S. operations, he had spent little time in his Houston office. Instead, he had traveled to different BP facilities and talked with workers, and he'd found that one issue kept coming up. Workers didn't feel that they could voice concerns, either because they'd be punished for questioning safety or because their concerns would simply be ignored. The issue became a key focus of Malone's efforts to reform BP's troubled U.S. operations.

Overall, the Baker Report came with a dose of public relations polish, a veneer of criticism that, while it may have appeared "savage," was still largely acceptable to BP. After all, what company can't improve safety? What chief executive would argue against embracing practices that will set a new industry standard? In Washington, Carolyn Merritt, the head of the CSB, knew that the Baker Commission hadn't gone far enough. BP had acted on her recommendation that it appoint an independent panel, but it had also largely controlled the scope of the investigation, and she feared that the limitations were deliberate. BP's upper management seemed to be walling itself off from the crisis that was growing within the company. "Something was very wrong, not just at Texas City but in the corporation itself," she would say later. "It goes back to the culture of the corporation that was driving for maximum profits over everything else."

The CSB released the results of its own investigation two months later. This time there was no BP press conference, no video link to Browne's office, no one-on-one interviews with BP executives, and no promises to accept the findings. In fact, Browne later admitted that he never even read the report.[6] The CSB called a public hearing in Texas City that drew about 200 people, many of whom submitted public comments. Its 300-page report and 200-page appendix of key documents (without three-ring binders or glossy paper) was the most exhaustive the agency had ever undertaken, and its findings were far more stinging than anything Baker's group had uncovered. "The combination of cost-cutting, production pressures and failure to invest caused a progressive deterioration of safety at the refinery," Merritt declared. The key difference in the findings of the two investigations was the role that cost cutting played in the Texas City tragedy. The CSB found that Browne's mandate to cut 25 percent across the board in 1999 and again in 2004, coming after Amoco's cuts earlier in the decade, had directly contributed to the accident and that the cuts were made even as BP's own internal surveys were revealing increasing safety concerns at the refinery.

The cost cuts had reduced the refinery's staff to a critical level. Without the technology improvements, the refinery's operations depended more than ever on front-line personnel; yet the report found that those were the same workers whom BP was cutting. At the same time, BP had cut its annual training budget in half, to about $1.5 million, and reduced its training staff from 28 to 8. With fewer trainers, BP switched to computer-based training sessions, which the head of that department told investigators was "a business decision to minimize costs."

In the first round of cuts in 1999, BP hoped to eliminate almost $1.5 billion in costs from its worldwide refining business.

At Texas City, managers had slashed a range of programs, including safety and maintenance, and laid off or outsourced engineers, supervisors, and inspection staff. The report found that, by late 2002, BP's refining results were worse than its top managers had expected, and they declared that the division was in "crisis mode" to reduce costs further.

BP failed to assess the impact of the repeated budget cuts on an aging facility. Some of the most fatal decisions involved the "blowdown drum," the stack from which workers at the refinery had first noticed clear liquid spewing just prior to the explosion. The drum was a 1950s-era safety valve, used long past its prime. Had BP spent the money—about $150,000—to install a flare system, the explosion either wouldn't have happened or would have been far less severe, the CSB found. As far back as 1991, refinery officials had considered installing flares, but had decided against it because of the expense. The refinery had had an accident in 1994, when Amoco still owned it, that presaged the 2005 disaster. The isom unit's distillation tower was overfilled, and the level monitors failed to sound a warning. In 2002, a consultant suggested that BP install a flare system, but BP rejected the proposal because it hadn't conducted inspections on the unit that would have been required to install the flare.

OSHA had criticized the use of blowdown drums and a vent stack for more than a decade before the explosion. In 1992, it had deemed a blowdown drum and stack on another unit unsafe and recommended that the unit be fitted with a flare. Even then, blowdown drums were considered technological dinosaurs in the refining industry, and few companies other than BP still used them. At the time, BP had a total of 22 blowdown drums at its five U.S. refineries.

The CSB also criticized BP's practice of placing trailers at various places inside the refinery, especially when units were being restarted. The location of the trailer in which Lorena Cruz-Alexander, Morris King, and others died violated BP's own policies, which called for them to be set no closer than 350 feet from equipment like blowdown stacks. The trailer flattened in the 2005 explosion was just 120 feet from the isom unit. CSB investigators were so disturbed by the trailer's proximity to operating equipment that in October 2005 they urged the petrochemical industry to review trailer placement at refineries nationwide and suggested that any distance under 600 feet was unsafe. Two weeks after the blast, BP revised its own policy to 500 feet.

—————⊗∞⊗—————

The CSB didn't stop with its criticism of BP. It also turned a harsh light on the Occupational Safety and Health Administration (OSHA), the government agency charged with inspecting workplaces and protecting workers. In the aftermath of the explosion, OSHA cited BP for 300 "willful violations" at the refinery and slapped it with a fine of almost $21.5 million, which was a record for the agency at the time. The CSB pointed out, however, that OSHA hadn't conducted a planned inspection of the refinery in six years, and a *Houston Chronicle* review of OSHA records had found that unplanned, or "surprise," inspections at BP and other Houston-area refineries had lapsed for five years.

Before the 2005 explosion, "we were not paying enough attention to refinery safety," said Jordan Barab, OSHA's deputy director, who worked for the CSB at the time of the explosion. The CSB called on OSHA to bolster its refining industry oversight. The CSB also chastised OSHA for refusing to turn over key information about its inspection history at the plant. "We want OSHA to step up its inspection and enforcement at BP and all U.S. refineries and chemical plants, and to require those corporations to evaluate the safety impact of mergers, reorganizations, downsizing and budget cuts," Merritt said.

───∞∞∞───

The CSB report was a stinging rebuke of BP's leadership during the Browne era, laying the Texas City disaster squarely at his feet. It revealed a company that chased profits and Wall Street–pleasing financial performance without sufficient regard for how its operations were carried out. It ended up placing its workers at risk to save money. A BP spokesman said that the company had "strong disagreement with some of the content of the CSB report, particularly many of the findings and conclusions." Unlike the Baker Report, the CSB's findings were largely brushed aside by BP officials. In his autobiography, Browne discusses the Baker Commission's findings in detail but makes no mention of the CSB.

Others, though, were taking notice. The victims' families and the United Steelworkers applauded the breadth of the investigation, which went far beyond the limited scope of the Baker Report. On the same day that the CSB report was released, the U.S. Attorney's Office in Houston confirmed that, months earlier, it had launched a criminal investigation into the accident. Charges were imminent. BP, already facing two other criminal investigations into its trading business and Alaskan pipeline operations, now found itself the subject of a prosecutorial hat trick.

CHAPTER 9

THE
FALL OF
THE SUN
KING

Darkness descended on the Sun King in the form of a judge's scolding. Lord Browne of Madingley wasn't used to being addressed in such a manner, even by a member of the judiciary in his native England. The words were blunt and lacking in appreciation for his stature as head of one of the world's largest corporations.

In careful judicial language, High Court Justice David Eady called Browne a liar and a bully and accused him of trying to smear the reputation of a former lover. The judge had reason to be angry. Browne, by his own admission, had lied two weeks earlier about how he'd met the young man, a 27-year-old Canadian former prostitute named Jeff Chevalier.

Browne and Chevalier had been lovers for four years, and the dark-haired Canadian had become the executive's frequent companion, accompanying him at social functions and on business trips worldwide. Now, not only was a London newspaper about to reveal Browne's homosexuality to the world, but it was accusing the chief executive of misusing BP funds to support his young lover. Chevalier had had the use of Browne's secretary to keep his schedule, book dental appointments, and upgrade his airline tickets, even when he traveled alone. A BP employee was once dispatched to Toronto on Browne's orders with $5,000 in cash to give to Chevalier so that he could buy a last-minute ticket to return to London. Browne had helped Chevalier set up a business selling cell phone ringtones and had tapped his contacts at some of London's top law and accounting firms to handle the paperwork. He then persuaded BP executives to sit on the company's board, Chevalier claimed.[1]

Browne had gone to court, asking the judge to prevent a London tabloid, the *Mail on Sunday*, from printing the allegations and the details of his affair with Chevalier, but in answering a few simple questions, Browne was less than truthful. He'd told Eady that he had met Chevalier in Battersea Park, his favorite jogging spot, across the Thames from his Chelsea home. That was the story that Browne and Chevalier had agreed upon during their four years together, a lovers' ruse to shield Browne from the embarrassing truth: The two men had met through an online escort service, Booted and Suited, that catered to a high-class, if closeted, clientele. No one could know the truth of how they met, Browne insisted. Instead, he concocted the jogging story and so convinced himself that it was true that even when he and Chevalier wound up on opposite sides of a court battle, he believed that his former lover would honor the fiction.[2]

———— ∞ ————

Browne saw himself as a master at dealing with probabilities, but his life, both personal and professional, was spinning out of control. BP was steeped in legal troubles in America, where rabid trial lawyers were hoping to get rich by connecting Browne directly to the explosion in Texas City. They wanted him to give a deposition, which he had no intention of doing. BP's lawyers were fighting it, arguing that Browne was too far removed from the events in Texas City to provide any worthwhile testimony. But the case was on its way to the Texas Supreme Court, and even though the justices had a reputation for being business-friendly, he'd hoped that the issue would have been resolved much earlier. Other business leaders had come to his defense. Industry trade groups in the state had filed friend-of-the-court briefs arguing that allowing high-level executives of global companies to be deposed so easily would "set back Texas' efforts to attract business to the state."[3] Even so, things were getting messy in courtrooms on both sides of the Atlantic.

Browne's relationship with Chevalier had deteriorated in what was about to become a very public manner. Their time together had been his first long-term relationship, which developed only after the death of Browne's mother in July 2000. For almost two decades, his mother had been his constant companion, sharing his home and following him to his different postings in the United States and Britain. She accompanied him to dinner parties and other social functions. He never told his mother that he was gay; although he tried a few times, she seemed not to want to hear it. Having survived the Third Reich, his mother knew something of public intolerance, and she'd admonished Browne from an early age: "Don't trust people with your secrets."[4] Those words helped him keep his homosexuality hidden and any relationships clandestine for most of his life. Once his mother was gone, he was overwhelmed by loneliness. In many ways, BP itself had become his real love, the relationship that mattered most in his life. The round-the-clock demands of running a global company, though, only seemed to underscore the depths of the emptiness in his personal life.[5]

Nine months after he'd found Chevalier through the escort service, the young man moved into Browne's £5 million flat, which occupied an entire floor of the building on Cheyne Walk. Chevalier quickly assimilated into the jet-setting lifestyle that, until then, he could only imagine. He joined Browne in dining with British Prime Minister Tony Blair, hobnobbing with celebrities like rock singer Elton John, and attending the opera in Salzburg and Venice in the private boxes of royalty. He followed Browne to the executive's other favorite hangouts, a flat on Venice's Grand Canal and a friend's villa in Barbados. Together, they shared private jets, cars, and a personal butler.

For the first couple of years, Chevalier was awash in luxury, sipping fine wines, eating extravagant meals, and jetting from one exclusive party to another. But his role as Browne's companion became awkward. He was introduced to countless celebrities, political leaders, business luminaries, and other dignitaries, but his role remained oddly vague. No one seemed to ask about his relationship with Browne, and Browne never offered an explanation. Oddly, Browne's high-profile socializing with a young man in tow failed to lead to any public speculation about his sexuality. Friends like Blair, who once had a private dinner at the Chelsea flat with Browne and Chevalier, must have known, but they said nothing. Others either were oblivious or didn't care. When Browne bought the apartment in a palazzo on Venice's Grand Canal, 1,200 guests were invited to the housewarming party. Princess Michael of Kent, who had met Chevalier on several earlier occasions, seemed confused about his role. She told him, "You must be a brilliant pianist." When he said he wasn't, she replied, "Well, whatever you do I am sure you are brilliant."[6]

Browne's constant socializing, his embrace of a world that still felt foreign to Chevalier, became increasingly stifling to the

younger man. "After a while, it became almost unbearable. Bil-
lionaires remembered me, but I did not remember them," he
would say later.[7] The pressure to remember Browne's friends
and business associates weighed on the young Canadian, and he
began to have panic attacks. Browne didn't understand why his
lover couldn't adapt to his lifestyle.

Chevalier felt trapped, as if he were another ornament in
the library of luxuries with which Browne surrounded himself.
Browne told him what to wear, what parties to attend, and how
to act. "Virtually every aspect of my life was managed by other
people," he said. "I felt like a puppet." As Chevalier began refusing to attend certain functions, the friction between the two
men grew.[8]

─────⊗☙⊙─────

It was Browne who ended the relationship, casting Chevalier
from the upper echelon of high society to which he'd grown accustomed, even as he detested it. Chevalier returned to Canada,
suddenly penniless. In mid-2006, as the Alaskan pipeline corrosion crisis unfolded, Browne agreed to "assist in the first year
of me transitioning from living in multimillion-pound homes
around the world, flying in private jets, five-star hotels, 2,000
pound suits, and so on, to a less-than-modest life in Canada,"
Chevalier claimed in court documents.

Browne had already given Chevalier money to set up
the ringtone business, but the company quickly faltered. He
continued to support him in the months after the relationship ended, but as Chevalier's demands for money continued,
Browne finally decided that enough was enough. On Christmas
Eve 2006, Chevalier sent a final, desperate plea via e-mail: "I
have nothing left to lose," he wrote. "I am facing hunger and
homelessness after four years of sharing your lifestyle. . . . The

least I am asking for is some assistance. . . . Please respond. . . .
I do not want to embarrass you in any way, but I am being cor-
nered by your lack of response to my myriad attempts at com-
munication."[9] Browne saw this as a veiled threat, which it was.
He had no intention of supporting Chevalier forever, and he
decided to ignore the e-mail. When he didn't get a response,
Chevalier sold his story to the *Mail on Sunday*, which contacted
BP, saying that it was looking for a comment from Browne. BP's
chief press officer reached Browne in Barbados and told him
that the story was supposed to run the following week. The
paper wanted a comment in the next few hours.[10]

Browne panicked. He felt suddenly vulnerable. The threat
of a tell-all story about his private life was opening "the cup-
boards of the past, full of ghosts," he would later tell the BBC.
"I was still terrified about being known as being gay. Even then,
I was actually terrified about being known as having a boy-
friend, widely."[11]

Browne's closest advisors within BP, fearing just such an
outcome, had urged Browne to reveal his homosexuality publicly, and had even scheduled a radio appearance for him to do
it, but he couldn't go through with it. Now, Browne's reluctance
to address his sexuality had become a pure instinct to protect
himself no matter what. He felt that he'd been betrayed. He'd
trusted someone with his secrets, and now those secrets would
be used against him. He hired a law firm and got an injunction to
halt publication of the story. On the phone from Barbados with
his London lawyers, Browne was asked to recount the details
of the relationship. How had he and Chevalier met?[12] Browne
had really never come to terms with the duality of his life, even
though many of his BP associates knew or suspected that he was
gay. "I had never openly admitted to strangers that I was gay and
now I was talking to a lawyer whom I did not know, on a long-

distance phone call, with my Barbados host in earshot. I just could not bring myself to tell the truth." Ashamed and embarrassed, with the situation spinning out of control, Browne stuck to the story that the two men had agreed to for so long: They'd met while jogging in Battersea Park.[13] Using Britain's strict privacy laws, Browne's attorneys won an injunction against the paper, delaying publication of Chevalier's story. The paper appealed, and the case moved forward quietly for months in the spring of 2007. Browne's efforts to separate his personal travails from his work at BP were collapsing. Even as the Chevalier case was headed to court, Browne was under pressure from BP's board, and especially its chairman, Peter Sutherland, to retire.

⸺◈⸺

Browne had been quarreling with BP's mandatory retirement age for several years. In April 2006, he gave a defiant speech entitled "Beyond Retirement," arguing that "a truly civilized society is one in which people have genuine choices unfettered by their origins, their color or their age." He likened mandatory retirement to racism because it essentially denied someone a job once that person reached a certain age.[14] BP, he believed, should abandon its policy of mandatory retirement for top executives. Ultimately, Browne and the company reached a compromise. He would remain as CEO until December 2008, eight months past his sixtieth birthday and long enough to oversee the centennial of George Bernard Reynolds's first oil strike in Persia.

As the showdown with Chevalier mushroomed in early 2007, Browne announced that he was moving his departure up a year. With the court case still secret, the timing of the announcement seemed to foreshadow the release of the Baker Commission report four days later. Had Browne's handpicked investigator implicated Browne's leadership? Baker had vowed to let the chips fall where they may, and Browne's resignation seemed like a big chip. Despite the appearances, however, the report's findings had nothing to do with Browne's early departure.

In fighting the appeal in the Chevalier case, Browne's attorneys claimed that publishing the former prostitute's tale was an invasion of Browne's privacy. The *Mail on Sunday* countered that its story wasn't really about his private life with Chevalier, but about his misuse of BP assets to which he had given Chevalier access, especially its computers. Browne then tried to use his celebrity and prestige to win the court's favor, portraying Chevalier as a drug addict and an alcoholic, which Chevalier denied. Browne declared he had never given his lover access to BP's computers. The paper responded by producing medical records that showed that Chevalier had never been treated for any addiction, and one of the paper's reporters found that Chevalier's sister had been given a computer from Browne that bore a BP logo. Another machine was still connected to BP's servers, and Chevalier was able to log in using Browne's name and password, revealing about 400 of Browne's e-mails. Some of them contained sensitive information, including details of a consulting contract and a discussion of plans to sell BP's Malaysian operations, the paper said.[15]

Those findings were compounded by Browne's own confession to the court, just three days after the Baker Commission press conference, that he had lied about how he had met Chevalier. "My initial witness statements . . . contained an untruthful account of how I first met Jeff," Browne would later say in his only official comment about the incident. "This account, prompted by embarrassment and shock at the revelations, is a matter of deep regret."[16] Eady was unsympathetic. Browne, the tyrannical CEO, was about to get a dose of his own medicine.

The judge declared that while the matter of how the two men met was relatively insignificant in the scope of the case, Browne clearly thought that it was important and "quite deliberately, and casually, chose to lie to the court about it." The lie was especially inexcusable given that Browne had cited his reputation and governmental honors in arguing that his version of events should be believed over Chevalier's. Eady then admonished Browne for willingly trashing Chevalier's reputation in an effort to discredit him before the court.[17]

———⁂———

Had Browne been honest about his relationship with Chevalier, he might have been embarrassed publicly, but in all likelihood he would have been able to retire on his own terms. After all, Browne's sexuality didn't take away from his accomplishments as the man who'd transformed BP and in the process earned a reputation as a British business icon. Yet that little lie would hasten the end of one of the most celebrated careers in the country's business history. Soon after he decided to fight Chevalier in court, it became clear to Browne himself that his days of running BP were numbered. By May, the situation was even direr. Not only had Browne been humiliated by the court's decision, but Eady's ruling raised the possibility of criminal perjury charges. Ultimately, the judge decided not to refer the case for prosecution, stating, "It is probably sufficient penalty that the claimant's behavior has had to be mentioned in this judgment."[18] Browne may have lied to the court because he was embarrassed about his homosexuality coming to light, especially in such an unceremonious manner, but his court fight endured even after he confessed his lie about the Battersea Park story to the judge. Chevalier could do more damage than simply embarrass his former lover; he could attack the one thing

that Browne loved perhaps more than anything else: BP. Chevalier knew, for example, that Browne had considered moving BP's
global headquarters to Chicago, Amoco's hometown, from London to save money on corporate taxes.[19] BP is one of the United
Kingdom's biggest corporate taxpayers. From 2001 to 2006,
it paid almost £4 billion (more than $6 billion) in taxes to the
British government. The move would have had a huge psychological impact in Britain, where BP was still considered "British Petroleum," an icon of the country's prewar imperial glory.
In many ways, BP's legacy of government ownership made it a
central pillar of the British economy, harboring billions of dollars in worker pension funds and being relied on to pay steady
dividends. Leaving the country would be akin to heresy.

Chevalier knew other secrets about BP as well. Browne had
told him how the company weighed the value of workers' lives
against the cost of safety measures at its facilities. "I had asked
John how BP calculated human life and John told me a value of
$20 million. According to John this was what BP was prepared
to spend ensuring people were not dying while not displeasing
their shareholders," Chevalier said in his newspaper interview.[20]
Browne's comment to Chevalier implied that if safety measures
cost more than the value assigned to workers' lives, BP would
sacrifice them in the name of saving money. Chevalier's claims
were backed by internal e-mails, one of which examined different disaster scenarios like the houses built in the *Three Little
Pigs*. It was a chilling analysis of the cost of human life versus
the cost of capital investment. All major corporations engage in
this ghoulish calculus, and Browne bragged to Chevalier that
BP's number was the highest that any company placed on its
workers' lives—higher than those used by other private corporations or the government.

For Browne and BP, though, the possibility that Chevalier could reveal this information couldn't have come at a worse time. The company was embroiled in class-action lawsuits over the Texas City explosion—it had already paid to settle more than 1,000 individual suits—and three criminal investigations, and was facing the release of both the Baker Report and the CSB investigation. The information would give powerful ammunition to the company's adversaries.

———⊚⊛⊚———

Browne lost the case, lost the appeal, and even tried to involve the House of Lords, of which he was a member, but to no avail. On May 1, the court ruling was made public, and Browne resigned. Rather than wait, the *Mail on Sunday* ceded its scoop to its daily affiliate, the *Daily Mail*, which ran the interview with Chevalier.

Browne's plan for a graceful end to his career, to a legacy as perhaps the United Kingdom's most distinguished executive, evaporated with one stroke of a judge's pen. His reputation was in tatters. Some British journalists argued that Browne was being unfairly persecuted because he was gay, that such a "white lie" under other circumstances would have been overlooked, especially for a man of his business stature. But Eady seemed most annoyed by the fact that Browne had used that stature in an attempt to curry favor with the court, as if Chevalier's claims shouldn't have any standing simply because he was a nobody, a discarded rent boy.

For Brent Coon, the lead plaintiff's attorney representing Texas City victims and family members, the Chevalier case was a gift. Browne's resignation meant that he could no longer hide from legal scrutiny behind his CEO title. A British court had called him a liar, and his former lover had claimed that Browne did indeed have direct knowledge of BP's cost analysis that presaged the Texas City explosion. Coon immediately stepped up his efforts to get Browne to testify in the civil cases that were still pending in Texas. Browne's courtroom humiliation was far from over.

His resignation, coming as it did amid the court cases and regulatory investigations, cast a shadow over Browne's legacy. BP had grown exponentially under his leadership, and that growth had rewarded the company's shareholders, but as the investigations unfolded, it was becoming clear that Browne hadn't been the great visionary he fancied himself to be. He had cobbled together big companies, but as so often happens with large corporate mergers, he had failed to integrate them. BP wasn't so much one company as pieces of others, and the whole didn't equal the sum of the parts. Browne hadn't delivered strong returns through operational prowess. BP had grown simply by buying other companies, and its impressive run of profits was due more to relentless cost cutting than to meaningful growth. The Sun King's luster was beginning to fade.

BP did its best to stand behind Browne, to assert a sense of dignity and even indignation at the circumstances that clouded his departure. BP's chairman, Peter Sutherland, who had clashed with Browne over his grandiose plans to buy Shell and who had insisted that Browne stick to the company's mandatory retirement age, now tried to paint the CEO's downfall with a tinge of melancholy.

"It is a tragedy that he should be compelled by his sense of honor to resign in these painful circumstances," Sutherland said.[21] His words rang hollow, as if echoing off the tombstones of those who died in Texas City.

CHAPTER 10

NOT ENOUGH

The federal courthouse in downtown Houston looks more like a bunker than a hall of justice. Gray and blocky, its concrete walls are pocked with windows that resemble square portholes. The building is perhaps best known as the venue where a jury found boxer Muhammad Ali guilty of evading the military draft in 1967 and where Enron leaders Ken Lay and Jeff Skilling were convicted in 2006. Now, almost two years later, a more mundane proceeding was under way. U.S. District Judge Lee Rosenthal had called a hearing on a proposed plea agreement between BP's operating subsidiary that ran the Texas City refinery and the U.S. Justice Department. Prosecutors had accused the company of violating the Clean Air Act, an antipollution law that had been amended in 1990 to broaden its scope and put new restrictions on fuel emissions. Using this law, they had ensnared BP over the release of hazardous gases from the Texas City refinery explosion. BP agreed to accept a record $50 million fine, the largest ever assessed under the law. The judge expressed some concerns about BP's safety history, but allowed the proceeding to go forward.

Family members of those killed in Texas City saw the charges as an insult. After all, 15 people had died in the 2005 accident, and almost 200 more had been injured, yet all the feds could do was charge the company with polluting the air? It was, in some ways, among the most powerful weapons that Washington could invoke against wayward corporations, but it seemed wholly inadequate. For a company BP's size, the fine was negligible. No individuals were held accountable. State officials and the local district attorney never opened a case. The refinery was still operating, and three more people had died working there in three separate accidents since the explosion.

Inside the courtroom, Keith Casey stepped to the podium. Casey was a large man with meaty hands and close-cropped black hair, already receding despite his only 41 years. A mustache was crimped between his ruddy cheeks. He had round, dark eyes that tended to enhance the sincerity of everything he said. Casey had taken over as head of BP's Texas City refinery just a month before the hearing. He'd come to the company more than two years after the explosion from Motiva Enterprises, a joint venture between Shell and a division of Saudi Aramco, Saudi Arabia's national oil company. Casey had run Motiva's refinery in Norco, Louisiana, which had about half the daily output of BP's Texas City operation.

Bob Malone was trying to break the toxic stalemate between workers and managers at the refinery, to build trust and allow "bad news to travel fast" up the chain of command. Safe operations, he knew, stemmed from empowering front-line workers to voice their concerns without fear of reprisals. That was especially difficult because of BP's fragmented management structure, which tended to dispel accountability. Malone wanted to streamline communications from the refinery floor to the executive offices, but the first step was finding a plant manager whom everybody could trust. Casey fit the bill. One of his first initiatives was a program called "what you say matters," designed to encourage workers to ask the boss "tough questions."

Malone was still troubled by the persistent problem of workers knowing about safety problems but feeling that management was unwilling to listen to them. He needed a conduit who would invite employees to voice their concerns without fear of reprisals. He hired a retired federal judge, Stanley Sporkin, an expert on corporate governance and ethical business practices, to act as an impartial conduit, investigating claims and passing on the information to Malone. As a judge, Sporkin had presided over the case in which Chuck Hamel, the former oil broker and whistle-blower on behalf of BP employees in Alaska, had accused the Alyeska consortium of spying on him and his wife. Sporkin blasted Alyeska's behavior from the bench. The consortium later settled the case and apologized to Hamel.

The first outsider to run the refinery since BP's acquisition of it, Casey brought a solid track record for operations, which he had maintained while guiding the Norco refinery and its workforce through the ravages of Hurricane Katrina in 2005. The facility was shuttered and evacuated in advance of the storm, then repaired and restarted after it passed. His workforce was scattered, and communications and power were out across southern Louisiana. Almost a third of the refinery's workers lost their homes in the storm. Casey's own house was flooded, and his family was displaced for nine months. With power still out across most of the region, he set out in his own boat, navigating the bayous and floodwaters to check on his refinery's employees. Slowly, he assembled enough workers who could make it to the plant, and they began the tedious process of restarting the refinery. Many of the workers slept on cots at the site.[1]

Casey grew up on a California grape farm and picked up enough welding skills working on farm equipment to be able to get an industry job. From there, he worked his way up through power plants and eventually wound up in the refinery business.[2] He agreed to take on the massive task of turning around BP's Texas City refinery on one condition: that his requests for the people, money, or resources to do the job properly and, most important, safely would never be questioned. He also brought a philosophy that quickly crumbled: "Somebody else owns the past; I own the future." Unfortunately, BP's past wasn't so easily buried. Now, a month into the job, Casey was facing a federal judge and admitting a felony on behalf of his company. The new guy was being asked to atone for the company's past sins.

"We plead guilty," he said, acknowledging that BP waived its right to appeal and accepted three years' probation. The company's subsidiary, BP Products North America, was now a corporate felon. Casey read a prepared statement to the judge, saying that the company accepted responsibility for the accident and that it was sorry. "Our guilty plea is an admission that we failed to meet our own standards and the requirements of the law," he said. "The result was a terrible tragedy that could have been avoided."

———— ∞∞∞ ————

Not only had disaster not been avoided on March 23, 2005, but death had continued to stalk the refinery in the ensuing years. A contractor, Ronnie Graves, was crushed to death in 2006. Richard Leining, an electrician and the cousin of David Leining, who was pulled from the wreckage of the trailer in the 2005 explosion, was electrocuted in 2007. Just three weeks before the hearing, in January 2008, William Joseph Gracia, a veteran BP supervisor, was working in an ultracracker unit, used to make raw materials for processing gasoline, when a metal lid bolted on the water filtration system blew off as the unit was being restarted, spewing gray water heated to more than 100 degrees Fahrenheit. The 500-pound lid struck Gracia in the head, killing him.

BP's refining unit had paid $20 million in OSHA fines and had spent more than $1 billion improving the facility, yet workers were still dying with disturbing regularity inside the refinery's fence. A contractor, Ramon SiFuentes, would die in October 2008, after being crushed by a backhoe. Three years after the explosion, the refinery remained the most lethal in the United States. Two workers also died at BP's refinery in Cherry Point, Washington, during that time, making BP's refineries the deadliest in the country. The 146 other U.S. refineries had only nine fatalities combined during the same period.[3] Not only had the deaths at BP's plants continued, but they were occurring at a faster rate than in the years leading up to the explosion. Less than a year after it issued its final report in the 2005 explosion, the CSB opened a new investigation into BP's refining operations.

Joe Gracia and his wife, Robbie, were high school sweethearts, and together they'd raised two children during their 35 years of marriage. Gracia had begun making plans to retire in about two years. Robbie was too upset to tell the judge the story, so her daughter read a prepared statement that included the heart-wrenching description of how they'd covered Joe's head with a baseball cap at his funeral to hide the massive head injuries that the morticians couldn't repair.

"He was loyal. BP repaid his loyalty by failing to ensure the safety of their workers," Robbie's statement said. "I am mad that my husband died and how he died. BP will not do what is needed unless the court forces it to do so. BP sucked every penny of profit out of that plant to the point it was an unsafe place to work. Now, BP claims it has made major safety changes at the plant. Joe's death proves that BP has not done nearly enough."

OSHA levied a $28,000 fine related to Gracia's death as part of a settlement with BP Products North America, the unit that ran the refinery. OSHA found that the company had used substandard bolts to secure the lid, which gave way as pressure built in the water system during the start-up. It also found that BP didn't document safe operating limits and start-up procedures for the ultracracker unit. Three years after the refinery explosion—with new management, a massive upgrade program, and vows to make safety paramount—the problems persisted.

———— ∞ ————

Judge Rosenthal, though, ultimately accepted the plea agreement. While Robbie Gracia and other victims' family members were incensed, the judge had little choice. The plea dealt with a narrow issue of air pollution violations, and it was outside the scope of the case before her to consider whether BP should have been accused of other crimes.

Among those watching Casey read the guilty plea inside the Houston courtroom was Eva Rowe, who was 20 when her parents, James and Linda, died in the Texas City refinery blast. Eva Rowe sued BP, and her case could have been just one of the thousands that the company settled in the wake of the blast. Instead, she teamed up with Brent Coon, a trial lawyer from Beaumont, Texas, and together they became the oil company's worst nightmare. Coon was the lead attorney handling the civil litigation, but in Eva he had something unique—a young client from a small town in Louisiana, just over the Texas border, who was filled with the blunt sense of right and wrong that small towns tend to nurture. Eva was somewhat of a rebellious teen who'd moved from job to job since high school.

Eva's father used to describe her as a "pit bull."[4] The death of her parents, though, awakened something in Eva, a sense of indignation that arose from a loss so profound that it replaced her rebelliousness with purpose. The rebel now had a cause.

Eva Rowe did, eventually, settle her case, but not before getting BP to donate millions to charitable causes in the names of the victims. Even after she settled, Rowe wasn't finished with BP. A CNN film crew followed her to London in 2006 as she tried to corner Browne at One St. James's Square. She attended the Texas Supreme Court hearings aimed at compelling Browne's testimony, just as she sat in the audience in downtown Houston, waiting to hear the company she blamed for her parents' death admit its guilt.

When it came time for the victims and their families to speak, Eva implored Rosenthal to see the unfairness of the plea agreement through the eyes of the victims. The harrowing stories from her and from other family members of those who died seemed oddly disconnected from the cold legal calculus of environmental violations. "My mother had to be identified by DNA because there was not much of her left. She had been severely burned and decapitated during the blast," Eva told the judge. "I will never forget seeing my father's blood-soaked face with the lines running from his eyes down his cheeks from the tears that he cried before he died. I often wonder what he was thinking at that moment." Outside the court after objecting to the plea deal, she drove home her point with reporters: "BP took my parents from me forever. Was pollution BP's greatest sin?"

BP's three-pronged plea agreement had come together months earlier, in late 2007, as part of a sweeping pact with the Justice Department to settle all of the company's outstanding criminal investigations. In addition to the Texas City case, a BP subsidiary in Alaska pleaded guilty to misdemeanor violations of the Clean Water Act related to the pipeline leaks, admitting that its corrosion monitoring and oversight had been inadequate. The company also agreed to pay a $12 million fine, accept three years' probation, and pay $4 million in restitution in the form of funding for environmental research. In the trading case, BP America admitted that it had manipulated propane prices in 2004, had attempted to do so in 2003, and had failed to properly oversee its trading operation. Its fines, penalties, and restitution in that case exceeded $300 million, more than six times the fine for the Texas City explosion. The company also accepted a three-year deferred prosecution agreement.

In Seattle, Scott West was furious. He was a year and a half into his investigation at the time, and he'd become convinced that the case was far bigger than he'd first thought. He saw the potential for it to lead high into BP's corporate leadership. His bosses in the EPA told him that it was one of the agency's top cases in the country. A grand jury was interviewing witnesses, and he'd assembled a multiagency task force that included the Federal Bureau of Investigation and state investigators in Alaska. Completing the case, though, might take as long as five years.

In July 2007, the U.S. attorney called a meeting and asked what West could prove if he had to take the case to trial right then. His investigation was still in the early stages. West thought that he was being asked to give a simple progress report, not realizing that the Justice Department was close to cutting a deal. His answer was matter of fact: He could prove a corporate misdemeanor with no charges against individuals. That's what BP had agreed to plead to, he was told, and so the case was over. BP wanted to settle all three of the criminal cases at once.

"I was shocked. It was surreal," West said. He begged for more time to finish the job, but he was told no. Almost three years later, sitting in his living room in Seattle, he saw news of the *Deepwater Horizon* explosion on the television. At the time, the news reports hadn't yet identified the companies involved. "I looked at my wife, and I said, 'I bet you that's a BP rig.' I just expected it based on what I'd learned about BP's operations," he said. "It just had all the earmarks."

———∞———

As Keith Casey returned to his seat in the Houston courtroom, though, the procedures with which West had become so familiar were supposed to be a thing of the past. Malone, who'd already made countless apologies on behalf of the company, flew to Washington, went before Congress, and apologized again. His message: "We get it." The company would change. Lawmakers were furious that by shutting down the Alaskan pipelines, Malone had singlehandedly caused gasoline prices to rise. Malone saw it differently. He felt that he'd done the right thing. If a pipeline leaked, he had to stop the leak and fix the problem. Would Congress have preferred that he keep the oil flowing through dangerously corroded pipes? He was willing to take the criticism. No more fuzzy accountability. He was ultimately responsible for BP's operations in America, and he'd made the tough call.

This was, Malone hoped, the dawn of a new BP. In Texas City, flares now towered over the blown-out site where the isom unit had been. The melted pipes still hung like old shoelaces, ringing the area where the blowdown drum had been. The slabs where the trailers had been remained vacant. But change was evident throughout the plant. BP refurbished an abandoned Walmart store in downtown Texas City, turning it into offices for those nonessential personnel who didn't need to be inside the refinery fence. No personal vehicles were allowed inside anymore. Employee parking was moved across the street. The refinery's 27-mile steam system was replaced and upgraded.

Malone ushered in a new era of openness, in which workers were encouraged to speak up about their concerns. He flew to Pittsburgh to meet with Leo Gerard, head of the United Steelworkers, which represented many of the employees at the refinery. The two men had something in common. Malone, who had a degree in metallurgical engineering, had begun his career in an East Texas steel mill. Gerard had started work at a nickel smelter in Ontario, Canada. Gerard proposed a ten-point plan for improving process safety at BP's refineries, and Malone agreed to all of them. They created a joint committee to implement the plan, with union leaders and management working side by side on safety. Years of lax government oversight and cost-cutting demands from London had resulted in what amounted to voluntary compliance with many safety standards. Maintenance that should have been done in one year was pushed to two, and so forth. BP agreed to hire 400 additional maintenance workers to get the repair schedule back on track and make sure it stayed up to date. Gerard believed that they were finally making progress, that BP might be taking safety seriously, rather than giving it the lip service it had been given under Browne. "Malone was seriously trying to do things," Gerard said.

Cultural change in an organization the size of BP, which has almost 90,000 employees worldwide, is slow, and it has to come from the top. It's a tone set by the chief executive and reiterated by all the executives below. Under Browne, safety may have been talked about, but cost cutting and profits were re-warded. Gerard had met Browne several years earlier, and he hadn't been impressed. "He had a level of self-importance that I think was unwarranted," he said. "His tremendous marketing skill gave the impression that he was transforming BP, but his management skills were very traditional—chop, chop, chop."

Now, Browne was gone, and BP appeared to be chastened by its round of guilty pleas and fines. Tony Hayward, one of Browne's former turtles, had ascended to his mentor's role, vowing to undo the culture that rewarded more for less. The company was making progress, but it still had much to do. Hay-ward knew it would take time. Just implementing the Baker panel's recommendations could take five years, he said. He'd get only three.

CHAPTER 11

"A BURNING PLATFORM"

Tony Hayward shifted in his chair just slightly as he thought about what he was going to say. The soft-spoken Englishman liked to choose his words carefully. Sitting in Bob Malone's office at BP's office tower in west Houston, Hayward was giving one of his first press interviews as chief executive, six weeks after taking over from his mentor, John Browne. Wearing a pink shirt that was open at the collar and dress slacks, Hayward leaned back in the black leather chair and crossed his legs. He seemed both relaxed and reticent, as if he knew that his words would form the foundation for rebuilding BP.

Even before Browne's career ended in scandal, as he was fighting BP's mandatory retirement rules, Browne had tapped Hayward as his successor. Hayward had been one of Browne's turtles, and, like Browne, he'd spent much of his career moving between the company's finance and exploration operations. He'd been head of BP's vaunted global exploration and production division for four years, overseeing the company's crown jewel as it searched for some of the world's biggest oil discoveries in some of its most hard-to-reach places.

Hayward's face was framed by protruding ears and set with blue eyes that rested atop cheeks that appeared perpetually sunburned. His thin features gave him a boyish appearance despite his 50 years. He was a company man through and through, just as Browne had been. Both had spent their entire careers at BP. The oldest of seven children, Hayward had been educated in public schools and had studied geology, first at Aston University in Birmingham, then later earning a doctorate from the University of Edinburgh. Like Browne, he had shuttled among BP postings all over the globe—London, France, China, Scotland—but it was a chance meeting in a place far removed from the global oil industry that altered the trajectory of Hayward's career. In 1990, Hayward helped to organize a leadership conference in Phoenix, Arizona, and Browne put in an appearance. Browne was so impressed that he asked Hayward to become one of his personal assistants, an inner circle of rising executives that Browne was grooming for bigger responsibilities. For Hayward, who'd been focused solely on the exploration side of the business, this meant an education in finance.

After a couple of years under Browne's tutelage, Hayward was dispatched to Colombia, where BP was tapping the huge Cusiana field, and then later to Venezuela. He spent almost five years in South America, and his time there shaped his views of how BP should operate. As BP's top executive in Venezuela, he attended the funeral of a young worker who had been killed in a BP oilfield. At the end of the service, the man's mother approached Hayward and began striking him on his chest, screaming, "Why did you let it happen?"[1]

───── ∞ ─────

Hayward may have been Browne's protégé, and their career paths may have had some similarities, but Hayward lacked

Browne's fondness for the limelight. In some ways, he was determined to be the opposite of Browne, insisting on a low profile. He wanted to focus on BP's operations, on improving safety across the company. There would be no *Vanity Fair* accolades, no "Sun King" profiles, no speeches before the World Economic Forum in Davos, Switzerland, where the monied elite mingle with celebrities and world leaders. He removed the artwork around the head office that Browne had accumulated. Hayward's focus, instead, was on making BP a "great operating company," and that primarily meant improving safety. "We have to have a work environment where people don't get injured or killed, period," he said. But at BP, that was easier said than done. Richard Leining's death at the Texas City refinery, just weeks after Hayward became chief executive, was "a vivid, tragic reminder that we still have a very long way to go."

BP, as the Baker Report found, spent a lot of money and effort on reducing personal injuries. In the parking garage outside BP's Houston offices, a five-mile-per-hour speed limit was strictly enforced. Employees were forbidden to talk on cell phones, even with hands-free devices, while driving on company business. But reducing accidents didn't address the broader process issues that could lead to catastrophes like the explosion at Texas City. Hayward knew that the company needed a different approach, an end to the "manage to failure" philosophy that had led to the Texas City blast and the corrosion problems in Alaska. It needed to invest in systems that would make the refineries safer even if workers made mistakes. Process safety, after all, was supposed to take human error into account.

Even before he'd been officially named CEO, Hayward set the tone that would distinguish his leadership from Browne's. In a "vision statement" published on BP's internal computer network months earlier, Hayward had made what many saw as

his pitch for the top job. He characterized employees' percep-
tion of BP's management as unresponsive and dictatorial and
said that if BP were going to fix its operational problems, it
would require "behavioural changes that will have to start at the
top of the organisation." He criticized a management style that
"made a virtue out of doing more for less."[2]

<hr>

Rarely had an energy company executive inherited such an
abysmal corporate track record. Lee Raymond, for example,
took over as chief executive of Exxon almost four years after
the 1989 spill in Alaska, and by then the company's cultural
turnaround was already under way. Long loathed by environmentalists for the *Valdez* spill, Exxon Mobil had reinvented itself, creating a culture that placed a priority on safety, even as
it turned out stunning financial results year after year. In the
ensuing two decades, Exxon built a reputation for exemplary
operations. As a result, in the previous three years, government
inspectors had found only a single safety violation at Exxon's
refineries, which include the country's two largest. At BP's, they
found more than 700. (BP's numbers were exaggerated because
of its repeated safety violations. OSHA now counted its violations differently from other companies'. At other refineries, 25
corroded valves would count as one violation. At BP it would
count as 25 separate ones. While this inflated BP's numbers, it
also underscored the magnitude of the task that Hayward had
inherited.)

Hayward also took office amid the three criminal investigations, and jump-starting the huge cultural change that his
fundamentally staid company needed fell squarely on him.
BP wasn't just shaking off recent history. For decades, it had
functioned more as a part of the British government than as

an independent company, and it still carried some of the plodding, bureaucratic characteristics of its heritage. Two months into his tenure, Hayward took full aim at the Browne era. BP's operations were too complex, he said, and they needed more transparency and accountability. The company had too many top managers, and he proposed eliminating 100 positions at the corporate headquarters. He unveiled plans to hire more than 1,000 engineers and improve BP's safety procedures worldwide.

He shuffled management, adopted new policies, invested in safety, and sought to make BP's operations the standard for the rest of the industry, much as Exxon Mobil had done after the *Valdez* spill.

One of Hayward's first acts as CEO was to replace the company's refining chief, John Manzoni. Hayward also scaled back Browne's green agenda. As a geologist, he knew that BP's future was still inextricably tied to fossil fuels. While research into alternative energy would continue, the company would drop the "Beyond Petroleum" slogan.

Hayward had a five-year plan for restoring BP's past glory, but he also couldn't lose sight of what had happened in the previous five years. He wanted to move the company beyond its past, to own a future that would learn from past mistakes and build an even stronger company. Sitting in Malone's office, Hayward fumbled for the right words to sum up BP's current state: "We know when we get it right, we can do really good stuff. I sort of say, BP's a little bit—when we're good, we're stunning, and when we're bad, we're really not very good at all."

Inside BP, though, the problems from the Browne era were taking their toll. Some midlevel managers were losing faith in the leadership, and the division between the British arm of the company and the American one seemed to be growing. Too many senior managers in London didn't seem to grasp the magnitude of the problems in the United States, or weren't willing to listen. While the U.S. leaders were emphasizing safety, the British managers discounted this initiative because it was coming from the Americans. The public statements that Hayward and other executives were making about improving safety weren't being fully implemented. Hayward himself failed to inspire BP's workforce in the way that Browne had. While his strategy of improving operations may have been exactly what BP needed from a management standpoint, he lacked the charisma to rally the troops. He was perceived "as an arrogant British schoolboy" by many in London, one midlevel manager said.

However, Hayward's turnaround plan got a boost from world events. By the time he became chief executive, global oil prices were beginning an ascent that would take them to a record $147 a barrel by the summer of 2008. The steadily rising prices enabled Hayward to fund increased safety measures without compromising BP's financial results. "Having high prices actually gave us a bit of a breathing space to get on and do what we needed to do," he would say later. "We would have been in much greater difficulty if we'd also been faced with a low price environment, so we had a bit of cover to get ourselves sorted." Unlike Browne, though, Hayward didn't enjoy a steadily rising stock price. BP shares traded in the same range for most of his tenure.

Hayward's broad strategy for BP wasn't all that different from Browne's. Though he would stress safety more—how could he not after everything that had happened?—his fundamental philosophy was the same as his mentor's. BP would continue to do what it did best: find the biggest and most lucrative oil and natural gas deposits in the world. That, Hayward believed, was the company's role as one of the world's biggest energy companies. Smaller firms could play it safe. BP and the other majors had to "live on the edge of the energy space," he said. "They should do the most challenging, the riskiest projects that need the biggest amount of technology and capability."

—————∞———————

However, BP didn't have the biggest amount of capability. It prided itself on its oil-finding prowess, and it had a long string of successes, but the Thunder Horse incident was a reminder that the company's engineering ranks had been depleted by Browne's cost cutting. If the company wanted to continue pushing the technological barriers, if it were going to continue drilling in ever-deeper water, it had to replenish that capability; it needed more engineers. Hayward launched a hiring push, but the effort was hampered by poor timing. With prices rising, energy companies were expanding, and the demand for engineers and other specialists had intensified. BP was trying to hire top talent at the peak of the market, and the company's recent operating problems were driving good candidates to its rivals. Nevertheless, Hayward managed to add hundreds of engineers and bolster maintenance personnel at BP's refineries and pipelines as well. To offset those increased costs, he slashed more than 7,000 jobs in other areas, many of them midlevel managers. As a government-controlled company, BP had grown top-heavy over the decades as jobs had been seen as lifetime appointments, without regard for whether they supported the actual business. Hayward wanted to turn the corporate structure on its head, to have overhead that supported operations, rather than having operations to support overhead.

By mid-2008, his efforts seemed to be working. The criminal cases were settled, making what he hoped would be a clean break from the past. The friction between managers and employees at the refineries seemed to be easing. Despite all the improvements, BP's costs hadn't changed from the previous year, and the company went on to report an annual profit of more than $21 billion, a decline from Browne's final years.

—⊶⊷—

While Hayward embraced the role of reformer, he was also a career insider, and his pride in BP ran deep. He could admit the company's mistakes, but he also never lost sight of its successes, and he still believed that the successes defined the company. Hayward, like Browne, was willing to embrace the Baker panel's report, going so far as to say that he considered it "a real gift for BP." The company would learn from its past. It understood that much needed to be done. It would make changes. But it wouldn't accept the root causes identified by the CSB. It wouldn't admit that the effort to control costs, which continued under Hayward, had any bearing on safety. "Everything that we can find suggests that the budget cuts per se did not contribute to either the tragedy at Texas City or the spill in Alaska," Hayward insisted. "We spent a lot of time looking at that and there is no way you can say there is a direct correlation."

That steadfast refusal to link the budget cuts to the disasters had become ingrained in BP's management mindset. To admit that a demand for cost cuts had led to more than a dozen deaths would, of course, only embolden the plaintiff's lawyers, who, despite more than $1 billion in settlements, were still pursuing the company. Hayward, like Browne before him, used the narrow scope of the Baker panel as a shield. Because the Baker panel didn't investigate how cost cutting at the corporate level affected refining operations, the company sought to focus on its findings and brush aside the CSB's.

Despite the difficulties under which Hayward became chief executive, his tenure had its triumphs. Hayward, who had run the exploration division and had had to break the news about Thunder Horse to Browne in 2005, got to oversee the platform's finally achieving "first oil" and beginning production. For many within BP, it became a symbol of the company's rebirth. "Finally. Finally. This is a triumph for technology, engineering and perseverance over what is a very very challenging operating environment," Hayward said. The company rolled out a video of the massive platform, set to the music of the Australian hard rock band AC/DC's "Thunderstruck." They printed shirts that declared, "The horse is loose," and "Let the thunder roll!" After three years of catastrophe and turmoil, BP finally had a triumph about which it could brag. The symbol of the company's problems was now a herald of future success.

Under Hayward, BP appeared, at least outwardly, to be making good on its promises to focus "like a laser" on improving safety as well. The Texas City refinery returned to its full capacity, with more than $1 billion worth of improvements, new safety systems, and a new attitude toward maintenance. Bob Malone, who had earned the respect of workers, managers, and union officials, retired in early 2009, convinced that the cultural changes in the U.S. operations were on track. To outsiders, it wasn't clear that this was the case. Three more workers had died at Texas City since the 2005 explosion, but the fact that the rate of fatal accidents hadn't slowed seemed to be overshadowed by a focus on everything that the company had done and spent on improvements and policy changes.

The death of Joe Gracia in 2008 was a reminder that "we still have a long way to go," Hayward said, but many of the sweeping changes at the refinery weren't prompted by its tragic track record. In the fall of 2005, months after the deadly explosion,

Hurricane Rita battered the Texas and Louisiana coasts, damaging the refinery and forcing BP to shut the plant down for the first time in 40 years. BP used the shutdown to begin "rebuilding the refinery piece by piece," Hayward said. Gradually, portions were brought back online, but the refinery didn't return to full capacity until the end of 2008. Hayward was pleased with the overall progress, even touting the vigor with which BP had embraced changes in process safety. To describe the company's progress, he used one of those awkward expressions for which he would soon become famous. "We created a burning platform internally in BP," he said. "I was pretty vocal about what the issues were and how we needed to change them. That was a burning platform."

Hayward's analogy seemed awkward, even before the *Deepwater Horizon* disaster. What's more, it wasn't entirely accurate. BP hadn't gained the momentum that Hayward liked to portray, and the "burning platform" of change masked the embers of familiar lapses that were still smoldering within the company.

CHAPTER 12

"WHO CARES, IT'S DONE"

Tony Hayward described it as "a monster." He meant it affectionately, but few who had been to the massive Thunder Horse platform could argue with the description. It was a steel behemoth, the biggest production platform ever built, floating in the open water more than 150 miles from New Orleans. Landing on the platform, visitors quickly forgot they were at sea. Its sprawling complex of offices and living quarters made it feel more like a building than a floating island. The unique dual derrick, which could drill two developmental wells simultaneously, towered over the massive main deck like a monument. The oil reservoir deep below the platform was vital to BP's future, a find so large that by itself it would almost double BP's daily production in the Gulf of Mexico. Bringing the platform into production, along with its sister project, Atlantis, would "make an enormous difference to BP's financial performance," Hayward predicted. Thunder Horse's delays in reaching "first oil" had been costly. Not only had the repairs been expensive, but the lost time meant that when the field began producing in July 2008, it had missed the

peak oil prices of the previous summer. Thunder Horse was
ready to run just as a global recession was taking hold, hobbling
worldwide demand for oil. Crude prices tumbled. No matter.
For BP, the benefits were as much psychological as financial.
Thunder Horse represented everything that BP employees,
from Hayward on down, wanted the company to be, the sort of
stunning undertaking for which BP wanted to be known. The
difficulties in bringing the massive complex online only seemed
to add to the achievement. Hayward called it "a triumph of
technology, engineering and perseverance," and declared once
production finally began that "it's proving to be quite a spectac-
ular success." By April 2009, Hayward stood before BP's shareholders at the company's annual meeting and said that the field
was producing the equivalent of 300,000 barrels of oil a day.[1]
Analysts predicted that the Thunder Horse field alone would
help BP offset the production declines that had bedeviled it and
other major oil companies for more than a decade. But deep beneath the water and more than a mile below the seafloor, in the
bowels of the reservoir, the fortunes of Thunder Horse were
about to turn again. The stunning success would be short-lived.
Thunder Horse was really two fields: a main one and one to
the north of it that entered production later. Production from the
main field rose steadily in 2008, and then began to decline
almost as rapidly. In January 2009, three months before Hayward spoke to shareholders, the main Thunder Horse field
produced almost 5.2 million barrels of oil, far less than the company had projected. From there, though, the oil production began to slip, and it continued to decline.[2] Even more disturbing,
as the oil production declined, the amount of water produced
from the well rose. In the industry, this is known as the "water
cut"—the ratio of water produced to the total volume of hydro-
carbon liquids. During the next 18 months, water production in

the Thunder Horse field rose sixfold, meaning that water from an underground reservoir or some other source had entered the oil zone and was bypassing the oil as it came out.

───── ∞ ─────

When an oil well is drilled, the drill bit punches through the different strata of the earth, like a toothpick pressed through the layers of a cake. As it hits the layer containing oil, the well bore is "perforated" (holes are blasted into the side), and the oil flows into the hole and up the pipe to the platform above. Sometimes water from another layer can leak in from the top or the bottom, and because water is lighter than oil, it cuts in front of the oil flow, like an impatient child in an amusement park line. When this happens early in production, as it apparently did with the main Thunder Horse field, the company typically slows the rate of production, which reduces the pressure and decreases the inflow of water. In deepwater drilling, though, the economics depend on a high flow rate of oil. The platform has to produce enough oil to cover the company's investment, which in Thunder Horse's case was more than $5 billion. BP doesn't acknowledge the production decline and, in fact, has rejected any notion that the Thunder Horse project is anything less than a fabulous triumph. Most deepwater wells tend to begin with a surge in production and then trail off. Because of the high costs of drilling such wells, companies look for deepwater reservoirs that will sustain their high initial flow rates. If enough oil can be produced quickly enough, the company can recover its large investment and make some money before the reservoir plays out. In Thunder Horse's case, the rise in water production means that the main field may have a much shorter life than BP expected, according to experts inside and outside the company, who describe the rising water production as troublesome.

"They've got a big problem," said an executive familiar with BP's operations. Matthew Simmons, a Houston investment banker who specialized in energy and had studied oil production worldwide, said before his death in August 2010 that the increase in water meant that the main section of the Thunder Horse field was collapsing. In the spring of 2010, BP said it had temporarily shut in some production from the field because of maintenance.

———<del>∞∞∞</del>———

Despite Hayward's vow to make safety a priority, and despite all the proclamations of the "new BP," the company continued to battle the same demons. Its management structure was still convoluted, accountability was hard to find, decisions were made by committee, and cost cutting and financial performance continued to overshadow operations. The changes that BP had made tended to be reactionary. It spent heavily on its refineries after the Texas City explosion, but in the crown jewel of its business, exploration, there was little recognition that the safety lapses in the "downstream" business had any relevance to the search for oil. Sure, the exploration business had had a setback with Thunder Horse, but that was an engineering problem. No one was injured or even in any danger.

———<del>∞∞∞</del>———

About 100 miles southwest of Thunder Horse, BP had brought another gigantic platform on line. Dubbed Atlantis, it floated in 7,000 feet of water, compared with Thunder Horse's 6,000. If BP's estimates were correct, Atlantis would produce about 600 million barrels of oil, making the reservoir under the platform the third-largest field in the Gulf of Mexico. If Thunder Horse was the symbol of BP's rebirth, then Atlantis was its encore, proof that the company was back on track after the problems of the previous three years.

The encore, though, was tinged with the same sour notes that had become BP's theme song: operational failures. In mid-2008, a piece of tubing ruptured, causing a minor oil spill. It was less than 200 barrels, hardly the environmental disaster BP would unleash on the Gulf two years later, but the reason for it was painfully familiar: The tubing was connected to a pump that had failed after BP managers had delayed maintenance on it. An internal report later found that the maintenance was postponed amid "the context of a tight cost budget," and none of the leaders overseeing the project seemed to question the impact that the delays might have on safety.[3] It was a familiar pattern, yet one that BP managers still wouldn't acknowledge. Instead, they boasted of Atlantis's operating efficiency by saying that it was 4 percent under budget in its first year of production.[4]

In April 2009, an engineer who'd worked as a contractor auditing the Atlantis project sued BP, claiming that the company didn't properly complete or document almost 90 percent of the necessary engineering inspections on the massive platform. The engineer, Kenneth Abbott, a 30-year veteran of the energy business, claimed that streamlining the process had enabled BP to speed Atlantis into production and save several million dollars. An independent engineer later reviewed Abbott's findings and concurred. E-mails unearthed in the case showed that BP employees were concerned about the lack of documentation as well. One warned that lack of proper documents could "lead to catastrophic operator errors."[5] BP's ombudsman office, the one set up by Bob Malone to field employee concerns, found that Abbott's claims were substantiated.[6] A year later, Abbott and a Washington nonprofit group, Food and Water Watch, sued the Minerals Management Service (MMS), asking that it halt the Atlantis's operations until BP could produce all the proper documents. BP insists that all the inspections were done properly and were thoroughly documented, and that safety on the platform has not been compromised.

∞

Hayward wanted to be known for bringing a safety culture to BP, but he, like Browne before him, responded most to the demands of investors. The plunge in oil prices in late 2008 and the global recession in 2009 prompted even more cost cutting. Hayward slashed $4 billion in expenses in 2009, and was on track for further reductions in 2010. Even his vow to implement the recommendations of the Baker panel within the refining division was coming up short. After Joe Gracia's death at Texas City, OSHA conducted a six-month inspection of the plant in 2009 that resulted in an $87 million fine. It was the biggest fine in OSHA's history, surpassing the one it had issued against the refinery in 2005. Almost two-thirds of the latest fine related to previously identified hazards that BP had failed to fix, OSHA said. "BP as a corporation has some pretty serious systemic safety problems. They have not paid enough attention to their management safety system," OSHA's Jordan Barab said.

The problems weren't all at Texas City. At BP's refinery in Toledo, Ohio, OSHA inspectors told the company in 2006 to replace pressure-relief valves. When it inspected the plant again two years later, refinery managers had replaced only those valves that OSHA had specifically mentioned, and the same deteriorating conditions were found on the same types of valves elsewhere in the refinery. Hayward's "laser" was so precise that it was able to separate the letter of the rules from the intent.

In August 2010, the BP subsidiary that runs the refinery, BP Products North America, agreed to pay more than

$50 million to settle OSHA's claims that it had failed to address previous safety problems, but it continued to contest the other $37 million in fines for new violations, including the problems with the pressure-relief valves. The fines put BP's operations at the top of a dubious list. The two largest fines in OSHA history had been levied against the company, and much of them related to the same persistent problems in the same places. "We are under no illusion that these fines are sufficiently high enough to impact BP's bottom line," Barab said. "Record fines of that size coming out of OSHA does send a message to BP. It does affect BP's reputation."

Things weren't any better in BP's other operating trouble spot, Alaska. After the leaks of 2006, the company spent a half-billion dollars replacing 16 miles of transit lines like the ones that had corroded. It tripled its inspections and increased its budget for safety. Yet problems persisted. In 2008, a high-pressure gas line exploded, blasting two pieces of pipe more than 900 feet across the tundra. BP crews had peeled back insulation on the pipeline in 1998 to check welds, but had never replaced it. Nor had they sealed the pipeline to protect it from moisture. No inspections of that section of pipe had been done in the decade since, according to Alaska's Petroleum Systems Integrity Office. The one time an inspection had been scheduled, that portion of the pipeline was covered in snow. BP never got around to checking it once the snow melted. The agency also found that BP was too slow in investigating the accident.[7] In late 2009, BP reported three pipeline leaks in a month, including one in which a two-foot gash in a BP pipeline spewed some 46,000 gallons of an oil-and-water mixture onto the tundra.[8]

As budgets tightened, signs of operational shortcuts similar to the ones that Kenneth Abbott saw on Atlantis began appearing in the company's other operations in the Gulf, the showcase for BP's exploration prowess. Internal e-mails revealed mounting safety worries, although the company didn't have a known lapse until the *Deepwater Horizon* explosion. The reasons were all too familiar. Workers talked of managers who were obsessed with hitting their performance targets, which determined their bonuses. Cost cutting was still the overriding order of the day. BP insisted that it had learned from its mistakes, that safety was now a priority, and that managers were rewarded for safe operations as well as for performance. Yet Harry Thierens, BP's vice president for drilling and completions, would later tell a government panel investigating the *Horizon* accident that he couldn't recall what BP had done to improve safety after the Texas City explosion. If the message wasn't reaching the vice-presidential level, it presumably wasn't getting through to the rig floor.

———✍———

The decisions that would ultimately engulf the *Deepwater Horizon* began hundreds of miles from the rig, inside BP's gleaming glass high-rise in west Houston. There, a team of engineers designed the plan for drilling the new Macondo well. BP had reorganized the drilling operations unit for the Gulf of Mexico in January 2010, and five of the engineering and operations personnel involved in the Macondo project were relatively new to the job. David Sims, the drilling operations manager, had been in that position just three weeks at the time of the disaster, although he had previously been involved in the well design. The vice president of completions had held that job for eight months.

The *Horizon* moved into position in February 2010. She had a stellar safety record and an impressive list of wells completed to her name, having been under contract to BP in the Gulf for about three years. But the *Horizon* was also the least-efficient rig in BP's contracted fleet. Because deepwater rigs are so expensive, companies like BP that hire them measure productivity in "rig days." More than 40 percent of the *Horizon's* rig days were nonproductive by the spring of 2010, meaning that BP was paying millions for what amounted to downtime. The Macondo well was a difficult one, having been plagued by setbacks since a previous rig, the *Marianas*, had been damaged in a hurricane the previous fall and had been removed. BP brought in the *Horizon* to finish the job, and the well suffered kicks and other problems related to gas flowing up the well. In March, about a month after the *Horizon* resumed drilling where the *Marianas* had left off, hydrocarbons flowed into the hole from a sand layer thousands of feet above the oil reservoir. Then a piece of drill pipe became stuck in the hole. The *Horizon* crew left it there and drilled around it. By early April, the crew members were confronting a new problem: the loss of drilling mud in the well that Stephen Stone and others had noted in the weeks leading up to the disaster. The delays were adding up. The *Horizon* was 43 days behind schedule. She was supposed to have moved on to another well by now, yet the Macondo well wasn't finished. The well cost, which BP had budgeted at $96 million, was now at least $40 million higher. The engineering team exchanged a flurry of e-mails that included references to time delays or costs. "Every conversation, every decision has a cost factor," Sims later testified. In the case of Macondo, as with so many other BP operations, key decisions tended to favor the fastest and the cheapest. Greg Walz, another engineer, would later testify that his team even discussed abandoning the well because of the runaway costs.

When the project began, it used a widely accepted well design, but as the time and budget pressures mounted, BP began changing the plan in ways that raised eyebrows among drilling experts inside and outside the company. On April 15, BP changed the details of the well's design three times in a day, filing multiple requests with the federal Minerals Management Service, which approved them all.

We tend to think of an oil well as a shaft of metal piercing the ground and drilling downward until it strikes oil, but modern wells (especially those drilled far offshore) are far more complex. The inside of the Macondo well bore looked more like a pirate's spyglass, with each outer casing extending from inside the previous one, getting narrower the farther underground it went. The final design used what's known as a "long string," a single tube running through the center of the well bore from 13,000 feet underground up to the seafloor. The single tube, or drill string, hung in the middle of the narrowing hole. This design meant that gases could enter the hole and flow up the space between the sides of the hole and the drill string. The only barrier would be a single line of specially made cement.

One of the premier companies providing cement to offshore rigs was Halliburton, the oft-maligned former defense contractor. Halliburton had blasted from the obscurity of the oil patch in 1995, when it hired former defense secretary Dick Cheney to run the company. The company's board wanted Cheney's contacts in the international community to help it expand its oilfield work overseas. Instead, he became a lightning rod for controversy. Halliburton owned an engineering and construction firm that did defense work, and it had been awarded a long-running contract to provide a range of services—such as catering, construction, and fuel transport—for the U.S. troops. Cheney left the company in 2001 to become U.S. vice president, and Halliburton's contract was expanded to include billions of dollars in work for the military operations in Afghanistan and Iraq. By the time of the *Horizon* accident, Halliburton had spun off its engineering unit and its military contracts, and returned to focusing solely on the business for which the company had been founded in 1919: oilfield services. Cement was its specialty. It had largely invented the techniques for using cement to seal wells. On the *Horizon*, Halliburton's job was to pump cement into the hole and seal it. The company ran computer models that questioned whether BP's design would result in a weak seal between the drill string and the well walls.

To prevent blowouts, most drilling experts favor using a shorter tube, known as a liner, that runs up from the bottom of the hole about 1,500 feet. There, it hangs from a slightly larger tube above it, which then runs the rest of the way up the hole. Where the two tubes meet, cement is used to "pack off" or seal the hole, providing a second buffer against gases building up inside the well. Documents released as part of an investigation by the U.S. Coast Guard and MMS show that BP had planned to use this "tie-back" method, but it would have cost $10 million more than the long string. "Not running the tie back saves a good deal of time/money," Brian Morel, one of the drilling engineers, wrote in an e-mail.

Although the long string was cheaper and faster than a tie-back, nothing was inherently wrong with the design. Thousands of wells in the Gulf had been drilled without incident using the long-string method. Of the more than 200 wells drilled between 2003 and the time of the *Deepwater Horizon* disaster, 26 percent used a long string. No other major oil company, though, used the design as frequently as BP.[9]

Halliburton's analysis of the revised well design determined that the long string wouldn't necessarily be a problem. The company said that it could still get a good cement job provided BP used 21 centralizers, devices that positioned the drill string evenly in the center of the hole. That was important to ensure that the cement filled in all sides of the hole equally, much like steadying a fence post in a hole in the ground before setting it in concrete. If the drill string isn't centered, it can leave some portions of the cement thinner or weaker than others, increasing the chances that the weaker portions will break loose under the intense pressures from the gas and oil in the reservoir below. BP engineers, though, believed the cement job would be just as effective using only six centralizers. That worried Jesse Gagliano, a Halliburton engineer who was assigned to BP's Houston office. He managed to convince several BP engineers that more centralizers were crucial before cementing the Macondo. One of them warned BP's well team leader, John Guide, that it wasn't the first time a BP well had been drilled with too few centralizers and an abundance of hope. At least one well in the Atlantis field had been handled in a similar manner, and the engineer warned BP about repeating "the last Atlantis job with questionable centralizers going into the hole."[10]

Sims, the drilling operations manager, shared the concerns and had 15 additional centralizers sent to the *Horizon*. Guide, however, believed that they didn't have the right fittings to hold them in place. There'd been enough delays already. Besides, even if the additional centralizers did fit, it would take ten more hours to install them, Guide noted in an e-mail.

Halliburton ran another model on the impending cement job, this time showing just the six centralizers. The results, Gagliano warned in his report to BP managers, showed that "the well is considered to have a severe gas flow problem."

Given the resistance he'd already encountered, Gagliano didn't press the point. The worst that could happen, he figured, was that his Halliburton team would have to do a remedial cement job to fix the problem. Just like using a long string, using too few centralizers wasn't typically an ingredient for disaster; it merely increased the potential for a mistake that would have to be fixed.

Ultimately, the cement job proceeded, over Halliburton's objections, with only six centralizers in place, but it's not clear who made the decision. One of the senior drilling engineers, Mark Hafle, wasn't aware of why the number of centralizers was changed, but noted that such a decision, like so many others within BP, wouldn't be the responsibility of one person. "It's a team decision on engineering decisions," Hafle told investigators probing the *Horizon* accident. "We make recommendations and people sign off on that, approve those design changes. It's not usually a single person making a decision for a change on a well of this magnitude." Asked who would have the ultimate responsibility for changing the number of centralizers in the well design, Hafle said he didn't know. "I'm not sure why a change was required. I mean, somebody made that determination," he said. "I don't believe it was made by a single person, but I don't really have the facts as to who made that decision that day."

—————⊗⊗⊗—————

Regardless, that fateful decision was compounded by another troubling characteristic of the Macondo well: the previously mentioned loss of drilling mud that had persisted during the drilling of the well. The "loss of circulation"—meaning that not all the mud that was pumped into the hole was coming back out, as it was designed to—increased the chances that the single cement job wouldn't hold, drilling experts said. A unique set of circumstances was building. Decisions made by engineers in Houston set in motion two fateful procedures that would combine with the lack of circulation to "essentially set up your Halliburton cementer for failure," John McCarroll, an inspector supervisor with the MMS, would later tell Hafle at a hearing investigating the *Horizon* disaster.

At the time, though, even the engineers who disagreed with using fewer centralizers shrugged off the decision. "Who cares, it's done, end of story, will probably be fine," one wrote in an e-mail.[11] It wouldn't be. The decisions made on the well design weren't the only problems that developed. Other decisions compounded the severity of BP's shortcuts, none of which, by itself, should have resulted in disaster. Taken together, though, they set the *Deepwater Horizon* on a catastrophic course, dooming 11 members of her crew. The story that Hayward thought he was writing—the rebirth of BP—was indeed nearing its end, but it wasn't the success story he'd envisioned. It was about to become a tragedy, and BP was about to become the most reviled company in America.

CHAPTER 13

PRELUDE TO DISASTER

The day was waning over the drilling floor of the *Deepwater Horizon*. Late April in the northern Gulf of Mexico can feel like summer, as the advent of the warmer months tends to race ahead of the calendar. The *Horizon* was a flurry of activity. A group of executives from BP and Transocean had arrived earlier that day, and the Transocean crew was already making plans to move the rig off the Macondo well and prepare for its next assignment. A small group huddled near the driller's shack discussing the next and hopefully final steps and finishing the current job.

Chris Pleasant had flown to the rig on a helicopter just before midday and gone straight to his bunk. He worked nights as a subsea supervisor for Transocean, which meant that he was in charge of the equipment on the seafloor. Pleasant's shift didn't start until six o'clock in the evening. He woke up about five, had some dinner, and was on the drilling floor shortly before his shift began. Pleasant's responsibilities included the five-story blowout preventer, a series of valves that could cut through the drill pipe and close off the well in an emergency. As the name implies, it was the last line of defense against a blowout, the ultimate life preserver for the 126 people aboard the rig.

Using the various valves and control systems on the blowout preventer and other equipment, Pleasant could adjust the pressure inside the well. That was crucial in testing the integrity of the cement that had been pumped into the hole to seal it. The seal would prevent oil and gas, under intense pressure from deep beneath the earth, from shooting up the well. Cementing a well a mile below the surface of the water is as much art as science. The cement itself is a unique mixture that, in the *Horizon*'s case, included a foam injected with nitrogen. It is pumped through a tube and spread at particular points. The Halliburton technicians aboard the *Deepwater Horizon* couldn't visually inspect their handiwork. They couldn't see whether the cement was in the right place or whether it was bonding to the sides of the well the way it was supposed to. For that, they relied on a battery of tests that would determine the strength of the cement job.

One of the best tests for assessing a cement job is a cement bond log. It uses sonic tools and computer software to evaluate the integrity of the cement and determine whether it is adhering to the side of the well casing. Because the BP engineers in Houston had opted for the long-string design, they ordered a bond log to ensure that the solitary cement barrier in the well would hold. A crew from Schlumberger, an oilfield services company that performs such tests, was standing by on the *Horizon*. However, Halliburton's pumping of the cement appeared successful. None of it escaped when it was poured into the hole. The BP engineers thus decided that a bond log wasn't necessary and sent the Schlumberger crew home on the late-morning helicopter, the return trip for the same chopper that had ferried Pleasant out to the rig.[1] Keeping the Schlumberger team on board to run the test would have cost BP about $100,000, as well as creating more delays while the team waited for the results of the time-consuming test. Had the test been run, it might have uncovered problems with the cement seal, but BP engineers testified later that cement bond logs were rarely done on this type of well. BP, after all, was plugging it only temporarily, until it could tie the well into a pipeline and begin pumping oil from the field. Like the other decisions in the prelude to the impending disaster, skipping the cement bond log wasn't an oversight, or even something that the crew aboard the *Horizon* gave much thought to at the time. It was simply one more safeguard that slipped away. Now, only two key decisions and one massive piece of machinery stood between the *Horizon* crew and catastrophe. None of these would protect them.

While Pleasant was talking to his supervisor, whom he was relieving, he overheard a discussion nearby among some of the crew members who handled the drilling operations. The drill team had conducted a negative-pressure test, which measures the upward pressure in the well, earlier in the day. If the test had been conclusive, it would have meant that the team was ready to take the final steps of replacing the expensive drilling mud in the hole with seawater, capping the well, and moving the *Horizon* to its next assignment. But the test results were muddled. About 60 barrels of mud had leaked through a valve in the blowout preventer. That was unusual, but it wasn't enough of a loss to indicate a definite problem.

As the group of visiting BP and Transocean executives made their way through the driller's shack on the tour, Jimmy Harrell, the offshore installation manager, and Randy Ezell, the senior toolpusher, peeled off from the group. Harrell suggested that the crew increase the pressure in the space between the outside of the hole and the casing at the center of the well, known as the "annulus." With the increased pressure, the mud loss stopped. Everything seemed to be OK.

One of the team members, Wyman Wheeler, was still convinced that something was wrong. Wheeler was also a toolpusher, the drilling crew member who oversees the materials and personnel and often serves as an advisor for the drilling process. The BP representative, or "company man," on the rig was Bob Kaluza, who had arrived on the *Horizon* from Thunder Horse just days earlier to fill in for the regular *Horizon* representative, who was attending a training course onshore. Thunder Horse was a production platform, and the sort of test results that Kaluza was now looking at weren't his area of expertise. He and some other members of the drill team thought that the inconclusive test result might be the result of "**U** tubing," a process in which downward pressure from the mud pushes seawater back up the drill pipe. Wheeler wasn't buying it, but his shift was ending, and his relief had arrived. The relief toolpusher, Jason Anderson, agreed with the **U**-tubing diagnosis. Wheeler left in a huff. "I guess we never had a clear understanding where the fluid went to," said Pleasant, who was still watching the conversation from nearby.

Kaluza decided to wait on a final decision until his own relief arrived. Don Vidrine had been a "company man," representing BP at well sites both off- and onshore, for 30 years. When Vidrine arrived, Anderson told him that he'd seen this sort of phenomenon before, calling it "annular compression."

Kaluza, Vidrine, and Anderson debated the test results for about an hour. Several members of the Transocean crew found their indecision humorous. After all, given the huge daily expense to keep the *Horizon* in place, the hour-long discussion cost BP about a half-million dollars. Eventually, Kaluza left to tell the BP engineers in Houston that they'd decided to do another negative-pressure test. Despite his experience, Vidrine was unfamiliar with annular compression, and he was wary of proceeding until he had conclusive results. "The toolpusher and the senior toolpusher told me it was this annular compression thing," he said. "I wanted to do another test."[2] As the discussion broke up, Ezell asked Anderson if he should stick around for the second test. "Man, you ain't got to do that," Anderson told him. "I've got this. Don't worry about it. If I have any problem at all with this test, I'll give you a call." Ezell and Anderson were both among the *Horizon*'s original crew, having served on the rig for about nine years. They'd worked together for a long time, and each knew what the other was thinking. "He was just like a brother," Ezell was to say later. Anderson didn't seem worried about the tests, so Ezell went to dinner. When he returned to his office, he called Anderson, who told him that the second test had gone well. "We watched it for 30 minutes and we had no flow," he said. "It's going fine."

No records of the second pressure test survived the fire that was soon to ravage the rig, but Vidrine later told Harrell that the results were good and didn't indicate any gas flow. Experts investigating the accident later questioned whether Vidrine or others had misinterpreted the results, or whether the test itself had been faulty.

Before he hung up the phone, Ezell asked again if Anderson needed his help. "No, man," Anderson said. "I've got this. Go to bed." With what they thought were good test results, the crew began the process of pumping mud out of the hole and replacing it with seawater.

———— ⚉ ————

As the sun slipped beyond the horizon and twilight washed over the Gulf, Pleasant left the drilling floor. He inspected a crane that would be used to raise the blowout preventer once the well was completed, and then returned to his office. Allen Seraille, an off-duty assistant driller, was in Pleasant's office watching television as Pleasant sat down at his desk and began entering the details of his crane inspection into his computer.

Vidrine, convinced that everything was fine, also left the drilling floor and went to his office. After 10 or 15 minutes, the phone rang. It was Anderson. Mud was shooting up from the hole. Something was terribly wrong. Vidrine grabbed his hard hat and started for the drilling floor. About the same time, Steve Curtis, the assistant driller, called Ezell in his cabin and told him that the well was blowing out.

Meanwhile, Pleasant, who was still filling out the crane inspection report, was interrupted by Seraille. "Chris, what's that water?" he asked. Seraille had been flipping through channels on the television and stopped at the onboard closed-circuit channel, which showed the drilling floor. Pleasant said it probably wasn't a big deal. Sometimes water gets displaced when the drill pipe is backed out of the hole. "I see mud," Seraille said. Pleasant looked up from his computer and saw the water and mud shooting out of the hole. He called down to the drill floor, but he got no answer. He tried another line. Then another. Nothing.

—— ∞∞∞ ——

Vidrine stepped outside onto the deck. "Mud and seawater were blowing everywhere." A film of slick drilling mud covered the deck. Then the first explosion rocked the rig, and Vidrine hunkered down. He was forward on the port side, and the blast had come from behind him, in the direction of the drilling floor. He grabbed a life vest and headed to the bridge.[3] Pleasant never heard the explosion, but when he couldn't reach the drilling floor by phone, he decided to head down and see what was happening. As he stood up, one of the visiting BP officials ran past his office door. "What's going on?" Pleasant asked. The official didn't know, but he told them that they needed to leave. Pleasant headed toward the drill floor. In the hallway outside his office, he ran into Chad Murray, the electrician. "Don't go that way," Murray told him. "Something bad just happened in there."

⸎

Pleasant turned around and followed Murray out on deck. "That's when I saw the fire," he said. Something bad had indeed happened. Something unthinkable was unfolding on the deck of the *Deepwater Horizon*. Some of the crew scrambled for the lifeboats. Others, terrified, simply jumped over the side. Pleasant made his way to the bridge, to the control panel for the emergency disconnect system, or EDS. By then, Vidrine was standing beside him. "I'm EDSing," Pleasant declared. "I'm getting off here." He hit the button to disconnect the rig from the well. The lights on the panel went through their sequence, indicating that the blowout preventer's heavy metal valves, known as "rams," had snapped shut, cutting through the drill pipe and severing the rig's connection to the well. But on the seafloor, nothing was happening.[4] The electronic controls had failed when the rig lost power, and the hydraulic systems were also dead. An automatic shutoff, which should have been triggered when the other systems failed, also hadn't worked. The rig's ultimate fail-safe, the final protection against disaster, had failed. No one on the bridge knew it, but 11 members of the crew—including Alexander and the other members of the drilling crew—were probably already dead, enveloped by the flames that were con-suming the drilling floor.

Still attached to the well, the *Deepwater Horizon* was doomed. Unable to break free, it remained tethered to the gas-fed fires that were now spewing forth on the deck outside. As Pleasant and his crewmates fled the rig any way they could—by lifeboat, by wayward raft, by jumping blindly into the water—the *Horizon* burned. The fires, fed by a below-ground bubble of energy big enough to power some of America's largest cities, raged for two days before the *Horizon's* melted, twisted remains finally sank. As the main deck slipped below the surface, quenching the blaze, the *Horizon* began her final journey. The massive steel city, now a lifeless derelict, crashed to the seafloor, the fi-nal resting place for the lost members of her crew.

The riser, the large pipe with a diameter the size of a manhole cover that connected the blowout preventer on the seafloor to the rig on the surface, buckled and bent like an old garden hose as the *Horizon* descended, coming to rest about half a mile from the well head. With nothing to stop the flow from the reser-voir below, oil began to press upward through the well, past the failed blowout preventer and out the kinks and cracks in the riser. Within days, it would become the worst oil spill ever in American waters, releasing the same amount of oil as the *Exxon Valdez* spill each week.

CHAPTER 14

DROPS
IN THE
BIG
OCEAN

The *Deepwater Horizon* burned for two days after the initial explosions had sent her crew scrambling for the lifeboats. The 11 who died would never be found; the flames and black smoke that could be seen as far as 70 miles away served as a funeral pyre against the expanse of the sea. Within days, what had initially appeared to be a tragic accident began evolving into a disaster. At first, as Coast Guard and company rescue crews searched for the missing, few were paying attention to the oil that was beginning to leak from the broken riser a mile below the surface. By the first weekend after the explosion, though, the looming environmental threat was coming into focus. For BP, the worst was yet to come.

It took a few days for the public to sort out the details. Transocean was virtually unknown to the general public, but it was the world's biggest offshore drilling contractor. Including the *Horizon*, it owned 138 vessels used in drilling for oil around the world, and more than 20 of them were designed for the ultra-deepwater. A dozen were deployed in the Gulf of Mexico. The company traced its history to the earliest days of the oil business in Louisiana, when Danciger Oil and Refining Co. bought its first drilling rig. Among the businesses that it acquired along the way was Southeastern Drilling Co., or Sedco, founded by a former Texas governor. Sedco's equipment was involved in the horrendous 1979 Ixtoc spill in Mexico's Bay of Campeche. Until the *Horizon* accident, Ixtoc had been the worst oil disaster in the Gulf, but although it had sullied the southernmost Texas beaches, the accident itself didn't occur in U.S. waters. In 2007, Transocean merged with GlobalSantaFe, combining the industry's two biggest players. Most of the company's operations were still based in Houston, but it moved its corporate headquarters first to the Cayman Islands and then to Switzerland, where it received more favorable tax treatment for its international profits.

———⊙⊙⊙———

Transocean has had its share of blemishes around the world. The U.S. Treasury Department is investigating a drilling project in Myanmar in which Transocean participated. The Myanmar regime is under trade sanctions from the United States. A freight forwarder shipped some of its drilling equipment through Iran on the way to Turkmenistan. Transocean has held a minority interest in a Libyan company that does business with Syria, although it sold its stake in 2009. The U.S. government prohibits companies from doing business with Iran and Syria, which it considers state sponsors of terrorism. Norwegian officials targeted the company in an investigation of possible tax fraud that could wind up costing it $500 million plus interest in back taxes and penalties. It has also faced tax probes in the United States and Brazil. Transocean disputes the tax claims, which are still pending.[1]

In recent years, BP had become Transocean's biggest customer, a relationship that was broken by the finger-pointing that followed the *Horizon* disaster. Transocean's motto is: "We're never out of our depth," but when it came to the public scrutiny it was about to face, it clearly was. Few drilling companies spend much time on public relations, because they have little direct contact with the public. Their customers are oil companies. The production of energy is an odd form of capitalism. The concept of competition is distorted, unlike the common rivalries among, say, retailers or restaurants that are familiar to consumers. Prices at all levels of the industry ultimately are based on oil prices, which are set not by the companies involved, but by the futures market, a global exchange of contracts among buyers and sellers.

Oil companies themselves collaborate more than they compete. On the Macondo well, BP shared its ownership with Anadarko Petroleum, one of the world's largest independent producers, which means that it explores for oil around the world, but doesn't refine it. Another Macondo partner was a division of the Mitsui Group, a Japanese conglomerate whose interests, in addition to energy, include shipbuilding, construction, mining, and chemicals. Together, the three companies paid to lease the drilling rights for specific areas of the Mississippi Canyon from the U.S. government. They also shared the investment in drilling the well. The three partners then hired a litany of contractors, including Transocean, Halliburton, and Schlumberger. These contractors, in turn, provide similar services for other oil companies. For contractors that specialize in activities at the forefront of technology, the number of companies that can afford the mammoth investments required to drill in the deepwater is small. A rig operator may have fewer than 20 customers worldwide.

Transocean owned the *Deepwater Horizon*, and 9 of the 11 people who died in the blowout were its employees. The other two worked for M-I-Swaco, which provided the drilling mud. BP didn't move to the forefront of the crisis until several days later. Inside BP, Hayward was demanding answers, but few were forthcoming. The company's early official response used Transocean as a shield. BP issued press statements saying that it "offered its full support" to the drilling contractor, and offered sympathy to the families of those who had been lost and were presumed dead. As the majority lease owner, however, BP was responsible for any pollution that resulted from the wrecked rig. Initial estimates put the amount of oil leaking from the mangled well at only about 1,000 barrels a day, a relatively modest amount that would mean that the well could leak for the better part of a year before matching the environmental damage from the *Exxon Valdez* spill. One of the conclusions of the commission that investigated the *Valdez* spill was that a spiller should not be in charge of the response.[2] Yet the Macondo well site, 40 miles from shore, was remote, and most of the early information about the damage was controlled by BP.

Oil spills occupy a prominent position in America's rogues' gallery of corporate villainy. Perhaps only the clubbing of baby seals is more detested by the public. America's revulsion with the damage from oil on the water predates the *Exxon Valdez* spill by almost two decades. In 1969, a Union Oil platform off the coast of Santa Barbara, California, blew out, and an attempt to cap it resulted in an even bigger disaster—the opening of a fault along the ocean floor that spewed oil into the Pacific.

About 200,000 gallons of oil created an 800-square-mile slick before workers were finally able to close the rupture 11 days later. The thick tar moved inland, staining some of California's famed beaches and killing shorebirds, dolphins, and seals.

What galvanized the public, though, wasn't just the impact of the spill, but the seeming indifference of the company responsible. Union Oil President Fred Hartley famously said that the accident didn't deserve to be called a disaster because no people died. Most of the victims—more than 3,600 of them—were birds. "I am always tremendously impressed at the publicity that death of birds receives versus the loss of people," Hartley said.[3]

Twenty years later, the *Exxon Valdez* ran aground on Bligh Reef in Alaska's Prince William Sound. Unaware of the Alyeska consortium's role in the slow response to the *Valdez* disaster, public anger was directed toward Exxon. The tanker spill was more than 50 times the size of the Santa Barbara accident, forever enshrining oil companies in the minds of many as enemies of the earth. As the Macondo well began shooting oil into the Gulf, BP, the "green" energy company, was determined to forestall any comparisons to the *Valdez* as long as possible.

In Tallahassee, Florida, Ian MacDonald was suspicious of the estimated flow rates that BP released in the days after the *Horizon* exploded. MacDonald, an oceanographer with Florida State University, is an expert on oil seeps that occur naturally from the ocean floor, especially in the Gulf of Mexico. One of his principal tools is satellite imaging. Within a week of the *Horizon* explosion, he and a colleague began to suspect that the spill was much larger than BP was saying. The government released maps based on the data that it had received from flyovers of the oil slick and satellite pictures. Without any other information, few people disputed the BP estimate, even after the company grudgingly raised it to 5,000 barrels a day, an estimate that was shared by the National Oceanic and Atmospheric Administration. MacDonald's analysis, though, found that the oil discharge was actually as much as six times greater, potentially 30,000 barrels a day. At that rate, the BP spill would surpass the *Valdez* in less than two weeks. MacDonald's estimate was the only other number available, and it quickly earned the nickname the "MacDonald minimum."

BP dismissed any contentions that the leak was larger than the company was saying. Tony Hayward argued that determining the true size of the discharge was impossible and, echoing BP's public relations mantra for the duration of the crisis, said that the company was more concerned with stopping the leak than with measuring its size. "A guesstimate is a guesstimate," he said, "and the guesstimate remains 5,000 barrels a day." Hayward characterized discussions of a larger flow of oil as "deeply theoretical," telling the *Houston Chronicle* that the company's assessment of the flow rate was the most accurate. "There's been no change in the flow since this started," he said, dismissing the entire issue as a "red herring."

MacDonald knew better. Government regulations require companies to assess the size of a spill as early and as accurately as possible. The Unified Command, the gaggle of federal agencies responding to the spill, never pressed BP for better numbers or, for that matter, insisted that BP reveal its method of determining the leak's size. As a result, the government's own estimates were flawed as well. The lack of adequate estimates may have affected the response, resulting in too few booms and skimmers being deployed in the early days after the accident.[4] In Washington, lawmakers' doubts about the accuracy of BP's estimate began to grow. Representative Edward Markey, a Massachusetts Democrat, ordered BP to release its live video from the wellhead under threat of congressional subpoena. When the feed was made public in mid-May, other experts began to weigh in. MacDonald's early projections, which were so much greater than what BP had been saying, now appeared to be low. Some estimates put the flow rate of oil as high as 70,000 barrels a day, meaning that the Macondo had released more oil than the *Exxon Valdez* in fewer than four days. Whatever had gone wrong with the Macondo, there was no denying BP's expertise at finding oil. The Macondo well had tapped into a huge reservoir.

⸻ ∞ ⸻

Despite its hopes of deflecting *Valdez* comparisons, BP wasn't just minimizing the spill for appearances' sake. The political backlash from the spill posed two threats to the company's future: the cost of its liability from the accident and the prospect of losing access to its lucrative oilfields in the Gulf. It still had dozens of potentially profitable deepwater prospects to explore, and it couldn't afford to allow the Obama administration to deny it new drilling permits or ban it from U.S. waters.

It also faced the potential for huge fines under the Clean Water Act, which regulates water pollution. The amount of the fine is determined by, among other things, the amount of oil that leaks. If the well was leaking 60,000 barrels a day and BP was found to be grossly negligent in its oversight of the spill, it could face fines of as much as $4,300 for each barrel—roughly $140 million for each day that the leak persisted. On top of that, it could also be liable for additional civil penalties under the Oil Pollution Act of as much as $25,000 a day and $1,000 for each barrel of oil spilled. BP's liabilities threatened to gut the company's financial performance. A week after the *Horizon* exploded, BP reported that first-quarter profit had almost doubled from a year earlier. After struggling through a global recession, BP had appeared to be on track for a record year. As it did after the Texas City tragedy, BP sought a response to the Macondo spill that would show that the company wasn't just another heartless oil company. The Oil Pollution Act, which Congress hadn't updated since it was passed in 1990, capped BP's liability to private parties at $75 million, a pittance for a company BP's size. The limit didn't mean that BP wouldn't have to pay billions in cleanup costs—it was still liable for those—but it limited how much BP could be forced to pay fishermen and business owners that had been harmed by the Macondo oil slick.

BP waived that limitation, saying that it would pay all reasonable third-party claims, thus proving that it was taking full responsibility for the accident. It set up claims offices along the Gulf Coast where business owners could come to apply for reimbursement checks. This was another financial calculation. The cleanup would cost billions, but the alternative might be losing access to its Gulf oil fields forever, a cost that could mean hundreds of billions in lost revenue over the lifetime of its reserves. BP's crisis response sought to differentiate the company from its peers and its own past. Exxon executives were criticized for not flying to Alaska quickly enough after the *Valdez* spill. The company appeared callous and uncaring. After the Texas City explosion, Browne made his appearance there, meeting with the families of the victims and then quickly left. While BP's response to the *Horizon* disaster may have been an improvement over Exxon's handling of the *Valdez*, it was tempered by John Manzoni's e-mail whining about his lost vacation day and, a few months later, the internal investigation that directed blame at the front-line workers while deflecting any criticism from BP executives. This time, it would be different. Hayward flew to the Gulf Coast and later set up camp at BP's crisis center in Houston, vowing, "I will stay here until we have fixed it."[5]

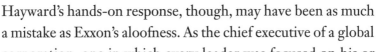

Hayward's hands-on response, though, may have been as much a mistake as Exxon's aloofness. As the chief executive of a global corporation, one in which every leader was focused on his or her own specific area, he was one of the few officials who were watching the overall operations of the company. Now his attention, too, was focused on one specific—although horrendous—problem. Even worse, Hayward himself handled some of the early television interviews. Inside BP, he was known for the occasional odd phrase or awkward comment; now this tendency of his would be on display for the world.

Just a few weeks after the *Horizon* sank, Hayward, attempting to put the size of the spill in context, told the United Kingdom's *Guardian* newspaper that "the Gulf of Mexico is a very big ocean" and that "the amount of . . . oil and dispersant we are putting into [it] is tiny in relation to the total water volume."[6]

A few days later, he told Britain's Sky News that the impact of the spill, already well on its way to being the worst ever in U.S. waters, would be "very, very modest."[7] His most famous gaffe came in late May, when he told reporters who were following him while he inspected a beach in Louisiana that BP was doing everything possible to clean up the oil. "There's no one who wants this thing over more than I do," he said in a segment that aired on NBC's *Today* show and elsewhere. "I'd like my life back." The seeming arrogance of the comment, more than anything else, was used against Hayward as the crisis dragged on through the summer. It infuriated Gulf Coast residents who were suffering economic hardship from the disaster and drowned out the company's efforts to clean up the spill and compensate victims. By early June, BP's $50 million ad campaign to show what it was doing to "make this right" was being derided as cynical even by President Obama.

"Tony's a good guy, bright guy, but he can't keep his mouth shut sometimes," said a retired oil company executive who had had numerous dealings with Hayward on exploration deals in South America. Hayward's gaffes turned him into a source of celebrity ridicule. He became the butt of late-night comedians, and comic newsman Stephen Colbert had an extended segment in which a likeness of Hayward was beaten, thrown from a roof, pecked by seabirds, and run over repeatedly by a semi truck driven by a sea turtle. The gossip Web site TMZ followed Hayward to a sports bar in Houston, perhaps the only time that a British oil executive was deemed worthy fodder for what is essentially a celebrity-chasing electronic tabloid in the United States.

———⊗⊗⊗———

BP's problems, though, were far greater than a chief executive with his foot in his mouth. The financial repercussions were spinning out of control. The stock market is a heartless forum. Investors care about returns, and any industrial disaster is looked at in terms of the company's potential liability. As one stock analyst noted, the markets don't care about the loss of life. Indeed, in the week after the Texas City refinery explosion, BP's stock price slipped less than 3½ percent in the week, then began rising again. With the smoldering remains of the *Horizon* heading for the seafloor, though, by the start of the following week, investors began to worry that BP's exposure could be far greater than it had first seemed. Its shares went into free fall, losing more than half their value by late June. Other companies associated with the disaster faced similar declines. Transocean and Anadarko, BP's far-smaller partner in the well, saw the value of their shares halved as well.

For BP, the falling stock price posed a direct threat to the company's survival. As the crisis progressed and the oil continued to leak, speculation grew that BP would be bought by a rival such as Exxon or even Shell, turning the tables on John Browne's own acquisition plans a few years earlier. In the United States, BP's market value—the worth of all its available stock—fell by $100 billion, making it the lowest among the "supermajor" oil companies. Exxon Mobil, by comparison, was worth more than three times as much. BP, though, still held some of the best oil and gas drilling prospects among the majors, and that created a dangerous market condition for the company. BP's assets were now worth far more than its stock price. For example, later in the summer, when BP began selling assets to raise money for cleanup costs, it reached a $7 billion deal with the Houston-based Apache Corporation for a package of oil and gas assets in places such as Egypt, Vietnam, and West Texas. Based on the sale price, all of BP's assets should have been worth more than $350 billion, but at the time, the stock market still valued the entire company at less than $130 billion. In other words, BP's parts were worth more than the whole.

Such a steep decline in stock value leaves a publicly traded company vulnerable. Rivals, seeing that they could buy the entire company on the cheap to get its properties, began looking at ways to do a deal. The problem was BP's huge open-ended liability from the Macondo disaster. Wall Street investment bankers, who collect big fees from takeovers, excel at solving such problems. They began working on scenarios to shield a prospective buyer from BP's Macondo liabilities. Speculation mounted that another oil company would make a hostile bid for BP in a transaction that would use a bankruptcy filing to corral the spill liabilities. The buyer would get BP's prime oil reserves while leaving a court to handle the spill cleanup.

Within weeks, Hayward had gone from the chief executive who was turning BP around to the executive who might oversee its demise. As investors fretted about the company's future, its engineers in Houston were working frantically to either cap the well or at least abate the flow of oil—anything that would end the environmental nightmare that was now playing out daily on newscasts and cable television shows. Everyone in the company knew that the best way to stop the slide in the stock price and preserve the company's future was to somehow stop the leak. But nothing worked. No well drilled to such depths had ever blown out before, and neither BP nor the industry was prepared to respond. Many of the methods (which had made-for-TV names like "top kill," "top hat," and "junk shot") had worked on land, but the pressure, water depth, and frigid temperatures at the Macondo wellhead frustrated the efforts. Containment devices were built from scratch and lowered over the well; new batches of mud were pumped in through the broken blowout preventer; a tube was inserted into the broken riser to siphon off some of the oil. The best BP crews could do was slow the flow of oil. To truly "kill" the well, the only option was to drill a second hole, known as a "relief well," which would intersect with the first. It meant positioning another rig near the site where the *Horizon* sank, drilling down 13,000 feet, angling the drill bit sideways, and then lining up two holes, seven inches in diameter, almost three miles below the surface of the water. Once the two wells intersected, engineers could use the new one to inject drilling mud and cement, permanently plugging the leak. BP well designers had drawn up plans for a relief well within days of the *Horizon* explosion, but drilling it would take at least three months.

Government officials began to doubt whether BP could ever get the well under control. "I was not comfortable they knew what they were doing," Interior Secretary Ken Salazar told the *New York Times*. Energy Secretary Stephen Chu turned to other oil companies such as Exxon Mobil and Shell for expertise, which insulted the BP engineers who were working long, frantic hours to cap the well.[8] Over time, the failed ideas permitted a solution to coalesce, allowing engineers to keep refining their designs toward a solution, known as a "capping stack," that would eventually cover the well.

Given the rapid decline in BP's share price and the mounting public anger over both the environmental and economic consequences of the spill, Hayward couldn't be sure that the company would survive long enough to complete a relief well. He decided that it would begin drilling two of them, with rigs provided by Transocean. In the meantime, teams of engineers would keep working on the other efforts to slow or plug the leaks, and BP teams across the Gulf Coast would keep paying the claims of fishermen and business owners whose livelihoods had been compromised by the spill. None of that, though, was enough.

Hayward needed more help. He got it from an unlikely source: the Obama administration. The president told the

Today show in early June that he would have fired Hayward if the BP executive had worked for him, and said that he wanted to know "whose ass to kick" over the spill.[9] The tough talk, though, masked a growing concern that the administration had appeared inept in its handling of the crisis. Relying on BP's predictions and its own flawed forecasts, it had appeared to defer to BP, letting the spiller clean up the spill. It needed to take charge. Its political desperation and BP's financial fears would dovetail into an agreement that would help them both.

CHAPTER 15

A FOX
IN THE
HENHOUSE

As the hulk that had been the *Deepwater Horizon* plunged like a wounded leviathan toward the seafloor, it ensnared President Barack Obama's energy agenda, dragging it into the depths of political uncertainty. In March 2010, less than a month before the disaster and a little more than a year into his presidency, Obama had announced that he wanted to open federal waters in the eastern Gulf of Mexico, along the eastern seaboard, and in parts of offshore Alaska to new offshore drilling. It was a concession to the oil industry, which had aligned against Obama's plan to limit greenhouse gases through an elaborate "cap-and-trade" system. Billed as a "free-market solution," the complicated process involved trading an ever-shrinking number of pollution credits on an exchange similar to that used for futures contracts. It was designed to create economic incentives for companies to reduce carbon emissions, but its structure placed much of the cost burden on companies that dealt in oil and gas, especially refiners. Cap and trade was the latest incarnation of the carbon-trading scheme that John Browne had championed within BP in the late 1990s and pitched to the Clinton administration. Obama had included it in his plan to promote alternative energy before political realities overtook it.

By early 2010, the cap-and-trade bill was languishing in Congress, and Obama needed the support of lawmakers from oil-producing states. The industry had long clamored for more access to offshore leases on both coasts. Former Alaska Governor Sarah Palin, the vice presidential candidate for Obama's opponent, John McCain, in the previous year's election, had summed up the industry's sentiment in her popular slogan, "Drill, baby, drill." Just three weeks before the *Horizon* blew up, Obama defended his plans to allow more offshore drilling. "It turns out, by the way, that oil rigs today generally don't cause spills," he said. "They are technologically very advanced."[1] The industry, though, remained wary. Despite his overtures, oil companies knew that Obama wasn't their friend. His predecessor, George W. Bush, had been considered an industry insider. While his own record in the oil patch of west Texas was spotty at best, Bush was receptive to oil companies' needs. What's more, he favored a soft touch with regulation, and the oil industry is among the country's most heavily regulated. Obama, by contrast, endorsed the allure of "green" energy. He wanted to take away long-standing tax credits and incentives for oil and gas production and shift them to subsidies for alternative fuels. Cap and trade was just another step in that process.

One oil company, though, was less concerned: BP. Obama had been a favorite of the company and its employees. During his time in the Senate and in his campaign for president, Obama was the biggest recipient of donations from BP's political action committee and individual employees, collecting more than $71,000. It was the largest slice of the more than $6.2 million that BP and its employees had given to federal candidates in the previous two decades, although the amount remained modest compared to that given by Obama's biggest donors.[2]

BP's financial connections to Obama's administration didn't end there. John Browne had set BP apart from other major oil companies with his 1997 speech at Stanford, acknowledging global warming and the role that oil companies played in it. Following the speech, BP had donated $20 million to solar research as the first step in a decade-long program of backing "green" energy research. By 2007, the program had expanded, and BP had awarded a $500 million grant to establish the Energy Biosciences Institute at the University of California, Berkeley. The institute funds dozens of research projects seeking what Tony Hayward described as the next generation of biofuels. Basically, the institute is attempting to find a more efficient fuel than ethanol, the corn-based gasoline additive.

"What the world needs is a plant that grows fast, doesn't need water, [and has] high cellulose lactose density, lots of sugar—so you can describe what you need. The task for the bioscience generally is to go and define it and create it," Hayward said soon after BP awarded the grant. "What we're trying to do with this Energy Biosciences Institute is create a sort of mission-based approach to science to say here's the task, draw on all the broad spectrum of functional science disciplines from biology to engineering to create what we need. That's what that's all about."

The institute was run by Dr. Stephen Chu, a Nobel Prize–winning researcher and a pioneer in the study of biofuels. Obama would later tap Chu to become his energy secretary, and Chu, in turn, would hire BP's top scientist, Steven Koonin, as the undersecretary for science. It was Koonin who made the decision, when he was still at BP, to direct the bulk of the grant establishing the biosciences institute to UC Berkeley and Chu.

Oil company executives love to complain about energy secretaries. A common refrain is that no administration—not even those of the two Bushes, both of whom had worked in the business—has ever chosen someone with energy industry experience to run the Department of Energy. Obama's selection of Chu, though, was seen as something even more dastardly. Far from being a detached bureaucrat, Chu had spent his career trying to develop alternatives to some of the biggest industries that he was supposed to oversee. Essentially, he had devoted his research to putting oil companies out of business. Now, he would be regulating them. BP didn't share the industry's concern. Inside its Houston offices, there was a sense of excitement, if not smug satisfaction, that someone that the company knew so well would now be in charge. It didn't work out that way. Although Chu was to play a role in the government's response to the *Horizon* spill, the Energy Department didn't oversee offshore drilling. Chu would grow increasingly disenchanted with BP's handling of the Gulf spill response as the summer wore on.

———— ∞∞ ————

Regulation of the offshore energy industry fell to the Interior Department's Minerals Management Service (MMS), a troubled agency whose name and structure were permanently changed by the *Horizon* disaster. The MMS, which approved BP's frantic well design alterations in the days before the rig blew up, was an agency whose very existence represented a potential conflict of interest between government and industry. Its job was to award offshore leases, collect royalty payments from energy companies on the oil and natural gas that they produced, and police offshore drilling. Both Washington and the state governments along the Gulf Coast welcomed the royalty revenues that poured in as offshore drilling activity increased in the 1990s. The influx of revenue to federal coffers combined with the post-Reagan philosophy of deregulation and the industry's own hubris about its technical advances to foster a system of lax oversight.

MMS rig inspectors lived in the same areas as the oilfield workers they oversaw. Many of them grew up in areas such as southern Louisiana, whose economy depends on the offshore industry, and many had worked in the oilfields themselves before joining the government. As one field office official, who had been an inspector for the *Deepwater Horizon*, said: "Obviously, we're all oil industry. We're all from the same part of the country. Almost all of our inspectors have worked for oil companies out on these same platforms. They grew up in the same towns. Some of these people, they've been friends with all their life. They've been with these people since they were kids. They've hunted together. They fish together. They skeet shoot together. . . . They do this all the time."[3] MMS employees often angled for industry jobs while still working for the agency. The MMS inspector general released a report a month after the *Horizon* explosion that focused on employees' behavior at the Lake Charles, Louisiana, field office from 2000 to 2008. It found that inspectors routinely accepted gifts from the oil industry—crawfish boils, hunting and fishing trips, skeet-shooting contests, and golf tournaments. Two employees and members of their families flew on an oil company jet to attend the 2005 Peach Bowl game in Atlanta, Georgia, to watch Louisiana State University's football team play. One of them told investigators that he knew the trip was wrong, but he justified it because he was a "big LSU fan."[4] The findings weren't too surprising. MMS had been running as an industry lapdog for years. Earlier investigations had found instances of favoritism and a litany of gifts from oil companies, including ski trips, tickets to sporting events, and golf outings. One report also found "a culture of substance abuse and promiscuity" involving regulators and the companies that they were charged with regulating. It detailed frequent social gatherings lubricated with alcohol, cocaine, and marijuana. Some women were dubbed "MMS chicks" by oil company employees, and one suggested that a female MMS worker meet him for a bubble bath before they attended a Houston Texans football game.[5]

Such revolving doors between regulators and the regulated weren't uncommon. In Texas, for example, BP hired a state engineer in 2003 after he'd spent the two previous years processing applications for BP's new air quality permit at the Texas City refinery. Once on board, the former regulator spent the next two years representing BP in the permit negotiations. BP and state officials said the hiring didn't violate state laws that restrict regulators from taking industry jobs because although the engineer was involved in some BP permit applications for Texas City, he didn't work on the specific one that was granted in 2005. Regardless, the move illustrated the economic power oil companies like BP have over regulators.

—— ⚬⚬⚬ ——

While MMS employees enjoyed the gratuities lavished on them by oil companies, the agency remained perpetually understaffed. It had a total of 55 inspectors to oversee about 3,000 offshore facilities in the Gulf. By comparison, on the West Coast, 5 MMS inspectors covered just 23 rigs.[6] Federal regulations call for each rig to be inspected monthly. As a result of the understaffing, many rigs in the Gulf fell behind on their inspection schedules. The *Deepwater Horizon*, for example, was inspected only six times in 2008, and at the time of the explosion, it had missed 16 scheduled inspections since 2005. When inspectors did make it to the rigs, they often focused on reviewing the paperwork on tests that the company had conducted earlier. Surprise inspections, although required, were almost never conducted. The last inspection of the *Deepwater Horizon*, which was completed less than three weeks before the accident, was done by an inspector who later would tell MMS and Coast Guard investigators that he had never done an inspection before and his only experience was four months of training, which he had just completed.

Perhaps it would have been physically possible for a single inspector to adequately supervise an average of 54 Gulf rigs if the inspectors had been properly trained, but many of them weren't. Half of those surveyed as part of an Interior Department internal investigation said that they felt they lacked sufficient training, and some said that they had so little understanding of what they were inspecting that they simply asked company representatives to explain it to them. As a result, the MMS collected less than $1 million in civil penalties for offshore safety violations, which an internal report noted equaled less than one day's production for a larger facility in the Gulf.[7] Even when it did question companies' records, the MMS rarely halted drilling or revoked permits for safety violations. As far back as 2003, the agency had questioned BP's safety record in the Gulf. The MMS had expressed concern about a rig fire the previous year and a pressure buildup in an unfinished well that had forced the evacuation of workers, saying that the incidents "raised questions about the ability of BP to safely conduct drilling operations in the Gulf of Mexico." Yet BP continued drilling with the agency's blessing.

While the MMS functioned as a regulator, its overriding concern was enabling drilling, not restricting it. With more than $10 billion in annual royalties being collected, the government had an incentive for offshore production to continue. That stream of revenue, combined with the Gulf's unique role as a vital source of domestic energy, led to a special set of policies, many of which minimized reviews and accelerated the issuance of drilling permits. As new drilling technology lured companies farther offshore in the 1990s, the MMS adopted a new system of safety rules designed to reduce human errors leading to accidents, but it made these rules voluntary. In 2009, when it proposed tightening its safety regulations and making them mandatory, BP and other oil companies opposed the move, suggesting how the rules should be written if the agency decided to move forward.[8] The former head of the MMS—Elizabeth Birnbaum, who was to lose her job over the *Horizon* disaster—told Congress that the rules would eliminate two-thirds of all offshore accidents. They still haven't been implemented.

———— ∞∞∞ ————

As drilling technology became more complex, the system of regulating it became more lax. MMS training couldn't keep up with the new equipment. After decades of safe operations, both the industry and the MMS began to believe that a blowout simply couldn't happen. But, the technology for drilling in a few hundred feet of water is vastly different from the technology for drilling in a few thousand feet. On shallower wells, for example, the blowout preventer, the fail-safe device that failed in the *Deepwater Horizon* disaster, sits on the deck, rather than a mile below the surface. Inspectors can see it when they tour a rig. The *Horizon's* was on the seafloor, a mile below the surface, and accessible only by remote underwater submarines.

As the knowledge gap between the industry and the inspectors grew, the MMS expanded the idea of voluntary compliance. Industry experts argued that only the companies themselves had the technical knowledge to regulate the business. Bureaucrats, being unfamiliar with the complexity of offshore drilling, would only inhibit production, leading to higher prices and a greater dependence on foreign oil. Rather than allowing Congress or the administration to make rules that it didn't understand, the industry's trade group, the American Petroleum Institute, outlined minimum operating standards for its members. In the budget- and time-constrained world of the MMS, the institute provided a way to speed rule making. The result was a system in which companies operating offshore didn't feel compelled to follow rules that many saw as voluntary.

In late August 2010, a panel of Coast Guard and MMS officials assembled in a hotel conference room in south Houston for the latest round of hearings into the *Horizon* disaster, which they had been conducting for most of the summer. Late on a Wednesday afternoon, investigators grilled a Transocean subsea superintendent on the arcane rules governing the maintenance of blowout preventers. Among many rules for offshore operations, the API had issued guidelines for how the preventers should be maintained. Transocean, however, didn't follow those rules because it didn't find them practical. Instead, it had its own set of policies based on its years of hands-on experience with the equipment, the supervisor said. At various times during the months of hearings, the panel's co-chair, Coast Guard Captain Hung Nguyen, appeared exasperated by the lack of clear procedures and a clear chain of command aboard the *Horizon*, lapses that are common in the industry. He asked, for example, how the crew knew when command shifted from the captain of the rig to the offshore installations manager, which is supposed to happen when the rig is connected to the well. There was no official transfer of command. The *Horizon*'s captain told him that everyone on board just knows. During another session, Nguyen questioned why companies weren't required to have backup systems that would trigger the blowout preventers if a rig lost power. An MMS official said that the agency "highly encouraged" such systems. "Highly encourage? How does that translate into enforcement?" Nguyen asked incredulously. "There is no enforcement," the official replied. Nguyen's disbelief at the lack not just of regulation but indeed of any meaningful oversight structure seemed to grow as the hearings progressed. Now, he interrupted the discussion again. The rules for inspecting blowout preventers seemed rather loose, he said. He found the "cavalier attitude" toward such a critical safety device disturbing.

The MMS regulations, he pointed out, codified the API guidelines as the rule, the minimum requirement for maintaining the preventers. "Now we have a company, Transocean or somebody else, deciding their program is better," he said. "What good's the regulation that sets the minimum standard when everybody's doing their own thing out there?" Transocean argued that since the API rule was voluntary, it didn't have to follow it. Nguyen countered that the government didn't adopt a regulation with the intent of its being optional. API's standards required the blowout preventer to be disassembled and inspected every five years. That would mean taking a rig out of commission for 90 days, the supervisor testified. At a half-million dollars a day in lost revenue, the inspection would cost the company $45 million. Its in-house procedure allowed it to keep the rig in operation.

⎯⎯ ∞∞∞ ⎯⎯

For its part, the MMS did little to ensure that the industry com-plied even with the voluntary rules because in the Gulf, unlike in other areas where offshore drilling took place, exceptions were the rule. As wells were drilled in deeper and deeper water, the rules that did exist were stretched. Many of them dated from the 1970s, when the deepest well was about 700 feet below the water's surface. The *Horizon* was drilling at a depth almost five times greater. BP had to apply for repeated exemptions when it switched to the long-string design, because it deviated from its own design standards and safety policies. It requested another exemption from testing the blowout preventer, even though it had malfunctioned weeks before the accident. The MMS granted all these exemptions, sometimes within minutes of the request.

Each offshore well is different, yet the MMS accepted blanket environmental plans for many of them. Known as the environmental impact statement, such a plan was supposed to outline the size and potential damage from a spill. Most ma-jor oil companies working in the Gulf used the same plan. As would later be revealed before Congress, among the contacts they listed was a national wildlife expert who had died four years before the plan was filed. They cited walruses, sea lions, and other animals that don't live in the Gulf as "sensitive bio-logical resources." One oil company executive admitted to law-makers that the plans were an embarrassment.

Yet even if the MMS staff had wanted to review these plans, it wouldn't have had the personnel necessary to wade through each study, which typically ran from 500 to 800 pages. John Hof-meister, the former president of Shell Oil, visited MMS's Washington headquarters in the summer of 2006 to determine why it was taking so long for the agency to approve a Shell environmental impact statement for drilling in the Beaufort and Chukchi seas off the coast of Alaska. The process was supposed to take 120 days, but at the end of that time, nothing had happened. Shell had a limited window of ice-free drilling days, and time was slipping away. Hofmeister, who had come to Shell as a human resources executive after working outside the industry for companies such as General Electric, thought he needed to understand the MMS permitting process better and arranged the headquarters visit. He found that preparing the paperwork involved reviewing hundreds of pages of documents and writing hundreds more. "Common sense told me that no one could put an eight-hundred-page permit together in four months. They acknowledged as much, knew what the law said, and admitted they were in violation."[9] Congress had refused to extend the time requirement for granting the permit, so MMS simply ignored the time stipulation. Shell had spent $3.5 billion for its Chukchi and Beaufort leases, and four years later, it was still waiting for permits. Yet in the Gulf, the MMS was issuing as many as a thousand new drilling permits a year.

⎯⎯∞⎯⎯

The offshore oil industry was awash in its own hubris. Oil executives frequently pointed out that tens of thousands of wells had been drilled in the Gulf without a major accident, all done under the auspices of the industry's self-regulation. While this was technically true, the industry's much-vaunted safety record involved some public relations veneer. Although they weren't considered major accidents, 18 workers—excluding the 11 who died aboard the *Horizon*—had been killed while working offshore since 1979. In the past decade, blowouts and other "well control incidents" had caused 5 rig explosions and 17 evacuations.[10] That's still a low incident rate compared with the number of wells drilled, but after most of the accidents, the MMS proposed new rules, such as improved cementing techniques or better-equipped blowout preventers. In each case, the industry said that such measures were unnecessary and too costly. Some changes were eventually implemented; others weren't.

Exploration for oil in the Gulf of Mexico had become ruled by the engineers' conceit that the industry's technology was impeccable and by the financial arrogance that argued that safety would never be compromised because the fallout from a disaster would be so great that companies would never cut corners. The companies never asked the key questions: What happens if the technology doesn't save you? What if workers have been lulled into complacency and fail to recognize how their decisions could lead to disaster?

It was against this backdrop of fractured regulations that Obama made his call for lifting some of the long-standing federal bans on offshore drilling. The move drew an immediate rebuke from some members of his own party and from environmental groups that included key supporters. The *Horizon* disaster, coming just weeks later, erupted on the political front like a flaming chorus of "I told you so." Obama struggled for months to express the proper amount of outrage, to capture the public's anger, and to prove to his party faithful that he was willing to stand up to oil companies. One of his first decisions in response to the disaster, though, came on May 12. He abolished the MMS, splitting it into three agencies. One would issue leases, one would collect royalties, and a third would supervise offshore drilling and production. His second major decision came a few weeks later: All new drilling in the Gulf of Mexico, America's most prolific and promising reserve of domestic energy, would cease immediately.

CHAPTER 16

REEFS
OF RUIN

S outhern Louisiana isn't really land and
isn't really sea. It's a giant ecological sponge,
miles upon miles of wetlands that stretch out across the Mississippi Delta in an ever-thinning web of land and water. The
pores of soil and water collect the fresh water that flows down
the Mississippi River as it mingles with the saltwater of the Gulf
of Mexico, producing a brackish liquid that creates one of the
world's most prolific breeding grounds for shellfish. Louisiana
is the largest supplier of seafood in the United States—blue
crabs, redfish, and shrimp the size of crescent rolls. Most of
all, though, it's known for oysters, huge succulent bivalves that
beckon diners from the half shell. In 2008, the oyster industry of
southern Louisiana produced more than 11 million pounds
of the shellfish, worth about $34 million. The delicate mix of
salt- and fresh water in the Delta creates a unique breeding
ground, one that Dale Chaisson has fished for most of his life.

Chaisson bought his first boat at age 11, and he's roamed
the oyster reefs around Pointe-Aux-Chenes, 70 miles southwest of New Orleans, in the 37 years since then. His father,
grandfather, great-grandfather, and ancestors several greats

beyond that all fished for oysters and shrimp. For two centuries, oystermen like Chaisson have prowled the marshlands, interrupted only by the occasional hurricane. The past ten years had been a bad decade for storms, though. Along the bayou Pointe-Aux-Chenes, lifeless trees snake skyward, their leaves stripped bare. Between the occupied homes, crumbled houses remain, victims of Katrina or Rita or Gustav or the other storms that have blown through with such disturbing regularity that residents can't remember which one destroyed what. The harvest for 2010, though, was looking better. Chaisson and his brothers and nephews and cousins—oystermen all—were hauling up big clusters of shellfish, the sign of an abundant crop. Then the *Deepwater Horizon* exploded 40 miles offshore, and Chaisson and his family found themselves waiting for the inevitable influx of oil that would kill at least the current season and perhaps many more seasons to come. "Last year, the storm took it away from us. This year, BP took it away," he said. Chaisson has a linebacker's physique and a jockey's height. His black hair recedes from a widow's peak. He has meaty, rough hands scarred from years of handling ragged-shelled oysters and an easy smile that spreads out from under a thick mustache.

As the oil approached in early May, government inspectors closed the reefs to fishing. Chaisson's five boats sat idle, moored in the bayou, waiting. He eventually leased one of them to BP for spill clean-up work, but what he received didn't come close to covering what he could have made with a good harvest. BP was paying about $1,700 for each day it used the boat, which wasn't a bad rate except that he still had four boats sitting idle. Each would normally haul 40 sacks of oysters weighing 110 pounds each, and heading into the harvest a sack was selling for $30. With all five boats working every day, he would have brought in five times what BP was paying him. Besides, BP used

his boat only intermittently, even though it required partici-
pants in the cleanup program to keep their vessels ready at all
times in case the company decided that it wanted them. "The
boats belong to them right now," Chaisson said. The process
was chaotic. BP representatives weren't consistent in the rules
they relayed to the fishermen about the "vessels of opportunity"
program, and rumors ran rampant through the bayous. Some
of the boat owners were signing contracts even though they
couldn't read. Others didn't receive copies of their contracts.
Those who did often didn't read all the provisions, one of which
stated that if the fishermen developed a viable spill-fighting
technology, the idea belonged to, and could be patented by, BP.

The economic ripples from the encroaching oil slick spread
quickly. On the nearby Isle de Jean Charles, Chaisson's cousin
Tio runs a small marina. In midsummer, the lot should have
been full of boats heading out to the reefs, but the empty asphalt
served as a stark reminder of the leaking oil's price. A few miles
away, BP rented an entire marina as a staging area for cleanup
boats. Along the bayou Pointe-Aux-Chenes, shrimp sheds that
normally would be lined with boats unloading their catch were
deserted. Along the Gulf Coast, from Louisiana to the Florida
Panhandle, similar tales of economic hardship began to grow as
the oil moved in. Tar balls washed up on the shores of Florida's
white sand beaches, and owners of vacation homes struggled to
attract beachgoers to their properties. The annual fishing rodeo
on Dauphin Island, Alabama—the small community's biggest
tourist attraction of the year—was canceled and replaced with a
sparsely attended "liar's contest."

All along the Gulf, the public anger toward BP grew as the
money became tighter and tighter. In Grand Isle, Louisiana,

one of BP's staging areas for cleanup work, a homeowner set an old toilet by the side of the road and hung a sign over it that said "BP headquarters." Nearby, the beaches were closed as cleanup crews worked behind orange booms to scoop up contaminated sand. On the inland side of the island, oil oozed into the marsh grass, leaving its stalks stained from the waterline down when the tide went out, like a dirty ring left in a draining bathtub.

In New Orleans, P&J Oysters, the oldest oyster processor in the United States, shut down after 134 years in business, its supply strangled by the advance of BP's oil. In New Iberia, about 130 miles away, Bill Parker closed his Pearl Reef Oyster Co., which he'd founded 36 years earlier. Parker, affable and soft-spoken, had weathered a host of hardships during his three decades in business—hurricanes, floods, a fire at a processing plant, and even embezzlement by an employee that almost put him out of business. The oysters, though, he could always count on to be there. Sometimes he marveled at nature's resilience, at how the reefs could recover from natural disasters. Now, they faced a far greater threat—not just the influx of crude, but also the chemical dispersants that BP was using to break down the oil on the water. Oysters are filters of the sea. They suck in everything, and they hold on to impurities, which affect their taste. Parker worried that one glob of oil in the reef would taint the entire crop because the taste of oil can spread so quickly among the shellfish. He'd seen what petroleum in an oyster reef could do. The marshes of Louisiana are crisscrossed with pipelines, and occasionally there's a leak. A few drops of petroleum can ruin a sack of oysters and any other sacks with which it comes in contact.

By mid-May, Parker had laid off his 100 employees, parked his fleet of trucks, and told fishermen, including Chaisson, to moor their boats. "We've been knocked down so many times, and we never shut down completely," he lamented. Gil LaCour, who had been Pearl Reef's marketing director, worried that the encroaching oil would mean "the death of the oyster culture." LaCour, a towering man with dark hair and a beard, became visibly agitated when talking about how BP crippled his industry. In the sticky heat of the southern Louisiana summer, his glasses slid down his nose, and he pushed them back up as he spoke, leaving the lenses smudged. Fishermen like Chaisson, he pointed out, have known only fishing, skills passed down through generations, skills that they intended to pass on to their children and grandchildren. "What do you pay for a lost culture?" he asked.

Parker would keep Pearl Reef closed through the summer and into the fall. By October, his smallest leases near the Texas border would reopen, and he would plan to restart with about 20 percent of his previous business. Parker's main reefs would remain closed, however, and the outlook wasn't good. To keep the oil away from shore, BP and the government devised a plan to open locks near the mouth of the Mississippi, flooding the marshes with fresh water and disrupting the delicate brackish recipe oysters need to thrive. It's known as a "freshwater kill." The oysters that remained were small and brown, and Parker worried that even if they were free of dispersants, it would take at least two years for them to recover from the flood of river water.

—❧—

Parker leased more than 26,000 acres of reefs, mostly around Grand Isle, and he leased most of it from the Apache Corporation, the Houston energy company. The arrangement underscores the economic irony of southern Louisiana: Just about everyone either fishes or works in the oil industry, and many do both. Water inundates the land, but so does oil. It's carried by the pipelines that run through the marshes like a cross-hatching of steel. In the six decades since Kerr-McGee drilled the first offshore well off the coast, energy has grown into an engine of jobs that provides the region with its economic foundation. Its impact is visible along the 20-mile stretch of highway between Lafayette and New Iberia, where the shining glass-and-stone buildings of oil company offices are interspersed with used car lots and gas station casinos. Just outside Lafayette, bright yellow helicopters hover like bumblebees over a landing strip as pilot trainees practice touch-and-go exercises at the offices of Petroleum Helicopters. The company is one of the primary shuttle services ferrying crews and supplies between land and rigs.

Drive on, and the energy company names pile up like mile markers—Baker Hughes, M-I Swaco, Pencor, GE Oil and Gas—the list grows as long as the highway itself. The seafood industry felt the brunt of the oil slick's arrival first, but the impact quickly spread to the area's other economic pillar, energy. The Obama administration's drilling moratorium was the second fist of what amounted to a one-two economic gut punch. Further down the road, in Des Allemands, Otto Candies III worried about his marine transport business, which provides services such as ferrying supplies and conducting underwater inspections for offshore rigs. His company, Otto Candies LLC, was founded by his grandfather in 1942 when Humble Oil Co., now Exxon Mobil, asked the company's namesake to clear water lilies from a small canal. The company grew into a global marine transport enterprise, specializing in moving big equipment. In 1972, NASA hired it to transport the Saturn V rocket to Cape Canaveral (at that time known as Cape Kennedy). It once moved an entire refinery from Houston to Puerto Rico, delivering 6,000 tons of cargo a week for almost a year and a

half. Now, Otto Candies III, the company's secretary and trea-
surer, wondered how he, his father, and his two brothers would
steer the family-run company through a shutdown of the Gulf,
which remained its lifeblood. The longer drilling remained
halted, the greater the chances that the big drilling companies
like Transocean would move their equipment to other oil hot
spots around the world, such as Brazil or West Africa. Once the
business left, he feared that it might not come back. "It's not
like six months and a day you throw the switch and everything
comes back on," he warned. "Big equipment that's going to
other places, that's not going to be coming back. All this does is
it takes an already bad economic situation and makes it worse."
Candies's company idled two of its biggest boats in the Gulf for
most of September, accepting lower rates. That kept them under contract and avoided layoffs for the crews, but it meant less
revenue for the firm heading into the traditionally slower winter season in the Gulf. For most of the summer and fall, though,
transport vessels, tugs, and other boats used as workhorses of
the offshore industry were moored as many as five deep along
some docks in southern Louisiana.

Residents had begun the summer furious at BP over the spill,
but now their anger shifted toward the Obama administration.
It had managed to make an untenable situation unthinkable.
Thousands gathered in places like Lafayette's Cajun dome sta-
dium to protest the moratorium. The Louisiana Oil and Gas
Association estimated that 150,000 jobs would be lost at a time
when the national unemployment rate was already hovering
above 9 percent. Drilling companies, echoing Candies's concern, threatened to pull their rigs from the Gulf.

As the summer wore on, the worry eased, but not the anger. Among the 30 or so deepwater projects that had been halted by the moratorium, most of the companies that owned the rigs worked with producers to keep the rigs in place and the crews occupied until drilling resumed. The mass exodus of rigs didn't happen, although a few rigs did move off to other areas. Most, though, were under long-term contracts, and none of the companies involved were willing to give up on the promise of the Gulf, even if it meant having to wait six months to proceed.

———— ∞∞∞ ————

The energy industry is tightly knit and insular. Companies are slow to publicly criticize one another, but executives were becoming increasingly frustrated that the entire industry was suffering for what they saw as BP's carelessness. If a company gets a reputation for having too many accidents or lapses in judgment, it becomes difficult for that company to find partners. The whole industry was disappointed in BP, but the industry also knew why the blowout had happened. Among its peers, BP was known for finding big deposits of oil, but it was also known for cutting corners and cutting costs. Now, its runaway well had brought the drilling moratorium to the Gulf, shutting down the entire industry. Long the industry outlier, BP found itself with few friends in the oil patch. In testimony before Congress, both Transocean and Halliburton executives pointed fingers at BP as the culprit in the blowout, even as BP tried to lay the blame on them. Executives of four major oil companies testified before a congressional committee in mid-June and stopped just short of blaming BP for the disaster. They made it clear, though, that they didn't agree with BP's methods of operation. "We would not have drilled the well the way they did," Exxon Mobil Chairman Rex Tillerson said.

The statements of the industry's most prominent executives emboldened BP's partners in the Macondo well to break ranks, too. Just days after the executives' testimony, Anadarko issued a public statement refusing to contribute to any of the cleanup costs and blaming BP for the disaster. "The mounting evidence clearly demonstrates that this tragedy was preventable and the direct result of BP's reckless decisions and actions," Anadarko's chief executive, Jim Hackett, said.[1] Hackett added that he was "shocked" to find that BP "operated unsafely and failed to monitor and react to several critical warning signs during the drilling of the Macondo well." It was a carefully crafted statement, invoking the legal language that would release Anadarko from its obligations under the Macondo contract, provided it could prove the allegations. The company had little choice. Its insurance would not come close to covering its share of the spill costs if it had to pay, and with its own stock price dragged down by the crisis, its future as an independent company was also in jeopardy. Although BP sent Anadarko and Mitsui bills for their share of the costs, neither of them agreed to pay.

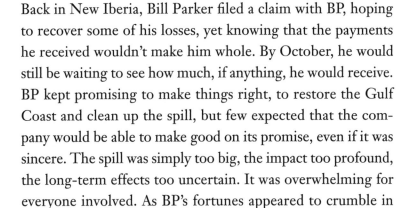

Back in New Iberia, Bill Parker filed a claim with BP, hoping to recover some of his losses, yet knowing that the payments he received wouldn't make him whole. By October, he would still be waiting to see how much, if anything, he would receive. BP kept promising to make things right, to restore the Gulf Coast and clean up the spill, but few expected that the company would be able to make good on its promise, even if it was sincere. The spill was simply too big, the impact too profound, the long-term effects too uncertain. It was overwhelming for everyone involved. As BP's fortunes appeared to crumble in June, the residents who were so angry with the oil company now had a new fear: that BP would pay the ultimate price for its sins. With their businesses shuttered or suffering, BP's claims process became a lifeline, and they worried that if the company went bankrupt, they would be left with nothing. Their futures depended on the very company that had ruined them. "The only hope that we have is BP now," Parker said.

In Washington, as the Obama administration watched the spreading economic devastation along the Gulf, a similar fear was growing. If BP reneged, how could the government, which was already running record deficits, avoid shouldering the financial burden for what was a private-sector mistake? The answer seemed clear: Make BP pay in advance.

CHAPTER 17

APOLOGIES
ALL AROUND

Tony Hayward stood before the long wooden table. Behind him, cameras clicked like popcorn. He was there to be called to account, to explain one of the worst environmental disasters in America's history. It had been almost two months since the blowout aboard the *Deepwater Horizon*. He sat down in front of a microphone, alone at the table, facing a hostile group of U.S. lawmakers who had summoned him to the wood-paneled hall for a venting of the public outrage that they represented. Congressional hearings are more political theater than fact-finding missions. The most revealing evidence tends to be released long before the first witness ever strides though the giant wooden doors and enters the chamber. This case was no different. The committee, led by Henry Waxman, a California Democrat whose disdain for oil companies was well known, had released BP e-mails that showed engineers debating the well design, especially the use of only six centralizers, but those facts weren't really what the committee members were after. They wanted to hurl the collective anger of their constituents at the man whom they deemed responsible. They wanted to show voters that they were holding someone—this man, this Mr. Hayward from Great Britain—accountable. They would demand answers. They would expect contrition. They would get neither.

Hayward maintained a sedate veneer, but his displeasure at the process was apparent. He had dealt with leaders the world over, but few political processes compared with the grilling he was about to endure. The hearing began with Waxman excoriating Hayward as an absentee executive who was deliberately blind to the dangers of the Macondo well and the shortcuts being taken by his subordinates to save time and money. One after another, the congressmen took their turns, revisiting the disaster in Texas City and the leaking pipelines in Alaska. One called for Hayward's resignation, which already seemed inevitable.

—⁂—

After an hour of this verbal flogging, Hayward raised his right hand and agreed to tell the truth. As he began to speak, a protester in the audience interrupted him. She raised hands stained with oil, shouting, "You need to be charged with a crime!" Hayward paused, but kept his eyes on the panel, blinking slowly. When security guards had removed the woman from the chambers, he began again, trying to set the tone that would assuage the anger of a nation. "I'm deeply sorry," he said. But the answers that the members of Congress wanted weren't forthcoming. As the day wore on, Hayward's testimony became pocked with excuses. It was too early to draw any conclusions about the cause of the accident, he insisted. The more the lawmakers asked, the more Hayward's responses underscored the lack of accountability in BP's management structure. He wasn't involved in the well design decisions. He wasn't a cement engineer. He wasn't a drilling engineer. "I'm not able to make a judgment as to whether the right decisions were made," he said.

What the lawmakers wanted from him—an explanation—was the one thing that he couldn't or wouldn't give. As the chief executive, Hayward clearly wasn't involved in the decisions on how to drill a specific well. He hadn't known at the time about the type of cement used or why the engineers opted for a long string rather than a tie-back on this particular well. However, in the months since, he hadn't bothered to find out, or if he had, he wasn't willing to share the information with the angry inquisition before him. In America, chief executives bear the ultimate responsibility for the companies they run. In Britain, the stopping of the buck is less well defined. Just as John Browne seemed surprised by the anger directed at him in the United States after the Texas City disaster, Hayward seemed to struggle with the notion that he personally should answer for what happened aboard the *Deepwater Horizon* or for the oil leaking from BP's runaway well.

The hearing ground on for seven hours, and Hayward began to appear increasingly evasive. It wasn't just that he didn't know specifics about the well; it was that he refused to put anything that happened in any sort of context. Pressed again and again on the cause of the accident and whether broader corporate policies, such as cost cutting, may have played a role, Hayward dodged and weaved. "None of us yet knows why it happened. I haven't drawn a conclusion."

If Hayward hadn't drawn conclusions, others had. Just days earlier, his counterparts at Exxon Mobil, Chevron, Conoco-Phillips, and Shell Oil had testified that they had concluded that BP's well design didn't follow the industry's best practices.

Anadarko, with its public admonishment of BP, had come to a similar conclusion. Hayward, though, refused to even go so far as to refer to BP's own document, submitted to the committee, outlining what might have happened based on the evidence that it had available at the time.

Four years earlier, as head of the company's exploration division, Hayward had openly criticized a BP leadership that had grown complacent, that failed to see the problems facing the company. He came into the chief executive's job as a reformer, as someone who would make sweeping changes. Yet as he sat in front of Waxman's committee, he sounded much like John Browne at the press conference for the Baker Commission report. For Hayward, the hearing was something to be endured. It wasn't a forum at which a chief executive could make his case. His job was to accept his public spanking, and with that done, he walked out of the chamber and slipped into a waiting sport-utility vehicle, which melded into the crush of the capital's rush hour. Besides, Hayward had already achieved his real purpose in coming to Washington, and it had nothing to do with Waxman's committee. He had made the deal the day before, and it was barely mentioned at the hearing except, oddly, in the opening comments from one Texas congressman.

—∞∞∞—

As the hearings began, Joe Barton, a Republican from the Texas town of Ennis, south of Dallas, opened by issuing an apology to the man who had come to issue an apology to the nation. Barton used his opening remarks to decry an agreement that had been made between BP and the Obama administration the day before that would create a $20 billion fund, paid for by BP and administered by the government, to handle claims related to the disaster. Barton made it clear that he was speaking only for himself, then said he thought it was "a tragedy of the first proportion that a private corporation can be subjected to what I would characterize as a shakedown, in this case a $20 billion shakedown." While he didn't question that BP should be liable for damages, or that many people thought that the company had compromised safety, he felt that the creation of the spill fund violated BP's due process. "I apologize," he said. "I do not want to live in a country where any time a citizen or a corporation does something that's legitimately wrong is subject to some sort of political pressure that is—again, in my words, amounts to a shakedown. So I apologize." Barton said he spoke on his own behalf, but the comments didn't seem to be his idea alone. The day before his apology, the Republican Study Committee, which consists of 114 congressmen from the party, floated the phrase "Chicago-style shakedown politics" in reference to the fund proposal.[1]

Barton, in an attempt to make political hay, missed the irony of the situation. He was an unlikely apologist. In 2006, when the Republicans controlled the House, Barton had led the committee that Waxman now chaired. He had criticized BP over the Alaskan pipeline corrosion and Bob Malone's decision to shut down the system, triggering a spike in gasoline prices. In a letter to John Browne, Barton had argued that BP's cost cutting had undermined the integrity of the pipeline system, referring to "substantial evidence that BP's chronic neglect directly contributed to the shutdown." Coming on the heels of the Texas City explosion and the Alaskan spill earlier that year, the pipeline shutdown "calls into question BP's commitment to safety" and "contradicts everything the committee has been told" about the lessons the company said it had learned from its mistakes, he said. "The fact that BP's consistent assurances were not well grounded is troubling and requires further examination."[2] Barton himself had overseen those examinations, running committee hearings and pressing BP executives to answer his charges of neglect. In response, BP's representative had offered a defense that bore a stunning similarity to Hayward's in its evasiveness: "I am not a pipeline expert." Barton concluded that BP had essentially "bet the company" on the premise that its fields in Alaska would be depleted before the pipeline failed. "BP's policies are as rusty as its pipelines," he said, adding that he was "concerned about BP's corporate culture of seeming indifference to safety and environmental issues, and this comes from a company that prides itself in their ads on protecting the environment. Shame, shame, shame."[3]

Yet four years later, it was as if Barton, still the committee's ranking member, had forgotten BP's track record and its "corporate culture of seeming indifference." He sat at the far corner of the committee bench, now a minority member, and issued his apology before Hayward had had a chance to speak. Hayward seemed stunned by Barton's comments, but he showed little reaction.[4] He began his own remarks by touting the very fund that Barton had criticized. It was proof, he said, that BP would honor its promise to make things right. The government's oversight would make the claims process more transparent and remove any suspicion about how BP was handling the claims. "We said all along that we would pay these costs," he said. "Now the American people can be confident that our word is good."

---⊗⊗⊗---

Ironically, the idea for a spill fund didn't begin at the White House. It was first proposed by a member of Barton's own party, Florida Senator George LeMieux. LeMieux had been proposing for more than a month that Congress should establish a revolving account to ensure that the money would be available for the states that needed it.[5] As BP's stock continued to slide during the month, the Obama administration began fleshing out the idea. The president summoned Hayward, BP Chairman Carl-Henric Svanberg, and managing director Bob Dudley to the White House to hammer out an agreement on how BP would pay for the fund. Some of the details continued to be negotiated throughout the summer, including exactly how BP would provide the funding. Initially, the company contributed $3 billion, and Obama appointed as the fund's administrator Kenneth Feinberg, who had been overseeing executive pay packages at financial firms that received federal bailout money. By the time Feinberg took over, in late August, BP had already paid almost $370 million in claims. From the government's standpoint, the fund would ensure that economic victims of the spill would be compensated, but it also offered benefits for BP.

While the administration made it clear that $20 billion wasn't a cap—BP might be forced to contribute more to the fund if claims exceeded that amount—it gave investors an element of certainty. As the summer wore on and the crisis eased, it seemed unlikely that BP would have to pay more. The company's stock began to recover, with the fund serving as a de facto estimate of BP's liability. For BP, the spill fund was anything but a shakedown. Not only did it offer the company some reprieve from the financial uncertainty that had been battering it for two months, but it allowed it to foist the administrative duties of paying claims onto the government. By mid-August, the company had handed off all responsibility for reviewing, paying, and rejecting claims to Feinberg. Almost immediately, he drew the ire of business owners by declaring that the amount that they would receive would be linked to the distance between their businesses and the beach.[6] Those who were closer would

get more. He also decided that any money that fishermen received for assisting in the cleanup effort would be deducted
from their claims, although he later said that he might change
his mind on the matter.

Feinberg had received public accolades for his handling of
the 9/11 victims' fund, set up to pay the families of those killed
in the 2001 terrorist attacks in New York and Washington.
The spill fund, though, was something entirely different. The
number of claims and claimants continued to grow. Feinberg
backed a provision that required claimants to agree not to sue
BP or other companies involved in the *Deepwater Horizon* accident, including Transocean, Halliburton, and Anadarko. It was
similar to a provision that he'd used in the 9/11 fund, but this
time, it invoked anger from Gulf Coast residents. "It is not in
your interest to tie up you and the courts in years of uncertain
protracted litigation when there is an alternative that has been
created," he said. "I take the position, if I don't find you eligible,
no court will find you eligible."[7] Many residents saw this as yet
another attempt to shield BP from liability.

⦿⦿⦿

The Gulf Coast had a new villain. No longer was it BP that
was frustrating their efforts to get compensated for their losses;
now it was the government. In September, Feinberg attended
a hearing in Houma, Louisiana, where the local civic center
was filled with residents looking for an explanation of how they
would be paid. One woman held a sign that read: "Hey, Feinberg, you make me miss FEMA," a reference to the federal relief agency that had bungled the response to Hurricane Katrina
five years earlier.

Meanwhile, BP had gained leverage. Having created the
fund and taken over responsibility for it, the government now

had to make sure that BP paid. With difficult elections looming in November and the country running record deficits, the
Obama administration couldn't afford, financially or politically,
to pay for BP's mistakes. The two sides continued to discuss
the funding structure throughout the summer, with the government looking for a guarantee on the remaining money—about
$17 billion—that BP had pledged to the fund. The administra-
tion wanted some sort of collateral to ensure that the program
would be funded, even if BP were unable to pay in cash. BP suggested posting revenue from its oilfields in the Gulf.

Earlier in the summer, George Miller, a California Democrat
in the House of Representatives, had proposed an amendment
to a bill that would prohibit the issuance of drilling permits to
companies that had had more than ten fatalities at drilling or
production facilities that resulted from violations of federal
or state law. The amendment was tailored for BP. The Texas
City explosion in 2005 exceeded the fatality threshold and had
resulted in a guilty plea to a federal felony. The bill passed the
House in late July, increasing the chances that BP might be
barred from the Gulf for years, cut off from its lucrative drilling
prospects, and denied its future revenue from the prolific fields
that it hoped to tap.

By pledging the Gulf production as collateral for the spill
fund, not only did BP give the government a short-term incentive to lift the moratorium, but it was gaining leverage in
its fight for continued access to U.S. waters. In early September, BP drove home the point, saying that if lawmakers suc-
ceeded in passing legislation that restricted its receipt of new
offshore permits, it might not have enough money to pay for
all the spill damages. Barton had it wrong. BP wasn't the victim

of a shakedown, but the perpetrator of one. The spill fund, the claims it had already paid, its waiver of the liability caps under the Oil Pollution Act, the money it gave to help Florida market its beaches after the spill, and the millions it donated to study the disaster's long-term environmental effects were all proof, BP liked to point out, that it had done more than was required to take responsibility for the disaster. Increasingly, though, it was becoming clear that those efforts were little more than bargaining chips in BP's ultimate endgame of resuming operations in the Gulf as soon as possible.

CHAPTER 18

MEET THE
NEW BOSS . . .

Perhaps it was appropriate that when the end came, Tony Hayward quoted Winston Churchill. After all, the famed British wartime leader had been singlehandedly responsible for keeping what became BP in business a century earlier. Hayward, in contrast, had presided over what had become the biggest threat to its existence since that time. The company, he conceded, couldn't move forward as long as he remained chief executive.

Things had begun to improve for BP by late July 2010, but nothing could save Hayward's career by then. Engineers working in Houston had failed in several earlier attempts to create a custom cap that would fit over the broken wellhead, but the previous failures had provided illumination on how to succeed. Using the remote-operated vehicles, they sliced through the bent riser pipe in early June and attached a cap over the jagged edge. The cap didn't stop the flow of oil, but it enabled BP to reduce it, siphoning more of the oil to collection ships on the surface. That design led to a better solution: the "capping stack" that was bolted over a flange for the riser, providing a tighter seal. Gradually, the engineers closed valves on the device, shutting down the flow of oil and monitoring the pressure from below. From the time of the blowout in April, engineers and geologists had been concerned that the integrity of the well bore itself might be in question, and that the pressure from capping the flow might cause it to collapse. However, the pressure held, and the final valve was closed. It wasn't a solution. Only the relief wells, which had been slowly churning for the past two months to intersect the well bore, could ensure that the Macondo was truly dead. The capping stack, though, meant that for the first time in three months, BP's oil wasn't adding to the pollution of the Gulf every day. It was a small victory in an otherwise dismal summer.

The end of Hayward's career began with yet another misstep on his part. Despite having vowed to stay in the Gulf until the crisis was resolved, Hayward decided to take a little time off. He'd barely been home since April, and he decided to spend a Saturday attending a yacht race around England's Isle of Wight, in which his 52-foot sailboat *Bob* was participating. The Round the Island Race is one of the world's biggest, with more than 1,700 boats competing on a course that spans 50 nautical miles. A photographer snapped a grainy picture of Hayward in the cockpit of the yacht, the port-side sheet—the line that controls the direction of the foresail—gripped firmly in his left hand. He wore dark glasses and a black baseball cap pulled down tight over his face. The collar of his windbreaker was flipped up straight, covering his ears, as if he were seeking anonymity at one of the world's most exclusive yachting events. BP's public relations team immediately went into damage control, saying that Hayward would be back at work fighting the runaway well in the Gulf of Mexico Monday morning. "He's spending a few hours with his family on a weekend. I'm sure that everyone would understand that," one spokesman said. No one did.

———∞∞∞———

Three days later, BP announced that Hayward would return to London and focus on running the rest of BP. Bob Dudley, the former Amoco executive who'd grown up in Mississippi, had already been tapped earlier in the month to take over the spill cleanup. Now, it was clear that BP wanted to distance Hayward from the spill and shift the focus to an American executive. Dudley was serving as a managing director, an ill-defined role that he'd been given when he had had to flee his post in Russia in 2008. The move was also the first clear sign that BP's indulgent board had finally given up on Hayward. Rumors quickly circulated that his long-expected departure was nigh and that Dudley would replace him.

———∞∞∞———

Dudley had a receding line of straight blond hair, blue eyes, and a tall, lanky appearance. He looked more comfortable in open-collared shirts than in suits, which seemed to hang off him as if they were a little too big. He had joined Amoco in 1979 and moved to BP after it acquired Amoco in 1998. Like Hayward and Browne before him, Dudley had been shuffled around the world by BP, with postings in the United States, Great Britain, the South China Sea, and Moscow. He became one of Browne's trusted inner circle, a turtle. After two years in Russia, Dudley technically left BP to become chief executive of TNK-BP, a joint venture between the company and a Russian concern controlled by a group of wealthy oligarchs.

John Browne had been angling for a way to push BP into Russia since soon after the fall of the Berlin Wall. The collapse of the Soviet Union created an opportunity for foreign oil companies, which saw a chance to tap Russia's huge and under-developed oil reserves. The early post-Soviet years, though, were marked by widespread corruption and economic chaos, as a once centrally controlled economy tried to understand the concept of a free market. Browne's early discussions yielded little more than a chain of BP gas stations in Moscow. As Russia moved to privatize its previously state-owned com-panies, the arcane process was understood by only a few in-dividuals, who used it to their advantage and assembled big portfolios of industrial assets on the cheap. In many cases, the government, facing mounting budget shortfalls, may have simply steered auctions so that assets went into the hands of a favored few. These oligarchs became a part of the new Russian power structure.

In late 1997, Browne signed a deal with one of the oligarchs at 10 Downing Street while his friend Prime Minister Tony Blair looked on approvingly. The $571 million venture was her-alded as one of United Kingdom's biggest investments in Russia at the time. But the deal, which gave BP a stake in a Russian company called Sidanco, quickly unraveled. Using Russia's new bankruptcy laws, competitors bought up Sidanco's debt, had its assets essentially declared worthless one by one, and then forced the sale of the assets for a fraction of their value. One of the best assets, which controlled prolific reserves in western Si-beria, was taken over by a company called Tyumenskaya Nefty-anaya Kompaniya, or TNK. "I was livid," Browne recalled. "I had signed the deal in front of Blair; BP had been made to look a fool."[1] The company lost more than $200 million on its investment in two years. Other Western oil companies were finding similar difficulties in Russia. Many decided to pull out.

Browne refused. "I knew if we allowed ourselves to get pushed out of Russia, we would probably never go back."[2]

Browne used his political connections to put pressure on TNK, and eventually the two companies reached a deal in which they would set up a fifty-fifty joint venture. Browne had wanted a 51 percent stake to give BP the upper hand, but the oligarch in charge of TNK, Mikhail Fridman, refused. Browne was adamant that BP wouldn't settle for a minority stake. He didn't want a repeat of the Sidanco fiasco. So they agreed to even shares, putting the assets of TNK, Sidanco, and BP's Moscow gas stations into the deal. Before it was signed, Russian President Vladimir Putin warned Browne: "It's up to you. An equal split never works."[3]

———— ∞ ————

BP invested $8 billion for its half of the deal. Fridman became the chairman, and BP gained the right to appoint the chief executive. For that post, Browne chose his American turtle, Bob Dudley. Its interest in the TNK venture made BP the world's second-largest oil producer, and the Russian venture now accounted for almost one-third of its reserves. For the first three years, the deal seemed to be working. BP boosted production by 30 percent by introducing Western oil technology. Profits soared. Hayward, soon after taking over as chief executive, declared the venture a "stunning success."

The task of melding the two distinct corporate cultures fell to Dudley. He quickly won over the combined workforce with a management style that was seen by employees as open and direct. He implemented "town hall"–style meetings, something that was almost unheard of in Russian companies, to encourage open discussions between management and workers. However, the fifty-fifty nature of the partnership meant that Dudley had to balance the interests of both BP and TNK without appearing to favor either. Dudley soon found himself caught between the venture's shareholders.

The oligarchs saw Dudley as BP's puppet, and they began to bristle at what they saw as BP's attempts to exert more control over the venture. To make matters worse, Browne, Hayward, and Dudley all failed to understand the complex stew of politics and business that were at work in Russia. Hayward dismissed the growing discontent of the Russian investors. "From time to time, there are little bumps in the road," he said. The oligarchs accused Dudley of impeding plans to expand TNK-BP's investments outside Russia. Increasingly, they wanted to buy into deals in Europe and other parts of the world that might have put the venture into competition with BP itself. To the Russian investors, BP had become the paternal corporation, dictating where and how the venture would grow, as if TNK-BP were just another BP subsidiary.

By late 2007, the oligarchs were demanding that BP fire Dudley, but Hayward refused. The oligarchs then used their political connections to increase the pressure. The government threatened to revoke Dudley's visa. Meanwhile, TNK-BP's Russian executives, who had sheltered the venture's BP employees from the vagaries of the Russian legal system, simply stopped shielding them. The expatriates were now at the mercy of Russia's complicated tax system, and many of them weren't in full compliance. One morning in early 2008, none of the venture's Russian employees reported for work, and soon after Dudley arrived, Russian agents stormed TNK-BP's office. A month later, about 150 work permits were suspended. Then there was another raid. Investors began to worry that BP would once again lose its entire investment in Russia.

As the political furor intensified across the international stage, Dudley got a warning that he would be arrested the next day. He immediately drove to the airport and caught a plane to Paris. He spent the next few months in hiding, moving around Europe, while still attempting to retain control of TNK-BP.[4] Eventually, Hayward struck a truce at a meeting in Prague: the partnership would sell 20 percent of its shares to the public, BP's ousted staff members in Moscow would not return, and the company would appoint an independent Russian chief executive. Putin's warning to Browne had been prescient. With equal shares, there was no "tiebreaker mechanism," no way to resolve disputes between the owners. The stock sale would alleviate that problem, and Hayward, while he bristled at the public nature of the dispute, remained steadfast in his commitment to the venture. "The premise on which the thing was structured was right," he said. "It's been the most successful investment BP has made in ten years—period."

It turned out that the new chief executive wouldn't be as independent as Hayward had believed. In 2009, the oligarch Fridman appointed himself to the job. However, Hayward had managed to salvage BP's Russian investment, even if the Russians were now calling the shots. At least its role in the venture was secure, and the company was able to continue booking big dividends from its stake.

Dudley remained in a sort of limbo. Technically, he hadn't been a BP employee since 2003, but the plan was clearly for him to return to the company. After all, regardless of the errors that he, Hayward, and Browne had made in Russia, Dudley had borne the brunt of the consequences. He had literally put himself in danger protecting BP's interests, and for that, he was considered a hero within the company. As Hayward saw it, "Bob Dudley did a fantastic job."

---∞∞∞---

Now, Dudley was stepping into another BP hot spot. Hayward, after his disastrous testimony before Congress, had become a lightning rod. A soft-spoken American with ties to the Gulf Coast might be just what the company needed to soften its image and ease public anger. Hayward, meanwhile, embarked on a self-imposed exile of sorts. BP's deteriorating finances were a growing concern. The company's stock had hit bottom in late June, but it remained well below its trading range before the *Horizon* accident. It announced plans to sell assets to help pay for the spill fund. It didn't have to pay the full $20 billion all at once. In the first year, it was required to put in just $7 billion. Setting aside the money and walling off its potential liabilities was just one step in securing BP's future. The second step was lining up enough friendly shareholders to discourage a hostile takeover.

Hayward traveled around the world, courting investments from foreign governments and winning assurances that they would vote against any buyout offers that BP might face because of its depressed stock price. He met with officials in Abu Dhabi to propose that the emirate buy 10 percent of BP's shares, and he wooed investments from Kuwait, Qatar, and Singapore. With BP's stock battered by the crisis, sovereign wealth funds suddenly started talking about buying double-digit stakes in BP. BP had signed a deal to drill off the Libyan coast, and Libya's oil minister said he recommended that the country's investment fund buy a stake in the company because "it's a good opportunity for bargain hunters."[5]

By the time Hayward returned to London and addressed shareholders on July 27, no oil had flowed into the Gulf for two weeks. Still, BP's crude had stained more than 800 miles of beaches along the Gulf Coast, and the company had paid more than 80,000 claims totaling more than $240 million. Hayward confirmed a month's worth of rumors, announcing that he would step down as chief executive on October 1, turning the job over to Dudley. "In the words of Churchill, it is not the end, not even the beginning of the end, but it is the end of the beginning," Hayward said.[6]

Dudley became the first American, indeed the first non-Briton, to run BP. Even a few years earlier, the notion that BP would be run by an American would have been almost unthinkable. For decades, dating to Churchill's time, the company bylaws required that all directors be British citizens. With BP facing punitive legislation, possible criminal investigations, and civil penalties in the United States, however, tapping an American to run the company was seen by many, especially in United Kingdom, as a decision that was prompted more by circumstance than by choice. Dudley, though, displayed many qualities that are respected in Britain. He was modest, yet he projected a steely air. He was tough, but he didn't appear arrogant.

Dudley announced plans to step up BP's asset sales, saying that the company would sell as much as $30 billion worth of properties. The BP that would emerge from the disaster would be a much smaller company, and, Dudley hoped, a more focused one. Browne's dream of building BP into the world's biggest oil company was now being dismantled piece by piece. Ironically, one of the buyers interested in some of the assets was TNK-BP, the venture that Browne had once feared would compete with BP's own global interests. In another touch of irony, Hayward's concession for leaving BP was his appointment as a BP representative to the venture's board. While bloggers sneered that

Hayward was being sent, literally, to Siberia, the posting meant that Hayward, who had understood the workings of Russian business and politics so poorly, would now be right in the thick of them.

BP's stock was rebounding, and the takeover concerns had eased. For the first time in months, BP had some breathing room. As Dudley prepared for his turn in the fifth-floor office at One St. James's Square, he sounded much like Hayward in 2007. BP's management team, he said, was guided by its determination to have safe and reliable operations. It had learned the lessons of the Texas City disaster, which "shook the company up deeply." When it came to the latest crisis, he stuck to the company's carefully crafted defense: The *Deepwater Horizon* explosion was an accident that no one could have anticipated. "There's no plan in the world by any government anywhere that plans and responds to something that's ongoing like this, and no one anticipated this," he told the *Houston Chronicle*. "No one could. It's not something you would normally anticipate." Just as Hayward had seen the recovery from Texas City as a chance to position BP as an industry leader in safety, so, too, did Dudley seem to externalize the implications of the *Horizon* disaster. "This is just a really tragic setback, and I think it's a wake-up call for the industry. I think it's a game-changing event in terms of the industry needing to understand certain equipment and how it functions and spill response."

One of Dudley's first statements to reporters was that the *Horizon* accident resulted from "a series of individual misjudgments by very experienced people and a multiple series of failures of equipment and process of using equipment that is going to involve multiple companies here." It was the introduction of a theme that BP would continue to return to throughout the summer and into the fall, as the various investigations progressed. It was also chillingly similar to Ross Pillari's comments that the Texas City explosion was the result of "surprising and deeply disturbing mistakes."

—⚬⚬⚬—

Despite all the talk of change, Dudley was sounding much like the company man he'd always been. BP's culture had remained fundamentally unchanged during Hayward's three years at the helm. As his career came to an end, it raised questions as to whether BP needed an outsider to infuse the sort of cultural shift that BP had been unable to achieve under Hayward, despite all his promises. Hayward—and BP's board—clung to the company's insular culture, believing that even long-serving executives could change their ways. "Everyone can learn irrespective of how long they've been in a role," Hayward said in 2007. "I'm not certain you always have to change out people to develop a different culture or behavior." In his reluctance to acknowledge the problem, he also underscored the nature of it. Dudley, with 20 years at BP and Amoco, was as much an insider as Hayward. While the company and its investors still wrestled to answer the question of just what had gone wrong aboard the *Deepwater Horizon*, BP now faced an even more troubling uncertainty: Under the new chief executive, would anything really change?

CHAPTER 19

LOST
FAITH

H ouston is defined both physically and
economically by energy. To its south, re-
fineries and petrochemical plants stretch along Galveston Bay;
to the west, the "energy corridor" is home to office complexes
housing companies like BP and ConocoPhillips. Exxon Mobil, Halliburton, Chevron, and Shell occupy floor upon floor
of downtown office towers, and the northernmost edge of the
sprawling metropolis is marked by the Anadarko building rising above the trees of the Woodlands, an entire suburb planned
by George Mitchell, one of Houston's preeminent oil entrepreneurs. Two hours to the east is the old Spindletop field, the
cradle of the modern oil industry, whose discovery a century
ago ushered in the age of liquid fuel and inspired speculators
worldwide, including BP's founder, William Knox D'Arcy.
Housing, employment, and even the arts are tied to petrodol-
lars, and despite attempts to diversify into medicine and technology, the city still clings to its nickname as the Energy Capital
of the World.

There are 25 companies in the Fortune 500 that are based
in Houston, and of those, 19 are involved in the oil business.[1]

Four of those on the list, which doesn't include BP or Transocean, had a role in the drilling of the Macondo well. The presence of so many energy companies has created a cottage industry of experts, retirees, and consultants, all of whom followed the emerging crisis in the Gulf of Mexico with increasing fascination. No sooner did word of the *Horizon* disaster reach the city than legions of industry insiders began to scour every detail in an attempt to determine what went wrong.

From large companies to sole proprietorships, these consultants were careful not to anger the companies that might someday hire them. Yet they seemed both captivated and mortified by the sinking of the *Deepwater Horizon*. They pored over publicly available data, analyzing video feeds, sharing diagrams, and gossiping in the way that only professionals can. If it had been possible to capture the e-mail traffic of Houston in a jar in the weeks after the accident, it would have been aglow, like the flickers of captured lightning bugs, with talk of what might have happened. For months, Houston's energy subculture buzzed with theories and speculation, but little was said publicly. Much of the discussion, though, centered on BP itself, the perpetual industry outlier. The company's reputation for cost cutting was blamed for yet another catastrophe. Criticism abounded: BP shouldn't have used the long string; it should have run the cement bond log; it should have used more centralizers. Well design aside, though, one problem continued to vex: Why hadn't the blowout preventer, or BOP, worked?

———— ✲✲✲ ————

The blowout preventer is often referred to as a fail-safe "device," which makes it sound small. It isn't. On the Macondo well, the blowout preventer was the size of a small building, five stories tall and weighing 450 tons. While the technology, like everything else involved in drilling for oil, had evolved over the decades, the basic design hadn't changed in 90 years. The Macondo's preventer had been built by Houston-based Cameron International, which claims to have invented the first such device in the 1920s.

Of all the things that may have gone wrong aboard the *Deepwater Horizon*, what most concerned the industry was the apparent failure of this key piece of equipment. The lives of everyone on every rig depend on it. It is the last line of defense on thousands of rigs around the world. Inside the massive steel box is a series of cutoff valves that close around the drill pipe and seal the well if hydrocarbons began to flow unexpectedly. For the worst cases, in which the rig above needs to move off the well quickly, it has "blind shear rams," which Transocean's rig leader, Jimmy Harrell, referred to as "pinchers." The rams are basically metal plates that can slam shut, slicing the drill pipe and sealing the well opening no matter what. Sitting on the bottom of the sea, atop the opening of the well, the blowout preventer isn't concerned with whether the gas flows up the outside of the well or the inside of the casing. It's designed to stop everything, or so the industry had long believed.

Blowout preventers, or BOPs, were first used on land and migrated to sea with the rest of the industry. As the wells got deeper, the blowout preventers were moved from the rig floor to the seabed, closer to the wellhead. Subsea technicians control them from the rig above by hydraulic and fiber optic lines that run to two control pods, one serving as a backup for the other.

———⧜———

While the industry praised the effectiveness of blowout preventers, some problems with the evolving design had arisen over the years. In 2003, Transocean released a paper discussing

problems with the hydraulic controls for the deepwater preventers in use by all companies, saying that the equipment was
being rushed into service without proper testing. Studies also
questioned whether the blind shear rams could slice through
some of the thicker drill pipes used in deepwater drilling. The
MMS had proposed more stringent rules for emergency backup
systems on blowout preventers, but almost a decade later, these
rules hadn't been implemented.[2] Once again, the industry relied on its safety record as an argument against future disaster.
After all, 50,000 wells had been drilled in the Gulf without a
major blowout. The preventers must work.

Now, the *Deepwater Horizon* had called that statement into
question. The apparent failure was a key element of BP's defense. Hayward mentioned it in his soft-shoe testimony before
Congress, it was a focus of BP's own internal investigation, it
was dissected in agonizing detail before the Coast Guard–MMS
hearings, and it was echoed by Bob Dudley when he took over
BP's spill response. "If you look at a rig like this, you're going to
have a terrible tragic accident with a loss of well control, a fire
and a rig sinking," he told the *Houston Chronicle*. "It was a terrible tragedy. But you also should have had blowout preventers
that close that should have prevented the oil spill." Hayward had
told Congress emphatically that the blowout preventer was the
ultimate fail-safe device; it was supposed to prevent exactly this
sort of disaster. In that, he was right. BP's strategy from the earliest days after the explosion had been to cast doubt on the contractors and the equipment, not its own decision making, but
clearly, the blowout preventer hadn't lived up to its billing.

———— ∞ ————

Why hadn't the rams closed? Once the *Horizon* lost power,
the crew could no longer control the preventer. When Chris

Pleasant, the subsea supervisor, stood before the panel on the bridge with the drilling floor already engulfed in flames, he was helpless. The hydraulic controls weren't working, and the electronics on the panel were giving a false reading that the rams were closed. Later hearings would raise questions about Transocean's maintenance of the preventer and whether one of the control pods had failed earlier. Like most systems on offshore rigs, though, the blowout preventer had redundancies in its control systems. Even if one pod failed, the second one should have closed the rams.

Transocean's internal drilling reports, sent from the rig seven hours before the explosion, showed that the crew had tested the preventer, including the blind shear rams, and everything worked properly. "The BOPs were clearly not the root cause of the explosion," Transocean's chief executive, Steven Newman, told a congressional committee investigating the *Horizon* accident. "We have no reason to believe that they were not operational."

The preventers have multiple rams to ensure that even if one set fails to close, another will. Across Houston, the volunteer drilling detectives sifting clues as to what went wrong scratched their collective heads. How could all the rams have failed at once? Some theorized that gas had entered the well when the cement plug failed, and that the pressure of the gas rushing up the hole had forced a chunk of the cement into the BOP, preventing the rams from closing completely. Ironically, this theory was supported by BP's misleading oil flow estimates in the early days after the *Horizon* exploded. If the flow was that low, it might mean that the rams were partially closed.

By midsummer, when BP sliced through the riser to cap the well, a new clue emerged. Two pieces of drill pipe were stuck side by side in the riser. No one could explain where the "second string" came from, but if a piece of pipe had been dislodged and blown into the BOP, it might have prevented the rams from closing. Questions had been raised years earlier about whether the rams could slice through one piece of thick pipe. They were never designed to slice through two. "No shear rams would have been able to cut and seal on two strings of pipe," one independent consultant said. "Moreover, none of the other preventers in the stack would have been able to seal on two strings of pipe." In late August, after BP had capped the well and was able to get a better look inside the blowout preventer, it found that there were actually *three* strings of pipe inside the machine.[3] The first was about 3,000 feet long, the second about 40 feet long, and the third about a foot, jammed crosswise inside the device. The discovery seemed to bolster the idea that the force of the explosion had split the drill pipe and jammed the additional pipe strings into the blowout preventer. One expert theorized that Pleasant was getting more response than he had thought from the rig's control panel. He suspected that the shear rams had closed and opened several times, like gnashing teeth, as Pleasant pounded on the controls. The first slice severed the pipe. When the rams reopened, pressure from below forced a new length up into the BOP. At the same time, the piece that was already cut dropped down just enough to prevent the rams from closing again.

———— ∞∞∞ ————

As the investigation by the Coast Guard and the MMS continued over the summer, much of the testimony focused on the blowout preventer. After all, Transocean had used its own maintenance schedule rather than the one recommended by industry guidelines and the MMS. The BOP had experienced hydraulic leaks, and Transocean had repeatedly modified its design during its ten years in service without properly documenting the changes. Most of the modifications were done by Transocean crews, not the manufacturer.

Those modifications frustrated efforts in the hours after the explosion to activate the preventer manually and shut in the well. In the days after the *Horizon* exploded, Harry Thierens, BP's vice president for drilling and completions, worked with Transocean and other experts using a remote submarine to trigger the rams through access ports on the outside of the BOP stack. For more than a week, the crews tried to close the rams, only to find out that they were using the wrong access port. Thierens thought that they were attempting to close the middle pipe rams, which should have shut down the flow of oil from the well. But in an earlier modification, Transocean had reversed the access ports. The ports they were trying to activate were test rams, which weren't designed to hold under the pressure coming up from the bottom of the well. Even the Transocean subsea engineer seemed surprised by the discovery, Thierens would later tell Coast Guard and MMS investigators. All their efforts to close the well had been vain. "I was quite frankly astonished that this could have happened," he said. "I lost all faith in the BOP stack."

Even after Thierens and his team discovered the problem, though, the engineers were unable to close the rams manually. Transocean officials insisted that the modifications had no bearing on the BOP's function, and wouldn't have been a contributing factor in its failure.

For its part, BP's internal investigation offered few suggestions as to what went wrong with the preventer. One of the control pods had a nearly dead battery, it found, but that alone shouldn't have impeded the device's function. BP investigators also concluded that the second string was inaccurate. Only one string was actually in the blowout preventer. The second pipe that had been seen earlier in the severed riser was actually above the BOP and fractured after the accident, they said.[4] That finding appears to contradict BP's own earlier finding of three pieces of drill bit being snarled in the mechanism.

———∞∞∞———

In September, with the well finally capped and holding and the relief wells nearing completion, the blowout preventer, one of the most crucial pieces of surviving physical evidence in the *Horizon* investigation, was hauled to the surface, carried by barge to shore, and turned over to NASA, the American space agency, for forensic study. Outside NASA's facility in eastern New Orleans, it sat on a barge for days, its worn amber columns of pipes and valves hovering over the water like a spaceship recently arrived from the planet Caterpillar. Extracting answers from its internal mechanisms, though, will probably take months. Regardless of the reasons for the preventer's failure, its position as a fail-safe device remains suspect.

CHAPTER 20

ALL FOR OIL

Death officially came to Macondo early in the morning on September 19, 2010. The notorious oil well took its name from the town in novelist Gabriel García Márquez's *One Hundred Years of Solitude*. In the novel, the town grows from an isolated settlement to a thriving community before being deluged by a four-year rainfall and obliterated by a giant windstorm. The death of the Macondo well arrived much less dramatically, almost anticlimactically, after months that seemed like years to residents of the Gulf Coast. For four months, on and off, the drill bit of the relief well had been churning on its intercept course. Finally, it had hit its mark. A final cement pressure test just before six o'clock confirmed that the well had done its job. The relief well had intersected Macondo some 13,000 feet underground three days before the final pronouncement of the well's death. Crews then pumped cement into the original well bore through the new hole, sealing them both. By the time the well was killed, it was largely a symbolic victory for BP. The well hadn't spewed oil in two months, since the installation of the temporary cap in July. Killing the well, though, was an important step for BP, proof that the company could honor its pledge to fix what had gone so terribly wrong.

The effort to bring a final end to Macondo fell to John Wright, a quiet, unassuming engineer who'd earned a reputation as the world's best runaway well assassin. Wright had swept-back gray hair and the top of his mouth was hidden by the bristles of a gray mustache. When he wasn't on a rig, his office attire, like many veterans of the front lines of the oil business, was jeans and cowboy boots. The intensity of oil well fires had created a cottage industry in the middle of the last century, as fearless entrepreneurs like Red Adair built companies that did nothing but combat the industry's most ferocious mistakes. Adair, immortalized in the John Wayne movie *Hellfighters*, died in 2004, but the techniques that he pioneered lived on. Wright worked for Boots & Coots, a well-control company formed by two of Adair's protégés, and his specialty was the drilling of relief wells. He'd been involved in 83 of them, including the one that killed the infamous Piper Alpha blowout in the North Sea in 1988. He had directed 40 projects himself and had never missed an intercept, and he had no intention of making Macondo his first miss.[1] His margin of error in trying to hit the Macondo well two miles underground was about 3½ inches. The process involves directional drilling, in which the drill bit is turned at an angle as it nears the problem well. Using electromagnetic testing and other high-tech imaging equipment, the drill bit gradually closes in on its mark.

Wright began drilling the first relief well on May 2, and he spent the next four months on one of the drill ships among the fleet that had assembled at the Macondo site.

When Wright began the project, he felt as if the eyes of the world were on him, counting on him to end the environmental nightmare. He wasn't used to such widespread attention. By the time Wright's relief well got close, though, much of the public pressure to kill the well had subsided. With no oil flowing, the desperation that had pervaded BP's efforts throughout the early part of the summer had eased.

The end came quietly. After months of determined drilling, there was no celebration. After all, 11 people had died, the Gulf had been compromised, and people's livelihoods, both along the coast and in his own industry, had been devastated. "Maybe it's like firefighters after they finish putting out a fire in an apartment where people are killed," Wright said. "I guess they feel satisfied they put the fire out, but it's not a celebratory-type feeling."[2] The same was true outside the industry. News of the well's death paled compared with the fervor of its initial explosion. "We can finally announce that the Macondo 252 well is effectively dead," retired Coast Guard Admiral Thad Allen, who oversaw the government's response effort, declared. "The Macondo well poses no continuing threat to the Gulf of Mexico." There was no press conference, no fanfare. Allen's statement was sent to reporters by e-mail.

The Macondo well, however, had left an indelible mark on the Gulf. The economic, political, and legal repercussions would continue for years. Lingering long after the slick had dissipated were questions about offshore drilling in general and BP more specifically. In the wake of the disaster, the government issued new regulations for shallow-water wells, and while the process technically allowed new drilling to move forward, the government issued few permits in the summer and fall. Oil companies struggled to sort through the new requirements.

In the deepwater, the government lifted the drilling moratorium in October, a month early, but drilling remains halted as companies sort out new regulations. A government report released in mid-September found that the industry's earlier fears that the moratorium would kill jobs were overblown. By mid-September, only four rigs had left the Gulf. Only 2,000 jobs on deepwater rigs had been lost temporarily, and the entire impact of the drilling ban would probably be less than 12,000 jobs in the Gulf region, the study found.

In the offshore industry, the administration's nonchalance felt like cold indifference, an attempt to avert political fallout while ignoring the economic reality that was unfolding in the Gulf. Many drilling companies had avoided layoffs by accepting lower day rates to keep their rigs in place. Other rigs had been brought ashore for maintenance. The result was that the rig owners, not the oil companies, were bearing the financial brunt of the drilling ban. Noble Corporation, one of the biggest drillers in the Gulf, estimated that it was losing more than a million dollars a day as a result of the moratorium, even though it hadn't laid off any workers. More than 200 jobs that it would have filled for projects that were coming on line were put on hold.

———⊗∞⊗———

While such costs may be borne by the drilling companies and their shareholders in the short term, the broader cost implications of the Macondo disaster are likely to affect every aspect of offshore drilling. Even the industry's primary mouthpiece, the American Petroleum Institute, agrees that stricter regulations are inevitable. Companies that operate in the Gulf now have to account for "political risk," the concept that another company's mistake could affect everyone's operations. That sort of unilateral and unpredictable government action is more typically associated with Third World countries. Now, oil companies, drillers, contractors, and transport companies will all have to factor it into their risk-reward ratios for operating in the Gulf. More regulation and more uncertainty mean more costs, and more costs in one of America's most prominent energy fields ultimately mean higher gasoline prices for American drivers. Had the United States not been crawling out of recession at the time the *Deepwater Horizon* exploded, consumers might already be feeling the effect.

Congress also has considered raising the spill liability cap under the Oil Pollution Act to $10 billion from the current $75 million. BP waived that limit and agreed to pay all reasonable spill-related expenses, but there's no guarantee that other oil companies would do the same if they were faced with a similar disaster. The higher cap, though, might scare away smaller oil companies. Even large independents like Anadarko have had to rethink their liability for drilling in the Gulf. Higher caps may mean that only the supermajors—such as Exxon Mobil, Shell, Chevron, and BP—will have the financial means to shoulder the risk of deepwater drilling in the future. In other words, in an attempt to ensure that oil companies pay more for spills, Congress may create an incentive not just against environmental disasters, but against drilling in general. The result would be a concentration of some of the Gulf's richest fields in the hands of just a few giant companies.

The industry bristles at such possibilities, grousing that its stellar safety record is being ignored because of the mistakes of at most a few companies, and especially because of BP's habit of cutting corners. As if to refute the argument, on September 2, an explosion rocked another Gulf rig, this time in shallow water. Thirteen workers evacuated into the water and were later rescued. No one was killed and no oil spilled, but the blast bolstered the critics of drilling and emboldened supporters of the moratorium. The rig was operated by Mariner Energy, which was being bought by Apache.

———— ∞∞∞ ————

While Congress mulls the policy response, the environmental impact of the spill also remains in dispute and may not be fully understood for decades. In late August, the government declared that most of the oil that had still been floating in the Gulf had disappeared. The warm waters, intense sun, and oil-eating microbes native to the area had broken it down. Many scientists found the numbers vague and overly optimistic. The government estimated that the Macondo well had released almost 5 million barrels of oil between late April and mid-July. Some of that had been captured during BP's early attempts to curb the flow from the leaking well. That still left almost 4 million barrels leaking into the sea, and, of that, almost 3 million were supposed to have been handled by skimming, burning, evaporation, and microbes. While those natural processes will break down oil, it doesn't typically happen that quickly. So where did it all go?

One theory is that it sank. Samantha Joye, a professor with the University of Georgia, collected sediment samples from the seafloor and found layers of oily material, some as much as two inches deep. The goo contained small tar balls that looked like "little microscopic cauliflower heads." Beneath the oily layer, her samples revealed dead shrimp, worms, and other tiny sea creatures. Joye believes that the material may have accumulated when BP had sprayed dispersants liberally on the slick to break up the oil earlier in the summer, or it may be mucus excreted from the oil-eating bacteria that feasted on the slick. The mucus is "kind of like a slime highway from the surface to the bottom, because the slime gets heavy, and it sinks."[3] Meanwhile, the efficiency of the microbes themselves is suspect. The study that led to the government's assertion that the microbes had eaten most of the oil was done by the Energy Biosciences Institute at the University of California, Berkeley.[4] That's the institute, formerly headed by Energy Secretary Stephen Chu, which was funded by BP.

Some of the worst fears about the spill—that it would kill the Gulf, that it would enter the loop current and be sucked around Florida and up the eastern seaboard, that a hurricane might stir up the slick and cause oil to rain down on land— never materialized. But scientists are concerned that sea life may be affected for generations. Meanwhile, seafood sales across the Gulf, even in areas that were not affected by the spill, remain sluggish amid public fears that all marine life was tainted by the oil slick. Seafood restaurants and wholesalers are among the litany of businesses that have sued BP over the spill.

Despite John Browne's efforts to build BP into a global oil power, it remained an industry stepchild, and its handling of the *Deepwater Horizon* disaster only reinforced the disdain of its peers. After the well was finally killed, Exxon Mobil Chairman Rex Tillerson, who had declared to Congress that his company would have never have drilled the well the way BP did, questioned the company's and the government's approach to plugging the well. Rather than try riskier measures that had a higher chance of success, BP engineers, with anxious government scientists looking over their shoulder and sometimes second-guessing their decisions, opted for safer options that had less chance of succeeding. "The lowest risk and lowest-chance-of-success options were chosen first," Tillerson said at a government forum on the spill response in late September. He stressed that the accident was preventable. "When you focus on safe operations and risk management, tragic accidents like this one that occurred in the Gulf of Mexico simply do not occur."

—ᨁᨁᨠ—

BP, despite all its talk of change and lessons that can be learned from the Gulf spill, seems to be following a familiar pattern. In early September, it released the results of its internal investigation into the cause of the disaster. In keeping with the statements of BP executives dating to early May, it found that a number of bad decisions, mostly by Transocean and Halliburton, had sealed the *Horizon*'s fate. BP investigators found that the cement job at the bottom of the well failed, allowing hydrocarbons to enter. They questioned the makeup of the cement as well. The gas flowed up the production casing, the innermost part of the well, meaning that the issues of the long string and the number of centralizers didn't matter, BP found. It blamed the Transocean rig crew for not recognizing that gas had entered the well during a 40-minute period before the explosion when they could have shut down the well and saved the rig. That 40-minute period happened to be when the BP company man on the rig was in his office. After the flow reached the surface, the crew sent it to a separator, designed to remove the drilling mud from the gas. Normally, that would have been the right decision, but given the intensity of the flow, it diverted the gas onto the floor of the rig rather than overboard, allowing it to get sucked into the *Horizon*'s diesel engines and ignite. The nettlesome blowout preventer should have activated automatically, even after the rig lost power, but it didn't. BP found "potential weaknesses" in the testing and maintenance of the preventer.

Yet the study ignored BP's responsibility, as the leaseholder, to ensure that proper maintenance procedures were followed. The report did cast some blame on BP's employees, noting that the company men on the rig, along with the Transocean crew members, failed to properly interpret the results of the negative-pressure tests before the explosion. It also blamed its drilling engineers in Houston for not exercising more oversight of the cement process.

Once again, the *Horizon* disaster had an eerie parallel to the Texas City refinery explosion. The report was reminiscent of the Mogford report that investigated the refinery blast. Both placed the blame on contractors and on midlevel BP managers. Once again, though, BP's investigation ignored the broader context, failing to ask why its employees weren't more diligent in their decision making. BP's engineers clearly were concerned about the cost overruns and time delays on Macondo. In compiling the internal report, investigators never explored whether those pressures might have trumped safety concerns. Nor does it address BP's fractured management system or the culture that talks about safety, yet emphasized profit.

⟨∞⟩

Across the company, the familiar pattern persists. About a month after the *Horizon* explosion, a pump station along the Trans-Alaska Pipeline, about 100 miles south of Fairbanks, was shut down after a test of the station's fire detection system caused a failure of both main and backup power. The power loss triggered an opening of relief valves, releasing about 100,000 gallons of oil from an overflow storage tank to a secondary containment area.[5] Compared with the oil flowing from the Macondo well, it was a pittance, but the pipeline operations continue to be dogged by allegations of poor maintenance from employees.

A few weeks before the *Horizon* disaster, a fire broke out in a hydrogen compressor at the Texas City refinery and compromised the seal on the ultracracker. This was the same unit that had been ravaged by fire in the summer of 2005 and prompted the Chemical Safety and Hazard Investigation Board to label the plant an "imminent hazard." The malfunction forced BP to flare off gases, including benzene, a known carcinogen. Rather than shut down the unit, plant officials kept it running for the next 40 days while the damage was repaired, releasing more than a half-million pounds of pollutants in the process. While BP filed the required "emissions event" report with state regulators, it never informed its workers or Texas City residents of the release. By early August, after the release had become public knowledge, thousands of residents, citing a variety of health concerns, jammed conference halls where local trial lawyers were signing up potential plaintiffs for what they expected would be a $10 billion civil class-action lawsuit. Lawyers called on the Houston judge, Lee Rosenthal, to revoke BP's probation for violating federal air pollution laws in 2005. The Texas attorney general's office sued BP Products North America over the benzene release, citing a pattern of bad practices and repeated violations at the refinery.

In late September 2010, BP agreed to pay yet another record fine, this time $15 million for pollution violations related to fires at the Texas City refinery in 2003 and 2004. Katherine Rodriguez, whose father Ray Gonzalez, died after being burned by superheated water in September 2004, wondered if the latest fines would have any more impact than the previous ones. "It's very frustrating for us to see it going on and on and on and nothing happens," she said. She has begun pressing for changes in workplace safety laws. The regulatory environment in the United States, though, remains tilted in companies' favor.

All of these incidents happened against a backdrop of record operating profits for BP. With the fallout from the *Horizon* accident straining the company's resources, BP's culture of getting more for less is likely to intensify the company's operational shortcomings. Perhaps the most consistent aspect of BP in the decade since it acquired Amoco and Arco, the bedrock of the safety lapses that pervade its operations, is management's stubborn refusal to see any connection between its cost cutting and the disasters that have become BP's hallmark.

In mid-September, Tony Hayward appeared before a committee of the British Parliament, which was considering imposing restrictions on offshore drilling as a result of the *Horizon* accident. Once again, as he and John Browne before him had done so many times, he rejected any connection between BP's woes and cost cutting. Despite the Texas City refinery explosion, the leaks in Alaska, the trading violations, the problems with Thunder Horse, the ongoing dispute with OSHA over work conditions at its refineries, the latest gas release in Texas City, and, most of all, the *Deepwater Horizon* disaster, Hayward clung to his company line.

"It's easy for some parties to suggest that this is a problem with BP. I emphatically do not believe that is the case," he said. It was one of his last public appearances as chief executive. Bob Dudley took over a couple of weeks later. Hayward's stubborn refusal to acknowledge the role of BP's culture, of its top-down focus on financial performance over operating performance, raised questions about whether Dudley would also parrot the company line of his predecessors. Would the company change? Had it really learned any of the "lessons" that it so frequently talked about? Had executives learned the terrible price of stressing financial performance over operations? Or would more employees be put at risk? "It's very dangerous to join up dots that may not be appropriate to join up," Hayward said.

Even without connecting the dots, the pattern is painfully clear. Hayward, like Browne before him, was blind to the consequences of his actions because, as Texas City firefighter David Teverbaugh noted, neither chief executive ever stood amid the charred rubble and burned flesh of their own decisions. To the company's management, BP's mistakes are always accidents that could happen to any oil company. But equipment changes and mea culpas don't address the underlying problem that has plagued BP for the past decade. Its culture has resisted change and has clung to fundamental principles that emphasize financial performance over safety, not overtly, but subtly. As it attempts to recover from the *Horizon* disaster, BP faces a financial outlook unlike anything that it has confronted since William Knox D'Arcy sought the investment of Burmah Oil to keep the company in business. If the relentless cost cutting under Browne and Hayward spawned a culture of disaster, what will happen when the inevitable next round of budget cuts are demanded of its managers?

———— ∞∞∞ ————

The tragedy of the *Deepwater Horizon* has few victories. The well was finally killed, but not before it had exacted a huge cost. BP, of course, has paid a financial price, and it has paid with its reputation. Tony Hayward and Andy Inglis, BP's exploration chief and a former Browne turtle, paid with their jobs. BP's shareholders, including thousands of British pensioners, have paid with lost investments and dividends. Gulf residents have paid with lost livelihood. The Obama administration and political leaders in the United States have paid with a loss of confidence in their ability to bring Big Oil to heel when it engages in practices that threaten the public welfare. Most of all, the 11 men who died aboard the *Deepwater Horizon* the night of April 20 paid with their lives. Their families will pay for a lifetime, as wives grow old without husbands and children grow up without fathers.

The pattern that Hayward emphatically refuses to see continues. As Bob Dudley prepared to take office in early October, he once again reshuffled management, ousting Andy Inglis, the former Browne turtle who had been running the exploration business at the time of the *Horizon* disaster. Dudley, in an e-mail to employees, vowed to realign company incentives to ensure "the right balance between the short and long term." He created a new safety division that would oversee operations worldwide and report to him. He announced a new management team that, once again, was drawn from among the insular ranks of longtime BP employees. Most had joined in the 1980s, and none has worked for BP fewer than 19 years.

Dudley will try once again to change BP's culture without changing the people, much as Hayward tried and failed to do. Yet after all that's happened, Dudley must recognize the deep and dangerous problems that plague BP, that remain a threat to both worker safety and the environment. His new safety initiative and executive reshuffle must, at least, be an admission of the company's past mistakes.

In an interview from London the day before he officially became chief executive, Dudley told the *Houston Chronicle* "I wouldn't describe it as an admission of anything."

SOURCES

Many of the interviews quoted in this book were based on those that I did as a columnist for the *Houston Chronicle* or that were done by colleagues who were reporting news stories for the paper. Any conclusions drawn from their reporting are mine alone.

I have attempted to interview Lord Browne, the former BP CEO, for five years. All of my requests, including one specifically for this book, have been ignored. Peter Sutherland, the former BP chairman, also declined an interview request.

Many of the survivors of the *Deepwater Horizon* declined to recount their stories again for this book, but referred me to the public testimony that they had already given. The accounts of the accident were built from that testimony, and several of those contacted were given the chance to review the account for accuracy.

Finally, I interviewed a number of current and former BP employees, contractors, and consultants who asked not to be named for fear of reprisals or lost business.

Other sources are noted on pages 262–271.

CHAPTER 1

1. E-mails from BP drilling engineers Mark Hafle and Brian Morel to Richard Miller, April 14, 2010.
2. Firsthand accounts were compiled from survivors' sworn testimony and television interviews. In some cases, survivors were given a chance to review this account for accuracy.

CHAPTER 2

1. Daniel Yergin, *The Prize: The Epic Quest for Oil, Money and Power* (New York: Simon & Schuster, 1992).
2. Ibid.
3. Anthony Sampson, *The Seven Sisters: The Great Oil Companies and the World They Shaped* (New York: Bantam Books, 1991).
4. Yergin, *The Prize.*
5. Sampson, *The Seven Sisters.*
6. Yergin, *The Prize.*
7. Ibid.
8. Henry Longhurst, *Adventure in Oil, The Story of British Petroleum* (London: Sidgwick and Jackson, 1959).
9. Ibid.
10. Sampson, *The Seven Sisters.*
11. Longhurst, *Adventure in Oil.*
12. Sampson, *The Seven Sisters.*
13. Stephen Kinzer, *All the Shah's Men: An American Coup and the Roots of Middle East Terror* (Hoboken, N.J.: John Wiley & Sons, 2008).
14. Jonathan C. Brown, *Oil and Revolution in Mexico* (Berkeley, California: University of California Press, 1993).
15. Kinzer, *All the Shah's Men.*
16. Ibid.
17. John Browne, *Beyond Business: An Inspirational Memoir from a Visionary Leader* (London: Weidenfeld & Nicolson, 2010).

CHAPTER 3

1. John Browne, *Beyond Business: An Inspirational Memoir from a Visionary Leader* (London: Weidenfeld & Nicolson, 2010).
2. Ibid.
3. Ibid.
4. John Browne interview, *BBC Today*, Feb. 8, 2010.
5. Browne, *Beyond Business.*
6. Ibid.
7. Ibid.
8. Tom Bower, *Oil: Money, Politics and Power in the 21ˢᵗ Century* (New York: Grand Central Publishing, 2009).
9. Browne, *Beyond Business.*
10. Alaska Oil Spill Commission, "Spill: The Wreck of the *Exxon Valdez*," final report, February 1990.
11. Browne, *Beyond Business.*
12. Ibid.
13. Tyler Priest, *The Offshore Imperative: Shell Oil's Search for Petroleum in Postwar America* (College Station, Texas: Texas A&M University Press, 2007).
14. Bower, *Oil.*
15. Dan Fisher, "Going Deep," *Forbes*, April 2, 2001.
16. Browne, *Beyond Business.*
17. Browne, "Breaking Ranks," speech to Stanford Business School, May 1997.
18. Bower, *Oil.*
19. Browne, *Beyond Business.*
20. Ibid.
21. Steven Prokesch, "Unleashing the Power of Learning," *Harvard Business Review*, Sept.–Oct. 1997.
22. Browne, *Beyond Business.*
23. Elizabeth Lambert, "Shaken and Stirred: An English House Starts Fresh—and Finds a New Identity," *Architectural Digest*, December 2003, 202.

24. Tobias Buck and David Buchan, "Sun King of the Oil Industry, *Financial Times*, July 2002 (reprinted Jan. 12, 2007, www.ft.com).

25. "The Future Is Green: Politics & Power," *Vanity Fair*, May 2006.

CHAPTER 4

1. U.K. Health and Safety Executive, "Major Incident Investigation Report, BP Grangemouth Scotland 29th May–10th June," published Aug. 18, 2003.

2. Lise Olsen and Gregory Katz, "Refineries under Stricter Rules Overseas," *Houston Chronicle*, April 5, 2005.

3. U.S. Chemical Safety and Hazard Investigation Board. "Investigation Report: Refinery Explosion and Fire (15 Killed, 180 Injured)." Final Draft for Board Vote, March 20, 2007; and "The Report of the BP U.S. Refineries Independent Safety Review Panel," January 2007.

4. OSHA regional news release, Aug. 25, 2004, www.osha.gov.

5. Telos Group, "BP Texas City Site Report of Findings," Jan. 21, 2005.

6. Brad Hem, "Witness: Few at BP Knew of 30-Year Death Toll," *Houston Chronicle*, Sept. 7, 2007.

7. "HSSE '05 Business Plan," internal BP document, November 2004.

CHAPTER 5

1. Some of the survivor accounts were drawn from interviews with the *Houston Chronicle* in the days after the accident.

2. U.S. Chemical Safety and Hazard Investigation Board press release, Aug. 17, 2005, www.csb.gov.

3. Lise Olsen, "BP Leads Nation in Refinery Fatalities," *Houston Chronicle*, May 15, 2005.

CHAPTER 6

1. Bill Minutaglio, *City on Fire: The Forgotten Disaster That Devastated a Town and Ignited a Landmark Legal Battle* (New York: HarperCollins, 2003).

2. John Browne, *Beyond Business: An Inspirational Memoir from a Visionary Leader* (London: Weidenfeld & Nicolson, 2010).

3. Kevin Moran, Dina Capiello, Allan Turner, Richard Stewart, Dale Lezon, Lynn Cook, Thom Marshall, Steve McVicker, "We All Want to Know What Happened and Why," *Houston Chronicle*, March 25, 2005.

4. Deposition of John Browne, *Miguel Arenazas et al. vs. BP Products North America et. al.*05cv0337-A, 212th Judicial District, Galveston County, Texas.

5. *Houston Chronicle*, March 25, 2005.

6. John Manzoni to Mark Linder, e-mail message, March 27, 2005.

7 Browne, *Beyond Business*.

8. BP press release, May 17, 2005 and "Fatal Accident Investigation Report, Isomerization Unit Explosion Interim Report," May 12, 2005.

9. Ross Pillari statement, Texas City Investigation Report Press Briefing, May 17, 2005.

10. Center for Chemical Process Safety, *Guidelines for Investigating Chemical Process Incidents* (2nd ed.), 2003.

11. U.S. General Accounting Office, "Chemical Safety Board: Improved Policies and Additional Oversight Are Needed," RCED-00-192, July 2000.

12. Kristen Hays, "Witness for BP Says Permit Request OK," *Houston Chronicle*, July 9, 2008.

13. Ross Vail to G TCS Superintendents Monday Meetings, e-mail message, May 27, 2005.

14. Browne, *Beyond Business*.

CHAPTER 7

1. *The Herald* (Glasgow), "Oil Giant Is Fined for False Trade," Oct.16, 1998.

2. Transcript of trader phone calls, *Amerigas Propane L.P. et. al. v. BP America Inc. et. al.*, Exhibit A, 1:08-cv-00981, United States District Court for the Northern District of Illinois, Eastern Division.

3. John Browne, *Beyond Business: An Inspirational Memoir from a Visionary Leader* (London: Weidenfeld & Nicolson, 2010).

CHAPTER 8

1. John Browne, *Beyond Business: An Inspirational Memoir from a Visionary Leader* (London: Weidenfeld & Nicolson, 2010).
2. Deposition of John Browne, *Miguel Arenazas et al. vs. BP Products North America et. al.*05cv0337-A, 212th Judicial District, Galveston County, Texas.
3. Browne, *Beyond Business.*
4. Stephen Bartlett to Scott Crewson, Susan Dio, Mike Elgin, Jared Pearl, e-mail message Aug. 26, 2004.
5. Browne, *Beyond Business.*
6. Browne deposition.

CHAPTER 9

1. Glen Owen, "Secret Documents Found on BP Computers That Browne Gave to His Lover," *Daily Mail*, May 6, 2007.
2. John Browne, *Beyond Business: An Inspirational Memoir from a Visionary Leader* (London: Weidenfeld & Nicolson, 2010).
3. Janet Elliott, "Court to Tackle BP Blast Issue," *Houston Chronicle*, Oct. 19, 2007.
4. Browne, *Beyond Business.*
5. Ibid.
6. Dennis Rice, "The True Story about Lord Browne—by Ex–Rent Boy Lover," *Daily Mail*, May 6, 2007.
7. Ibid.
8. Ibid.
9. Public judgment, *Lord Browne of Madingley and Associated Newspapers Limited*, in the Supreme Court of Judicature Court of Appeal (Civil Division), A2/2007/0402, London.
10. Browne, *Beyond Business.*
11. John Browne interview, *BBC Today*, Feb. 8, 2010.
12. Browne, *Beyond Business.*

13. Ibid.
14. John Browne, "Beyond Retirement," speech to the Young Foundation, London, April 6, 2006, www.bp.com.
15. Owen, *Daily Mail.*
16. BP press release, May 1, 2007.
17. Public judgment, *Browne and Associated Newspapers.*
18. Ibid.
19. Dennis Rice, "BP Boss: Threat That Would Devastate the City," *Daily Mail,* May 6, 2007.
20. Dennis Rice, "£10m: the Price of a Life to Browne's BP," *Daily Mail,* May 6, 2007.
21. BP press release, May 1, 2007.

CHAPTER 10

1. Brett Clanton, "Rebuilding Trust," *Houston Chronicle,* Feb. 3, 2007.
2. T.J. Aulds, "BP Refinery Manager No Stranger to Challenges," *Galveston Daily News,* Jan. 30, 2007.
3. Lise Olsen and Tom Fowler, "BP's Texas City Refinery Remains Deadliest in U.S.," *Houston Chronicle,* Feb. 24, 2008.
4. Mimi Swartz, "Eva vs. Goliath," *Texas Monthly,* July 2007, 118.

CHAPTER 11

1. "Profile: Tony Hayward," *Sunday Times,* June 6, 2010.
2. Sheila McNulty, "Hayward Outlines His 'Vision' for BP," *Financial Times,* Jan. 15, 2007.

CHAPTER 12

1. BP Annual Review, 2009, www.bp.com.
2. Monthly production data for the main Thunder Horse field filed with the Minerals Management Service (now the Bureau of Ocean Energy Management, Regulation and Enforcement), http://www.gomr.boemre.gov.
3. "BP Oil Spill: The Rise and Fall of Tony Hayward," *Telegraph,* July 27, 1010.

4. Guy Chazan, Benoit Faucon, and Ben Casselman, "As CEO Hayward Remade BP, Safety, Costs Drives Clashed," *Wall Street Journal*, June 29, 2010.

5. Michael E. Sawyer, "BP Atlantis Report," May 12, 2009, www.foodandwaterwatch.org.

6. Billie Pirner Garde, deputy ombudsman, letter to Kenneth Abbott, April 13, 2010.

7. State of Alaska Petroleum Systems Integrity Office, status report, "Investigation of Sept. 29, 2008, Y-Pad Artificial Lift Gas Pipeline Rupture," Feb. 20, 2009, http://www.dog.dnr.state.ak.us/oil/programs/psio/psio_main.html.

8. "BP Discovers Leak at Alaska Oil Pipe, No Output Hit," Reuters, Dec. 22, 2009, www.reuters.com.

9. Russell Gold and Tom McGinty, "BP Relied on Cheaper Wells," *Wall Street Journal*, June 19, 2010.

10. Gregory Walz to John Guide, e-mail message, April 16, 2010.

11. Brett Cocales to Brian Morel, e-mail message, April 16, 2010.

CHAPTER 13

1. Schlumberger Mississippi Canyon Block 252 Timeline.

2. Notes from an interview Vidrine conducted with BP investigators on April 27, 2010. He declined to testify before the MMS-Coast Guard hearings citing medical reasons.

3. Ibid.

4. Firsthand accounts of Ezell and Pleasant were compiled from their public testimony.

CHAPTER 14

1. Transocean 10-K annual report, filed with the U.S. Securities and Exchange Commission, Feb. 24, 2010.

2. Alaska Oil Spill Commission, "Spill: The Wreck of the *Exxon Valdez*, Implications for Safe Transportation of Oil," Final Report, Feb. 1990.

3. Robert Olney Easton, *Black Tide: The Santa Barbara Oil Spill and Its Consequences* (New York: Delacorte Press), 1972.

4. National Commission on the BP Deepwater Horizon Oil Spill and Offshore Drilling, "The Amount and Fate of the Oil," Staff Working Paper No. 3 (draft), released Oct. 6, 2010.

5. Robin Pagnamenta, "BP Chief Tony Hayward Flies Home after Promising to Stay in US until Spill Stops," *Sunday Times*, May 18, 2010.

6. Tim Webb, "BP Boss Admits Job On Line over Gulf Oil Spill," *The Guardian*, May 14, 2010.

7. Greg Milam, "BP Chief: Oil Spill Impact 'Very Modest,'" *Sky News*, May 18, 2010.

8. Clifford Krauss, Henry Fountain, and John M. Broder, "Behind the Scenes of Gulf Oil Spill: Acrimony and Stress," *New York Times*, Aug. 26, 2010.

9. Anna Driver and JoAnne Allen, "Obama Says Ready to 'Kick Ass' over Gulf Oil Spill," Reuters, June 8, 2010, www.reuters.com.

CHAPTER 15

1. John M. Broder and Michael Luo, "Reforms Slow to Arrive at Drilling Agency," *New York Times*, May 30, 2010.

2. Center for Responsive Politics, www.opensecrets.org.

3. U.S. Department of the Interior Office of the Inspector General, "Investigative Report, Island Operating Company et al.," March 31, 2010 (released May 25, 2010), www.doioig.gov.

4. Ibid.

5. U.S. Department of the Interior Office of the Inspector General, "Investigative Report of MMS Oil Marketing Group—Lakewood," Aug. 19, 2008, www.doioig.gov.

6. U.S. Department of the Interior Outer Continental Shelf Safety Oversight Board, "Report to Secretary of the Interior Ken Salazar," Sept. 1, 2010, www.doi.gov.

7. Ibid.

8. Richard Morrison, BP vice president for Gulf of Mexico production, letter to U.S. Department of the Interior, Sept. 14, 2009.

9. John Hofmeister, *Why We Hate the Oil Companies: Straight Talk from an Energy Insider* (New York: Palgrave Macmillan), 2010.

10. Eric Nalder, "Deadly Gulf Blowouts Persist," *Houston Chronicle*, July 19, 2010.

CHAPTER 16

1. Anadarko press release, June 18, 2010, www.anadarko.com.

CHAPTER 17

1. Republican Study Committee press release, June 16, 2010, http://rsc.tomprice.house.gov.

2. Joe Barton letter to Sir John Browne, Aug. 11, 2006, http://archives.energycommerce.house.gov.

3. Joe Barton, statement delivered to the Oversight and Investigations Subcommittee of the House Energy and Commerce Committee, Sept. 7, 2006, http://republicans.energycommerce.house.gov.

4. Despite the Republican Study Committee's earlier endorsement of the term "shakedown," Barton's fellow Republicans distanced themselves from his apology. Sen. Richard Shelby of Alabama called Barton's comment "dumb." Barton later issued a statement saying he regretted using the term "shakedown" and withdrew his apology to Hayward.

5. William Gibson, "Florida Senators Push for BP Spill Fund," *South Florida Sun Sentinel* "Florida Politics" blog, June 14, 2010, http://weblogs.sun-sentinel.com/news/politics/dcblog.

6. Feinberg would later drop this provision, after widespread outcry from business owners.

7. Kenneth Feinberg, conference call with reporters, Aug. 22, 2010.

CHAPTER 18

1. John Browne, *Beyond Business: An Inspirational Memoir from a Visionary Leader* (London: Weidenfeld & Nicolson, 2010).

2. Ibid.

3. Ibid.

4. Tom Bower, *Oil: Money, Politics and Power in the 21st Century* (New York: Grand Central Publishing, 2009).

5. Tahani Karrar-Lewsley, "Libya Oil Chief Sees Value as BP Shares Rise," *Wall Street Journal*, July 6, 2010.

6. Tony Hayward, transcript, BP second-quarter results conference call with analysts, July 27, 2010, www.bp.com.

CHAPTER 19

1. CNNMoney.com, Fortune 500 online, http://money.cnn.com/magazines/fortune/fortune500/2010.

2. Brett Clanton, "Today's Offshore Gear: Up to the Task?" *Houston Chronicle*, May 23, 2010.

3. Paula Dittrick, "BP Finds Three Pieces of Drill Pipe inside Macondo," *Oil & Gas Journal*, Aug. 23, 2010.

4. BP *Deepwater Horizon* Accident Investigation Report, Sept. 8, 2010.

CHAPTER 20

1. Monica Hatcher, "The Quiet Assassin," *Houston Chronicle*, July 11, 2010.

2. Monica Hatcher, "5-Month Mission Was a Success," *Houston Chronicle*, Oct. 2, 2010.

3. Samantha Joye interview, *All Things Considered*, National Public Radio, Sept. 10, 2010.

4. Marian Wang, "Take It with a Grain of (Sea) Salt: Gulf Microbe Study Was Funded by BP," ProPublica, Aug. 26, 2010, www.propublic.org.

5. Bill Rigby, "BP-Owned Alaska Oil Pipeline Shut after Spill," Reuters, May 25, 2010, www.reuters.com.

BIBLIOGRAPHY

Bower, Tom. *Oil: Money, Politics and Power in the 21ˢᵗ Century.* New York: Grand Central Publishing, 2009.

Brown, Jonathan C. *Oil and Revolution in Mexico.* Berkeley: University of California Press, 1993.

Browne, John. *Beyond Business: An Inspirational Memoir from a Visionary Leader.* London: Weidenfeld & Nicolson, 2010.

Csorba, Les. "The New Energy Executive: What the BP Oil Spill Reveals about the Essential and Defining Attributes of the Next Generation of Leadership." Hendrick & Struggles, 2010.

Easton, Robert. *Black Tide: The Santa Barbara Oil Spill and Its Consequences.* New York: Delacorte Press, 1972.

Hofmeister, John. *Why We Hate the Oil Companies: Straight Talk from an Energy Insider.* New York: Palgrave Macmillan, 2010.

Kinzer, Stephen. *All the Shah's Men: An American Coup and the Roots of Middle East Terror.* Hoboken, N.J.: John Wiley & Sons, 2008.

Longhurst, Henry. *Adventure in Oil, The Story of British Petroleum.* London: Sidgwick and Jackson, 1959.

Minutaglio, Bill. *City on Fire: The Forgotten Disaster That Devastated a Town and Ignited a Landmark Legal Battle.* New York: HarperCollins, 2003.

Pickens, T. Boone Jr. *Boone*. Boston: Houghton Mifflin Co., 1987.

Priest, Tyler. *The Offshore Imperative: Shell Oil's Search for Petroleum in Postwar America*. College Station: Texas A&M University Press, 2007.

The Report of the BP U.S. Refineries Independent Safety Review Panel, January 2007.

Sampson, Anthony. *The Seven Sisters: The Great Oil Companies and the World They Shaped*. New York: Bantam Books, 1991.

Simmons, Matthew R. *Twilight in the Desert: The Coming Saudi Oil Shock and the World Economy*. Hoboken, N.J.: John Wiley & Sons, 2005.

Solomon, Charlene M., and Michael S. Schell. *Managing across Cultures: The Seven Keys to Doing Business with a Global Mindset*. New York: McGraw-Hill, 2009.

Tarbell, Ida M. *The History of the Standard Oil Company*. Edited by David M. Chambers. Mineola, N.Y.: Dover Publications, 1966.

U.S. Chemical Safety and Hazard Investigation Board. *Investigation Report: Refinery Explosion and Fire (15 Killed, 180 Injured)*. Final Draft for Board Vote, March 20, 2007.

Yergin, Daniel. *The Prize: The Epic Quest for Oil, Money and Power*. New York: Simon & Schuster, 1992.

ACKNOWLEDGMENTS

Soon after I agreed to take on this project, a colleague came into my office and asked how I was going to pull it off. I told her that I had no idea, but at least I had gotten Anne Belli Perez to help me. "Oh," she said. "If you've got Anne, then I'm not worried. You'll get it done." Indeed, I did manage to get it done, in large part because of Anne's top-notch reporting and research skills. It has been an honor to be able to work with her again. I also relied on the research skills of Luke Manning in London, who offered an array of insights, sources, and ideas.

Even a project as seemingly obvious as this one needs something to get it going, and in this case, that something came from Payne Harrison. I have valued his help, advice, and friendship over the years, and I will be forever grateful that he happened to contact me at just the right moment and point out the forest that I'd seen only as trees.

For their help and support, I am indebted to my colleagues at the *Houston Chronicle*, including Brett Clanton, Tom Fowler, Jennifer Dlouhy, Monica Hatcher, Lise Olsen, Terri Langford, Eric Nalder, and Katherine Feser. They provided both assistance and reporting that helped lay the groundwork for this project. Jeff Cohen, George Haj, and Laura Goldberg were willing to juggle their editorial calendars during a major news story to give me time to complete it. David Kaplan and Suzanne Garofalo were a fount of title ideas.

I am indebted to my editor, Mary Glenn, at McGraw-Hill for her steady and understanding hand in guiding this project under what might otherwise have been stressful circumstances, and to my agent, Matthew Carnicelli at Trident Media Group, for finding the perfect publisher in record time. Ruth Mannino and her editing team worked diligently to make me sound more eloquent than I am.

I must also thank other friends and colleagues who lent their patient assistance, often at moments of my great desperation. They include Mimi Swartz, Rob Urban, and Igor Sergeyev. Invaluable assistance was provided by René Carayol, Brent Coon, Matt Resell, Christopher Dean, and David Perry.

Kristen Hays lent her journalistic advice, suggestions, and energy industry expertise in proofreading the manuscript, for which she deserves a nice "thank you" without a smart-ass comment.

Those who were willing to spend their time and share their stories, insights, and expertise made this book all that it is. They include Art Berman, John Hofmeister, Ian MacDonald, David Teverbaugh, Katherine Rodriguez, Dave Leining, Ralph Dean, Leo Gerard, Jordan Barab, Overton Houston, Bill Parker (who also lent his expertise in shelling blue crabs), Dale Chaisson, Otto Candies III, John Breed, Scott West, and Tyler Priest.

I also must thank the numerous experts and consultants, competitors of BP, and former and present employees who helped me on the condition that I would shield them from reprisals by not revealing their names. You know who you are, and you have my appreciation. I also want to thank the BP executives, engineers, and public relations representatives who,

5

for a time at least, were willing to share their insights about the company and its projects.

Finally, I must thank my family for putting up with me as I completed this project, especially in the last month, when I became little more than a disheveled, unshaven hermit who emerged from time to time to refill his coffee cup. My wife, Laura, shouldered her own job and a disproportionate share of the parenting, and still managed to find time to proofread the manuscript and keep the coffee brewing. At the outset, my brother David offered the mathematical equation for what it would take to complete this project, unknowingly providing the terrifying incentive that I needed to stay focused and get it done.

INDEX

ABOUT THE AUTHOR

Loren Steffy is the business columnist for the *Houston Chronicle*. He has been recognized by the Society of American Business Editors and Writers, the Associated Press Managing Editors, the Houston Press Club, and other societies and organizations. In addition, his work has been cited in publications, including the *New York Times*, the *Washington Post Online*, and *Texas Monthly*, and he's made numerous appearances on CNBC, FOX News, MSNBC, *The NewsHour with Jim Lehrer* and Court TV. He lives in The Woodlands, Texas.